IN SILENCE

Growing Up Hearing in a Deaf World

RUTH SIDRANSKY

Ballantine Books New York

Copyright © 1990 by Ruth Sidransky

All rights reserved under International and Pan-American Copyright Conventions. Published in the United States by Ballantine Books, a division of Random House, Inc., New York, and distributed in Canada by Random House of Canada Limited, Toronto.

This edition published by arrangement with St. Martin's Press, Inc.

Library of Congress Catalog Card Number: 91-91915

ISBN: 0-345-37425-8

Cover design by William Geller
Background photographs: The Bettmann Archive
Inset photograph from the author's collection

Manufactured in the United States of America

First Ballantine Books Edition: October 1991

10 9 8 7 6 5 4 3 2 1

To My Father Benjamin
To My Mother Miriam
And to all the Children of the Deaf

The Talmud says: A word is worth one coin, silence two.

Contents

Acknowledgments

*A*bove all I am grateful to the Deaf for a rich language. Sign. It is the language of my parents, my language, the language from which this writing bloomed.

I want to thank those who made this book possible. Andrew Bromberg, who suggested the book, Marvin Fredman, who listened to the stories, and Rhoda Brown, who encouraged me to continue the writing.

And to my son, Mark Hyman, and my daughter, Carrie Hyman, who gave gentle suggestions as they read the work in progress and who offered memories of their grandparents.

And to my husband, Richard Rosenberg, whose support served as a shelter and whose good humor while I wrote made life a pleasure.

I would like to offer special thanks to Berenice Hoffman, my agent, whose kindness sustained me over a two-year period and whose literary taste and skill helped me sculpt the manuscript. I wish to thank Robert Weil for his patient reading, for his faith, and for his invaluable insights into the editing of this book. Thanks also to Richard Romano, his assistant.

And to Benny and Mary, my father and mother, I doff my hat!

FAMILY TREE

Sidransky

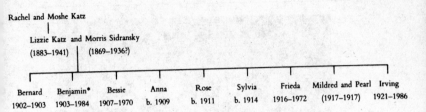

Rachel and Moshe Katz

Lizzie Katz and Morris Sidransky
(1883–1941)   (1869–1936?)

Bernard	Benjamin*	Bessie	Anna	Rose	Sylvia	Frieda	Mildred and Pearl	Irving
1902–1903	1903–1984	1907–1970	b. 1909	b. 1911	b. 1914	1916–1972	(1917–1917)	1921–1986

Bromberg

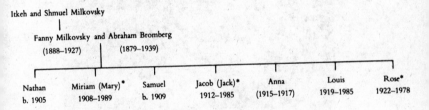

Itkeh and Shmuel Milkovsky

Fanny Milkovsky and Abraham Bromberg
(1888–1927)   (1879–1939)

Nathan	Miriam (Mary)*	Samuel	Jacob (Jack)*	Anna	Louis	Rose*
b. 1905	1908–1989	b. 1909	1912–1985	(1915–1917)	1919–1985	1922–1978

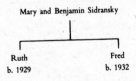

Mary and Benjamin Sidransky

Ruth	Fred
b. 1929	b. 1932

*Deaf

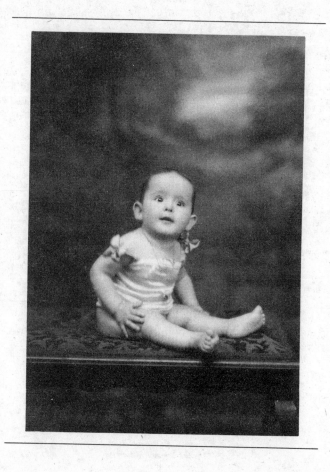

PROLOGUE

Keep silence before Me, O islands,
And let the peoples renew their strength;
Let them draw near, then let them speak; . . .

—Isaiah 41:1

*I*f there were a way, if I could, I would write this book in sign language. I cannot. Signs do not transpose to the printed page; they are understood only in the flesh, hand to hand, face to face. And so I write in universal printed English, words to conjure the magic of my first language—words my mother taught me, words my father taught me—words told by the flick of a finger, the sweep of a hand. Sentences, liquid, rising not from the human voice but from the human body.

My first memory is the memory of a word signed by my deaf mother. She signed the word *baby* for me, cradling an imaginary infant in her arms. She crooned the words with her voice, aloud, high-pitched and musical, to me. I was her baby, her firstborn. I can see her swaying, holding me to her, telling me to go to sleep. It was bedtime. Words fell from her hands and I learned them, imitating them like any child, in any language. My language, like my mother's, was in my hands. My spoken language, until I was five, was like hers, broken.

My father Benny's deaf voice was harsh to the hearing ear. But not to mine. He put me on his shoulders and danced me around the room, hands silent. He was holding my ankles. He sang. What it was I do not know. I can hear him, but I can't repeat his song. When he put me down he wanted to play. He teased and we laughed. All in sign.

We lived in two worlds as I was growing up, our private world and the "hearing" world outside. I was on intimate terms with silence and the language of silence. But my parents' oral words hit hearing ears like jagged stones on rooftops. And I, a small child, hung my head, unable to speak in clear sentences.

Benny stroked my head and signed, "Never mind, hearing not understand deaf words. Stupid people."

My ears tightened.

When I was a child we lived in isolation, celebrating life in our quiet enclave. My mother signed, "I have three nice rooms." And in those three nice rooms, with "good furnitures," I grew up. My younger brother Fred and I.

My mother washed clothes on a metal washboard on cold winter afternoons and created a festival.

"I make warm steam, make rooms warm for children, snow outside, but here I wash and you wring and we have small party for us alone."

Her mouth still, her fluent hands signaled, "Come use hands, I show you, together we do, and then you alone, Ruth."

With five-year-old hands I twisted the warm water from my undershirt. My mother said now, both in sign and voice, "Use hands harder, harder, use hands and squeeze to make a clothing dry." The language was perfect. Momma was perfect. Here she was not deaf, here no one stared at my mother's wonderful sign song. We were in harmony and I was warm. But not safe. I was sickly.

My mother explained, "You have tonsils infections, make you sick too often, running nose, coughing."

I looked at her in trust. And she signed, "Tomorrow we go to a hospital, nice place, there good doctor cut out bad tonsils, make you well and after you eat lots and lots cool ice cream."

My mother held my small obedient hand and led me to the hospital. I lay on the operating table and struggled to stay awake, to remain alive. I was frightened of the damp ether mask that put me to sleep. I awakened after the surgery with a cold, thick, red sausage-like ring around my neck. I vomited. I tried to speak.

"Momma," I signed, "I have no voice."

"You have voice. Be patient. Tomorrow you will speak. Today you will sign to me. I will tell nurse what you want. She will understand my speak words."

My voice did return but the fear of never being able to speak lingered on. I was confused. I had questions to ask, but I was too young to form them. I was afraid: afraid of silence, afraid of unknown sound, afraid of my distorted voice.

The years passed and more questions formed. I did not ask the questions; I kept them hidden as my mother did. She waited for me at the fifth-floor window when I arrived home from high school, waving me back into her life. When she wasn't at her window, I knew I would find her deep in conversation, alone.

I climbed the stairs to our apartment, opened the door with my key and paused to listen for my mother. I walked through the living room to her bedroom. She didn't sense my presence. I saw her shake her fist in the air twice. I saw her plead for an answer: "Why did you make me deaf? I am good person, why you punish me?" With her hands still signing the last words of her question, I touched her and signed, "Momma, who are you talking to?"

"I talk to God and ask why he make me to be deaf, to hear nothing for all my life, why I never hear the voice of my children?" Her hands were almost still as she spoke.

I tried to interrupt, but she went on. "I am angry with God today!"

"Momma," I tried again.

"Do not stop me," she blazed. "Tomorrow I will forgive God, not today. Why me, why my brother Jack, deaf, why my baby sister, Rose, deaf, suffer too much? Why can you hear and not me, your mother?"

I watched, too frightened to utter a sound or sign a word lest God strike sound from me too. Her anger entered me and I pressed it down into my childhood, my adolescence.

She looked at my face and her rage quieted. She shrugged and signed softly, "Nobody knows why, maybe it just happened."

Maybe she was right. I believe now that her deafness was random genetic chance. Maybe there is neither biological nor logical reason; maybe it was merely happenstance.

Many years later, during my first year of college, a year filled with learning, I attempted to explain the physical reason for her deafness. She discarded my words. Instead, she hinted at sin; she halfheartedly suggested that her father, Abraham, had a venereal disease. And so God punished him. She was looking for a cause, a reason to justify her deafness.

When I carefully outlined in simplified terms the Mendelian law of genetics, when I drew pictures of recessive and dominant genes for her, signing that deafness was a recessive one, she crumpled my biological diagram angrily in her hand. "You," she signed, "do not understand the ways of God."

The subject was forever closed. She could accept illness as a cause for her deafness but had difficulty with a God who made her eternally deaf. She turned from God, and asked me, as she did all the years of her life, to be her ears, her voice.

When I was no longer so afraid of sound, no longer sealed in solemn silence, I searched for the source of my voice through the sound of my mother's voice. What was the source of her voice? Was hers a voice that never heard sound, yet imitated words intelligibly for me, a voice that came out of nothingness, out of the void of human consciousness, or was it a voice of some immutable human genetic memory that spoke to the ages, that speaks for the ages? Was the simplicity with which she spoke related to a message that God meant to give me through her, or was I just searching, looking for more than there was? Was she simply deaf, mute in the nuance of the spoken word? Was that all it was? Was I searching for my own voice in the path of my mother's silence?

When I was still in high school, I walked the streets alone, my mother's fist echoing in my eyes. I walked as I always did, head high, and I called out with my hands, "God, can you hear me? Listen, God!" I shook my fist, "Listen to me. I am calling you. Speak to me!"

People passed in twos and threes. They stared and I shoved my hands into my coat pockets, but I kept my questions going, mouthing them internally. "God, do you speak English? Do you know sign language? I can teach you. God talk to me."

There was no answer.

I stopped talking to God, orally, in sign.

I spoke to my mother:

—Can you hear God's voice, Momma? Can I? I know that the hand of God calms me as your hand does. I like the sound of your voice. But you'll never hear mine, the sound of my voice.

I made a wish, the wish to hear satisfying speech, to hear Momma speak. I sent my own sounds ahead and tried to see them vibrating in the air. I wanted to see sound. I sat in perfect silence, thinking that the deaf must see sound, that sight and sound were somehow laced together; that maybe I too could see it.

I spread my voice over the air, playing with it, trying to sound like a man, like an infant, like a deep-throated woman. I played with my voice as I had once played with my dolls. I projected it, I swallowed it, whispered, pleaded, played with the tones. When I went to school, I relished telling others who asked me to sing in chorus, "Oh, I can't do that, I'm tone deaf." It connected me, anchored me to parental history. It was a lie. I wasn't tone deaf. I refused to hear music.

In my bed, in that space before sleep, when I was fully awake, I thought and the thoughts were loud. I addressed my mother once again:

—I can hear the exhalation of my breath, hear the beating of your heart when I press my head to your chest; I can hear the sound of my life. Why can't you hear yours? I hear myself sniff the perfumed aroma of a rose. I hear you snore. I hear the sound of my own voice as it reaches out across the enclosed room.

I can hear people speak. I have heard their words lifted across a crowded room full of scattered sound, full of energy, coming directly to me. I can hear the birds, even the flutter of winged birds in flight, swooping from the ground. Can I give you sound?

Your silence is a deep chasm, a hole I will fill with the embroidered pretense of sound. "Oh!" I hear you shout. "What was that? I hear something loud." "Loud," you say. "Do you know what loud is?"

I can ask you, as I did when I was young, "Momma, why does the ocean stop here? Why does the sea sound so loud?" Could you have answered these questions?

—Momma, you told me of horse-drawn sleighs and piles of winter snow lining the country lanes of your childhood. I wondered, did you hear the sleigh bells? You told me of the horse's breath steaming from his nostrils, but you never told me of the horses' hooves as they thudded to the snow-packed road. You told me of the fields of clean green grass but did you ever tell me how the growing grass sings in the wind?

Once, in hand-to-hand conversation, my mother asked if the yellow tulip had a sound of its own. I couldn't tell her that color was devoid of sound; she seemed convinced that color and sound were bonded. So I told her that red was loud like a summer sunset, that black had the sound of a thunder crack, that blue sounded like cool running water on her hands, that purple sounded like grapes, that silver sounded like moonrise, that pink was like red without the anger. She wanted to know about yellow. What could I tell her about yellow? I told her that yellow sounds like the soft morning sun that melts the winter ice.

My hands were flowing when she stopped me. "Does color really make noise?"

"No, it does not."

"To say truth, I never believe colors have noise, but nice to think so. Better, I feel color."

She smiled and her hands, slowly, one word at a time, signed, "I am jealous that people can hear and I cannot."

I held that sentence to me for years trying to help her hear visually, to help her hear with her own acute senses. It was no use.

When I wanted my mother to listen to my question, to see my eyes and hear my hands, I pulled at the hem of her dress, my fingers touching the warm crease behind her knee. She responded quickly, "You not little girl anymore."

I waited. I tapped her right elbow with my left hand poised for speech; she turned to face me and my hand attempted to ask a question; she answered before I could sign a word, "Don't bother me, I busy on cleaning rooms, must to dust furnitures."

I was rebuffed into silence. I wanted to ask only one question that I framed and reframed in her language. "Momma, explain to me what is no sound, what is quiet? How you understand what mean silence?"

When her work was done, her face washed, her arms rinsed of lather, her hair combed and recombed, her voice called out, singing my name. I had only to reach out and touch her shoulder. She signed, "You stand near to me, watch me clean myself in a sink. I not see you close to me. Not feel you. Now I ready listen you, what you want?"

She scanned my face. "You have thinking lots, not tell me what you want."

"Too hard, Momma. I think about angels who sing. You think angels are real?"

She raised her hands to speak: "Yes, of course angels are real. God's angels, and my angel; you are angel daughter Ruth."

My father, Benny, defied silence, ignored sound. He had his own words.

"The finger of God is in my fingers. You think I finger sign, no, it is God who go in my hands, in my fingers to make language so deaf can speak. God smart, he understand deaf words."

His eyes touched mine. "God and me, we touch hands to speak. He draw whole earth with his fingers; I draw language with fingers." Benny created the letter *L* in each hand, thumb out, index finger up, the other fingers curved into his palm. He danced his thumb tips together, moved his thumbs apart, his index fingers erect as he moved his hands to the full breadth of his arms. In this span he wave-signed the word language. It was a reverent description of his contact with God.

"Language is best." Benny wanted to speak well. And he spoke magnificently with his talking hands, his talking face and his talking body.

"God gave me fingers to be funny man, to make me laugh. You think God really true put his fingers to my head?"

He was asking me about God, waiting to see if I would divulge the secret that God spoke to me directly. He wanted to know why God touched the soundless with His hand and not with His voice.

I didn't say, "Daddy Ben, you stand in direct contact with God." In adolescence I had no signed vocabulary for "direct contact"; finger spelling was inadequate to the task. Instead my hands said, "You stand with God, close," each word described in its own sign, clear in his language.

"God bless you," he said.

He wrinkled his nose, leaned over and kissed me. I pushed him away. "Don't kiss so hard. Your mustache scratches my cheek!"

He had the wildness of the animals he taught me to know. Nothing stood between him and his God. His access was direct. He didn't know a single prayer or hymn. He signed, "Ruth, you hearing, you pray for father Ben. God understands what means I say through you."

I was responsible for him before God. But he had his own covenant, he had no need of me.

He had his own voice, a voice without imitation. At times it was soft and purring and when he tried to use his purring voice to sing a phrase or a melody he had watched on another's lips, I tried not to laugh. It was funny. His voice was purer than song. It was full of his own light. At times it was heavy, guttural, unintelligible even to me. But it was always the voice of a man, deep in the low registers, able to inflict anger, scorn and contempt. This was rare. It was a joyous voice, bounding with excitement, fingerpainting the passing person.

He signed, "See peoples in a street, learn what stories they tell, look at clothings, see if they have fat ass." And I laughed. Benny was filled with laughter. It was his walking stick.

He took me to watch the trains at Grand Central Station, to watch the people as they poured onto the platforms, scurrying to their lives. "See people with sad face, unhappy walk. Not me, not Ben. Faces show too much pain from their life."

He was undefeated. He transformed pain into humor, into a joke. His hands moved to say, "People out, train is out, gone from station." He played with his arms and hands; his arms chugged along the train track going nowhere, his nostrils snorted imaginary steam rising from the locomotive pulling life's passengers to their destination. "Train go nowhere, people not know where they go. Too bad. Better to laugh at life. Make easier hard time."

He was proud, defiant, servant to none. He made demands on himself and me. In exchange for my sustenance and his gift of life, I was his teacher, his translator when complex paragraphing gagged him. His spirit was voracious; it burned with curiosity.

"Hurry come see this." It was a shout I knew well, a shout to share something he had seen.

And on the ground a dead pigeon lay.

"See Ruth, it not die by self, it eat a poison, man put there. Too bad kill God's pigeon, stop wings to fly free."

I recoiled, hunched my shoulders. He pulled me to him, lifting my face to his hands, and signed, "Not bad see death,

God make life, must see all, know all. Life, death, all big thrill." I remembered his words when I saw him moments after his own death. He was blue, hair black, young again. My own view of his life was molded by his hands, his thoughts in his hands. He believed I was his teacher. He was mine. There were no frills to his teachings, nothing to veer me from fundamental knowledge.

He ordained acceptance. He preached rapture and never knew the word. When regret bit him, he put it aside. "Not important deaf, I am Ben," he said without reluctance. His consent was silent.

"Love to live, who know what life bring to each person, wait, watch and see." His hands moved and unerringly he prayed in tribute to his Maker. He did not suffer deafness. He was no Job.

"My name," he said in majestic sign again, "my name is Ben. And I can do what other man do. I support my family alone, nobody help me."

His attachment to life was erotic, to my mother passionate. When he was seventy-nine years old, we sat together and his hands remembered, "We have family, we have Momma Mary." He stood before her beauty, took pictures of her and called her "Queen." "You believe I have success to win Mary for wife."

Momma smiled at him, prodding him to continue. "Many people love your Momma Mary when she was young. So beautiful. She had another boy who like her, his first name Wolf, he ask her to go out. I am uneasy, but she find out he is two-faced, he is engaged to another girl. I feel better. I take Momma out on a canoe, we go in water, wonderful water, smooth lake. She not know how to swim, but I am not afraid, I swim strong enough for two people. We had some troubles, not tell you, all in past, long ago before you born, not your story, only story of me and Momma. We marry. Good times with Mary. Sometimes troubles, sometimes poor, work hard, but always Mary wait for me at home with good dinners, clean children."

My mother, still beautiful, watched his old hands, looked directly at me, her biographer, and signed, "I tell you many stories, often, on me and Daddy Ben, all long time ago. I have more story, one."

As my mother paused to collect her thoughts, to tell me yet another family tale, I remembered the times that she had told me of her frightened heart, her blank silence. I remembered her hands worn with work as she signed her memories, again and again for me. She questioned God about her deafness, but never said, "God grant me the power to hear." She said, "I know I am silent woman."

She asked questions. She wanted to know. "How does the voice of my son Fred sound? Tell me, is his voice hard like hammer? You are girl, is your voice soft like fur? Explain to me. Lift up hands, move your fingers. Tell me. The radio is warm. Are words from voice warm? Now you must tell me. Where does noise sound go? Far away?"

To me in these times of pleading she was the golden stranger, the alien without human sound. No voice penetrated her human awareness, but she had perception—her own warmth, her own knowing.

She stomped her foot on the floor for my attention. She turned to my father. "Ben, you watch me now. I am ready. I tell you now, story, I never, never tell before."

She began, "I am thirteen, fourteen years old. Rose not born yet. I am only girl in family. Nathan, oldest brother, sign, but not good. He not understand. Sometimes he put thumbs in ears and make sign of 'dummy.' I understand he not understand. I forgive, he young boy. My father not understand sign language, only few signs. I teach him to say 'Russia' his country. And Sam, my brother, younger than me, he learn more signs, like my father, but we not talk much. Sam in hospital long time. Bad legs. I not understand what family say—to me, to each other."

I had heard this part many times, the repetition etched into my brain. But this time she continued on, "I was alone in my home with my mother, Fanny. I ashamed tell you. She talk to me. More talk, sign something. I not understand what she say. I so angry that I punch her, punch her over and over again on arm. My mother say nothing, she not angry; she let me punch until I finish. Not long. She understand I do not understand. After finished she kissed me. I never do again, hurt me to hit my mother."

And with a long sweep of her hands rising from mid-chest she signed the word still with both hands and then the sentence, "Still not understand."

My father changed the subject, lightened the mood. "Forget past, it is over. Many years finished. I have other question here in newspaper, I have new word to learn." He grinned. "I ask you dictionary daughter Ruth, what means word *explicit*?"

"Explicit?" I repeated, signing each letter.

"Yes that word," and his words to me were oral.

"It means very, very clear, exact, clear."

Annoyed, he signed, "Why did not newspaper writer say that? So many hard words, makes not easy to understand what I read."

His white mustache lifted into his cheeks as he smiled; he was pleased, another word was added to his life.

My mother said, "I have word to ask too. I see in newspaper this morning." It was a rare request.

"What is the word, Momma?" I asked indulgently.

She pointed and said, "It is large word, *intuition*. Explain to me slow, right way. I want to understand."

I heard my response caught in my throat, unspoken.

—How can I tell you about intuition, you who kissed my tears away and said, "Cry is good, make you feel better, make hurt less."

Momma pushed my shoulder. "You quiet long time, you not know word, not very smart." Her face smiled at me. "You too serious now."

I signed quickly, "Intuition tells about understanding in the heart without words. It says, 'I know and I cannot explain how I know.' That is all, it is to know without language."

Satisfied with my answer, she said, in voice, "I go make lunch, you stay with Ben, keep company, talk lots." And she moved with grace from the room.

And in that space alone with my father as he read the newspaper, I remembered my own childhood, my own adolescence. I never spoke to anyone as I was growing up about my silent vista, my struggle with sound, not ever, not once. I held this blemish of creation to my chest. There was vastness to God's silence, an emptiness that reached across the earth, that spoke of eternal sorrow, Job's sorrow. I blundered into silence that bashed me with its darkness.

And in these dark moments when I was young, Benny rescued me, alive, always alive, pulsing with life.

He rushed to work, keys jangling in his pockets, arms waving behind his ears, signing the word hurry simultaneously in each hand: "I go to work, not be late, boss angry." The deaf are never late. I am never late. It is an internal clock that speaks to time.

My father gave me an alarm clock when I entered high school. "This for you, wake up right time, never be late for school." I hid the clock under my sweaters. I couldn't bear the incessant tick tock, the relentless noise. I rose from my bed each morning without the alarm startling me to the day's beginning.

"Where is clock I gave you? You must have!"

"I do not need it, Daddy, I wake up like you do. I have my inside clock same as you."

He laughed. "So you little bit deaf like me. Your body same as mine. But remember you are hearing girl, not deaf. You must listen to life, for you, for me, for Momma. Important you understand time in hearing world."

I was angry. I didn't want his time. I wanted my own, free of his need. His sense of time frayed me. He rushed time, anxious to please his boss, afraid that he would lose his upholstering job.

In age his temper was in tranquil time. His sense of rush gone, quiet. But the energy of his manhood is what I remember. His strength of hand, of will and body, permeated my childhood.

I can still see him now and he says, "Be strong, be a man. Ben strong." He clenches his fist, curls his arm, flexes his biceps and commands, "Touch father Ben, see father Ben, strong man, steel man."

I move away from his boasting. "I not show off; I tell you truth, who I am. Come touch Ben, true strong arm."

I reach out to touch him. "Wait," he says, putting both his hands up, palms flat, nearly touching my face, "I fix sleeve." He rolls up his sleeve to show me his rippling strength. The muscle quivers when I touch him.

"Watch Daddy Ben, make fun now." He places his hand on his head, flexes his muscle again, rolling it for me. I stroke his arms, undismayed now, and laugh with him.

"I told you, Ben strong, not afraid, never." He is free, fearless for the moment, and stone deaf. "Not afraid like you and Momma. You, Ruth, must not be afraid, you must be a man sometimes. Better for girls to know to be like a man. I know you not like this. I know you are girl, but girl must have man inside her too, make you brave person. This, I Ben, teach you."

I had been afraid; it was my mother's fear woven into me from infancy.

We fought once, my mother and I, many years later. She came to visit me, to see her grandchildren. And her eyes watched me as I talked to my daughter, my young son. My back was turned to her but she could see the children's oral response. She was momentarily excluded from my language, my facial expression. I turned immediately and apologized.

She turned to me and signed in bitterness, "Better you be deaf, Ruth. Then you and I could be friends." So great was my rage that she would curse me with her silence that I took her bodily and put her out of my house.

Hours later she came back and said, "I am sorry. Better you hear. I not mean what I say. Sometimes, I am lonely in big space. No one understand me."

And I asked aloud, "Who understands you Momma? Who understands me?"

She was abrupt. "Do not speak in mouth words. Sign to me. I want understand."

I signed my words.

She answered, "I understand you and you understand me. It takes all one's life to understand."

She put her arms around me. There were no tears.

"When you were little baby, even little girl, you were afraid to sleep alone. Do you remember?"

Yes, I remembered.

"I did not leave you alone in the night. I stay with you and rock you to sleep, until you were maybe seven, eight years old."

I nodded my head.

She continued, "When I take you home, little baby from

hospital, nobody there to help me hear you cry. I afraid you smother. So I take a long red ribbon, tie it to your wrist and my wrist. Your crib was next to my bed. When you move, my hand move too. I wake up to see what my baby need. I stay close to you."

It was the first time she spoke of my fear. I didn't tell her of the night sounds that struck my child's heart, that made me tremble under the bedcovers. I didn't tell her about the strange noises that assailed my acute hearing. I didn't tell her about the clang of metal garbage cans that woke me from restless sleep. It was enough that she knew I had been afraid, just as she had been.

Not Benny. I smiled at him sitting beside me. I touched him gently. He was old now.

His head came up with his hands. "Want to play new words, make up for fun, like before when you were little girl?"

Benny romanced language. It was the touchstone of his life. He demanded language, cajoled meanings from faces, from pages, from the dictionary, from confounding spoken words. At times the written sentence, the written word confounded my father more than the lips he strained to read. He circled one hand over the other, circled fingertips to fingertips, telling me of his confusion. The wider he signed the circles for the word confusion, the greater his confusion was.

He preferred the captioned photographs in *Life* magazine. The photographs, stark black and white, simply captioned, told the story. This he understood. He subscribed to the magazine, and each week on Fridays, during the years I lived at home, he gathered me to him with his oral words. "Come now, listen Ben read in loud voice from *Life* book. I practice plenty in bathroom."

His voice fractured sound. I pretended to understand the

pattern of all his vocalized sentences. Sometimes I understood only one. And then I said, "Now Daddy, tell me in sign what mean all words you read."

More eloquent than spoken words, he interpreted the meaning of the captioned photograph in accurate, untranslatable sign.

He pulled his chair closer to mine, pushed back his thick white hair and signed, "I tell you language is alive, like a person, like a river, always change, always new words. We make words. Hearing people not try to understand deaf language, but deaf try to understand hearing language. Not need to speak to know language. I late to learn my language, never really learn hearing language, to speak with tongue well, but sign language is real language, separate from English, separate from tongue language. It is first language from God, before man talk with mouth."

He paused to see if I understood his words. He nodded at my comprehending eyes and continued with his powerful hands. "I see more in one minute, understand more in deaf sign than you hear in speech words. You must wait for words to speak, one after the other, but I see meaning all at once in a face."

He was never confused in his own language.

The steep line of sign, the ascent of language as it rose from Benny's arms, created a mountaintop. It told of the perilous journey of a deaf man up a large mountain, told of his courage as he described the words, "Climb higher, higher to new life every day," with his hands in the air.

This is silence. This is how he taught me, the movement of movement; his language was motion and in his motion I understood the sweep of his daring. The signs were smooth, no jolting, no jarring, no snapping fingers. He pondered the meaning of life delicately with his square hands: "You go up a hill, always, up and up, sometimes fall down, but go up, hope is up."

Benedictions for Benny.

He knew language in a way that I never will. He danced it from his soul. To him language was a mantle, wearable. To Momma, language was tenderness, a protective touch, a means to tell me her stories, to hold me close to her life. And together, they brought me to a language beyond signed words.

Part One

MY BEGINNINGS

One

HANDS

Pleasant words are as a honeycomb,
Sweet to the soul, and health to the bones.
—*Proverbs 16:24*

I looked for my mother at the window. She waited for me to appear every afternoon on my return from school. I was five years old and warned not to cross the cobblestoned street until she waved me on in sign language. I raised my hand to the second story of our brownstone building to see her smile me home. She put her head out the window, looked both ways, and when she was certain that the South Eighth Street trolley car was nowhere in sight, she signed sharply in the language of the deaf, "Come now!"

I raced across the street secretly pleased that she did not scream as the other mothers did from Brooklyn windows. Her language was silent and did not shame me.

Men were standing in front of our building in small

groups, hands in their pockets, with nowhere to go, mothers with young husbands and babies, all waiting. I didn't understand that they were waiting for the Depression to end, that they had their own shame. I wanted to be invisible that afternoon.

When I went inside, I stopped at my grandparents' apartment, wanting to talk to one of my father's young sisters, wanting to keep the sound of speech with me a little longer. My Aunt Sylvia came to the door. "Hi, Ruthie, hurry upstairs, your mother is waiting for you, you don't want her to worry, do you?"

I was afraid of the dark wooden staircase but that wasn't why I lingered before climbing it. Once I entered our apartment, the door closed on the hearing world. My voice became the voice of my hands and I became a deaf little girl with ears that could hear.

I walked up the brown narrow flight of steps slowly, into the rooms we called home. The hallway was long and narrow, windowless. One naked ceiling bulb gave it light. I rushed past the bathroom, down the corridor, past the square skylit kitchen, into the light of the front room facing the street with two large windows, and into my mother's presence.

"Hello Momma," I mouthed. She read my lips.

She hugged me with her thick warm arms, smelling like Momma, sweet with the scent of Oxydol soap.

"I finished washing diapers. We go out soon. Fresh air good. I get baby Freddie."

"I have to pee, Momma."

"Hurry up, I need go shopping. You talk at meat store for me. Please tell butcher not cheat me, like last time. Too much fat."

I cringed at the unwanted burden of speech.

"All right," I signed, "I'll be quick." I didn't say what I felt. I couldn't name the feeling. Instead I smiled and walked with my mother to the door.

She settled my two-year-old brother into the faded blue wicker carriage, took my hand and said in her shrill voice, "Hold carriage here, we push together." Her strength bumped the carriage down the steps one at a time until we reached the street.

I loved our side of the street. The old brownstones nestled together. Mothers were out with their children. The older girls marked the street with chalk preparing the afternoon potsy game. It was years before I knew the game was a Brooklyn version of hopscotch. The boys knelt at the curbside playing with their prized marbles and called them "immies" and worried about their patched pants. Families lived their afternoon lives on the street. It was playtime. And South Eighth Street was a vast playground.

We walked down the street. My mother never stopped to speak to a neighbor; she moved regally, nodding her head, glancing at the familiar faces. She was dressed, coiffed, immaculate and beautiful. I was clean, but not beautiful. My tiny horn-rimmed glasses covered my crossed eyes. My mouth was closed to hide the missing front teeth I'd lost in an acrobatic somersault. My father tossed me in the air one night in play and I landed teeth-first on our brown enamel kitchen table.

I heard a neighbor say, "Hello, Mary, how are the children?"

I tugged at my mother's skirt. "Mrs. Eisen says to tell you hello."

Without breaking her stride, she lifted one hand from the carriage and said, "Tell her hello too. I hurry to store to buy foods for our supper."

As we walked, eyes were upon us. Voices spoke as though I were not there.

"Did you see Mrs. Sidransky? How does she do it? Raise two little children."

Another voice. "They look healthy. They're clean. The little girl talks. She can hear."

Yes, I could hear.

I hated the butcher shop. The smell of freshly killed chickens and cows clogged my nostrils in waves of nausea. The sawdust on the floor clung to my shoes on rainy afternoons. Blood and chicken entrails smeared the butcher's block. I watched wide-eyed as the heavy cleaver split the chicken. My mother never bought a chicken until she saw the healthy viscera sliding through the butcher's fingers. In one swift motion, he clutched and dropped the slime into a bucket half-filled with animal waste.

I clenched my teeth.

"It's your turn, girlie, what does your pretty mother want today?"

My mother signed, "Tell him neck bones for soup, no fat and one lung for stew meat. Tell him save me a good whole chicken for Friday, yellow skin."

I repeated her words in spoken English, adding some of her omitted words.

The butcher rubbed his solid blood-grimed hands across his aproned paunch. He spoke words to me. I cast my eyes down to the counter filled with steaks and veal chops, ground meat and curved lamb chops on chipped enamel trays. I did not speak again. My task was done. I had to save my words for the vegetable vendor, for the grocer.

When the shopping was done, our pace was leisurely until we arrived home. Safely flanked by 100 South Eighth Street, our home, my mother leaned against the building in the sunlight and signed, "You good girl, help Momma, now go play with friends."

I didn't want to leave her safe boundaries. She pushed me away from the carriage. "Go play, children must play." I left her sanctuary, wary of the girls jumping rope in front of the adjoining brownstone. I turned and looked at my mother, waiting for her to rescue me from these little hearing girls, with hearing mothers.

She was adamant. "Go play," she signed, "I watch you, not leave you alone."

I didn't move.

She raised her voice, and shouted to a child she recognized, "Anna, come take Ruthie play!" I understood her. I knew that Anna did not. Her unintelligible speech made my skin prickle, and I fled from the sound. Anna greeted me with, "What did your mother say?" I fumbled some words and said, "Can I jump rope with you?"

"Do you know Double Dutch?"

"Yes," I lied.

"You have to turn the ropes first and let Clara have her turn next."

I held the heavy ropes in my small hands, turning the two laundry lines in cadence. I didn't want the ropes to hurt my speaking hands.

I was playing. The minutes passed and my long, thin legs jumped in and out of the turning ropes. We were talking and laughing, and counting—"two, four, six, eight"—when my mother's voice pealed across my head: "Ruthie, come upstairs now, I cook supper."

"Open icebox, put meat inside. I put baby in crib."

"Hurry up, I late, four o'clock now. Louis K. come for supper. Wednesday night."

Louis Kazansky. How I loved him. He was my family's deaf uncle. My mother and father's friends came on regular days of the week. Some I know even now by the days of the week—Mr. Thursday came only on Thursdays after supper. I never learned his name, he never used his voice, and his signs were made without facial expression. I did not like him. He was undeaf.

But Louis K., as we called him, was my favorite. I waited for Louis at the threshold of our living room door every Wednesday. I watched the hands on the clock and advised my mother, "Louis K. coming soon. I go open door for him." At five sharp he was in the door. He picked me up in his short arms and hugged me. He put me down and we proceeded with our weekly ritual.

He clenched his fist and shoved it in my mouth—waiting for me to bite, to rage at every sound I heard, to punish him for every sound he did not. It was a fair exchange. My young teeth couldn't damage his nicotine-stained fist. We shared the pain of silent sound.

The void was terrible. There was no one at home with whom I could share the sound, no one to explain the meaning of sound, of this sound, of that sound. Is that the sound of a bird? Is that the sound of rain? I could not connect sound to movement. The rustle of leaves in a high wind terrified me.

Freddie was only two years old and he clung to me for comfort. The only sounds that comforted me were the off-pitch, guttural voices of the people who held me—my mother, my father, and their deaf friends who came on assigned days of the week for signed human companionship.

One night they held me in illness. It was a time before I entered school; it was a time before my brother was born. My nose was wet, my ears were wet and I was hot. The sound was running out of my ears.

The doctor came. And I heard muffled voices from my small bed. I was not yet three years old. I heard pencils scratching on paper, my mother asking questions, the doctor writing instructions.

He talked as he wrote. "Her ears are infected. You must drain the pus from them three times a day with warm oil."

I called, "Doctor, come."

He gently, but quickly, ripped the tape from my ears and soothed, "You will be fine Ruthie, do what your Momma tells you." He went back to the kitchen, and I heard voices and pencils: "Do not tape her ears to her head."

I heard the pencil again. And the doctor said, "Her ears

are not too big, they do not stick out, they are perfect." He said each word distinctly. And he left.

My mother picked me up and walked to the kitchen. Louis K. was sitting on the white wooden kitchen chair, ready to receive me with outstretched arms. I nuzzled him.

My mother placed a rubber sheet over my small body, while Louis held me tightly to him. She dipped an ear dropper into a vial of pungent oil and leaked searing hot liquid into my left ear.

I screamed, "Burn, too hot, too hot."

Louis K. crooned to me. "Good baby girl Ruth, good baby, good girl." I flailed and screamed, and he held me, until there was no more oil.

It was over and I was in bed again, safe. She sat beside me and sang in voice, her lullaby, until I fell into exhausted sleep. Years later when I repeated my memory of this incident to her, she looked at me in surprise and asked, "Why didn't you tell me the oil was too hot?" "Louis K. was holding my hands," I answered.

When my father came home there was laughter, rollicking, rolling laughter. He was strong and handsome; his thick black wavy hair fell into his black laughing eyes. When he kissed me, I pushed his bristled mustache from my tender skin. His hands, thick and squared off at the tips, smelled of the sweet horse hair at the upholstery factory. His fingernails carried the cotton lint he used to stuff overstuffed satin sofas. His fingers were so big that he could not button his shirts; my mother did this for him. Tired and worn out at the end of the long days of stuffing couch cushions, loveseat cushions and armchair cushions, he balled his hands into fists and smashed the walls with his talking hands—and said with his voice, proudly, "Ben strong, very strong."

He grabbed me, and tossed me in the air. He held me fast with his fingers, so fast that my arms were covered with black and blue marks the size of his fingertips. We spent little time together. He worked days and nights. He brought his money home and gave it to my mother to pay for the next day's meals. Some nights he found no extra work; on those joyous nights we had him at home.

Funny Benny. Strong Benny. He entertained us lavishly. He was a mime, he was a Chaplinesque artist.

He sat us down after our supper, very quietly, very still, and signed, "Stay there, no move. You watch Daddy Ben!" It was a command performance. "Lights out! You go, baby Ruth!" His hands and voice spoke together. When I heard him behind the door, I put the lights out, and crept, frightened of the dark, to my mother and brother on the sofa.

We waited. Out he came, with a squashed hat, a cane, splayed feet, jiggling shoulders, his jacket sleeves shoved up to his elbows, wiggling his mustached lips and nose, twirling his cane. My mother's hands were gleeful: "Look, look, Charlie Chaplin." He strutted across the room, miming the great sad mime.

He played the dumb fool, slyly, for each one of us. He paraded heroically, demanding attention. Back and forth he went across the room, mocking those who didn't know that neither he nor Chaplin was dumb. If the world saw him as a simpleton whose tongue could not speak, he knew he was a man of courage, the man who would, if he could speak, outsmart them all. Chaplin spoke to my father with his body and his mournful eyes. My father paid him tribute with his loving interpretations, charming us all with his body wit. When they were both old, my father saw a televised tribute to Chaplin and wept.

"Why you cry, Daddy?"

"He is old man now, die soon."

I invited my friends to our home; I invited only those who did not shrink at the sound of my father's voice. He reveled in the display of his talent for them. They loved him, applauded him with their small hands as he played the Little Tramp for each one of them.

"Don't clap now," I said, "he can't hear you. Wait until the lights go on; then he can see you." They clapped anyway.

When the performance was over, the girls and boys gathered around him as he patted their heads, gave one the cane, another his hat, another his slippers. Patiently, he taught them how to move, how to be sad like the great master. I refused to mime Chaplin. I would not play the dumb fool. I would speak my sadness. I was not dumb, nor was I deaf. I was a stranger, at home.

My mother, not to be outdone by my father, came grinning at us as we circled him. She took each of us by our hands and sat us at my father's feet. As she sat us down, she put her index finger over her curved mouth and whispered, "Shh, shh," with great mystery. "Wait, quiet," she shrilled. "No move."

All eyes were upon me as I repeated her words to the children as she left the room.

We sat expectantly.

In a moment, she was out the bedroom door, facing us. She turned her hands inward, thumbs tucked in, eight fingers open, pointing at her eyes. "Watch me. I dance for you."

I interrupted, "Want me put light out, Momma?"

"No, I want light, full light, so all children can see me," she signed.

She paused, looking down her heavy young body, demanding that we listen with our eyes. Her dress was short enough to see the lipsticked laughing faces she painted on her knees. Her silk stockings were rolled at the knee, fastened with a flapper twist. Certain that all eyes were on her she began to rhythmically, rambunctiously dance the Charleston. She abandoned herself to her musical feet. She danced a cappella. She sang music of her own creation, atonally, incomprehensibly perfect. Oh, how she danced! She flung her arms and snapped her fingers. She rolled her back down, grabbed her knees and crisscrossed her arms over them again and again with startling speed. She lifted her head slightly and we could see her eyes giggle. My father tapped his foot and clapped his hands with rapture.

My wonderful mother danced from child to child, lifting each one to her in turn until she had us all doing our own version of the Charleston. She alone was in rhythm. No one was frightened by her voice.

Our spontaneous party was a success.

"Come," she said, singing in voice, "I show you be sailors." My little friends understood her words. They moved with her in single file as she showed them how to hoist a sail up the "big, bigger mast in world." We heaved and grunted with our enormous work. We loved it. And I loved my mother.

I knew that these children would not stare at us in horror again. Like the others. In the street, at the park, on the bus, in the bowels of the subways, people stared. They turned their ugly heads, stopped and openly stared at my family, their mouths gaping. Those open mouths, which talked, said words that made me suck in my breath. I didn't understand all their foreign English sounds. But I knew they were repulsed and fascinated.

When my parents had their backs turned, I turned and stuck my tongue out at these men and women. I was adept at answering their wide-eyed stares, adept enough to put my thumb to my nose, fan out my fingers and present them with the vilest insult I knew. I never spoke. I pretended to be deaf. They glared at me, embarrassed, and turned their heads away. Most times my mother did not catch me.

Her eyes were keen and when she caught me, she grabbed

me by the offending hand and signed, "Shame on you, bad girl, not nice. Shame, shame." And my father said, "No more, not good girl. Stop it."

I never told my parents what the strangers said. They told me again and again, "You do it yourself. You hear. We deaf! No one help us, you help us. Do yourself, must do yourself. Forget stupid hearing words."

So I hearkened, heard the signs and remembered "Do it yourself."

Two

SCHOOL DAYS

LITTLE GIRL, BE CAREFUL WHAT YOU SAY

Little girl, be careful what you say
when you make talk with words, words—
for words are made of syllables
and syllables, child, are made of air—
and air is so thin—air is the breath of God—
air is finer than fire or mist,
finer than water or moonlight,
finer than spider-webs in the moon,
finer than water-flowers in the morning:
   and words are strong, too,
   stronger than rocks or steel
stronger than potatoes, corn, fish, cattle,
and soft, too, soft as little pigeon eggs,
soft as the music of hummingbird wings.
   So, little girl, when you speak greetings,
when you tell jokes, make wishes or prayers,
   be careful, be careless, be careful,
   be what you wish to be.

               —Carl Sandburg, Wind Song

*A*ll summer long my mother's hands lilted, preparing me for the first days of school. "Soon soon, September come, you go to big, wonderful school, be with hearing children, learn read, write, talk good English words."

"Ben," she signed to my father, "Ruth start school next week. We buy new dress. Important she pretty."

My crossed eyes wandered, scars left by measles, whooping cough and scarlet fever in rapid succession. My mother's early efforts to straighten my dark eyes with daily exercise failed; they moved at their own discretion toward the bridge of my small straight nose. My hands reached up continually, nervously smoothing my silky black hair down the sides of my face, covering my ears. Then, I was ashamed of my ears, pushing them close to my head with my small speaking fingers, remembering all the years they were taped to my skull. And those tiny hearing ears had to be perfectly formed for Momma's deaf eyes. Each time my hair pulled away with the adhesive tape, I winced, and my mother signed, "Don't worry, make you beautiful ears. We fix stick-out ears." Her signs were gentle and I hurt.

She could not hear my garbled speech. My language imitated hers, facsimiles of words she learned to say without the gift of sound. I understood all her words, the spoken ones and the signed ones. She never mastered the modulated pitch of normal speech, proclaiming her words just below the level of a shrill scream. Her sentences were signed, spoken in deaf shorthand, prepositions and conjunctions usually omitted. Strong verbs enunciated in the present tense; the words *today, yesterday,* and *tomorrow* added for absolute clarity. And it was all lyric.

I spoke as my mother spoke. But my speech, in that I tangled the words I heard, was more confusing than hers, clearer than hers, all mixed up. I spoke shyly. Oral words strained from my throat. I flinched when people did not understand my words, words stirred with the sounds of silence.

I longed for the great school that would teach me to be a hearing, speaking child.

'I remember my voice as a young child. Unsafe. I lurched in unstated loss, in sound I did not hear properly. My speech, like my eyes, was cockeyed, cross-eyed, my tongue twisted profoundly by deaf sound. I had a voice that blathered swollen English sounds, a voice that crumpled consonants too difficult for the deaf to pronounce.

I served as my mother's voice, shopping for fresh food. When I asked the green grocer for "one lib domadoes," his eyes squinted, and I recognized the pinched narrow face that didn't understand. I pointed to the soft red mound piled high and my finger indicated the words of my mouth. He recognized my mother and me, and was usually quick to serve us, but when he was busy he shouted, "Girlie, speak right. I'm loaded with customers here. I have no time for you. Come back when I'm not so busy!"

My throat lumped when my mother asked, "Why he not wait on me now, I must go finish shoppings. What take so long time?"

I shrugged without speech, not a sign, not a verbal mouthing.

"I come first before that fat women, tell man, it is my turn now."

I remained silent. My mother, irritated, shouted at me with her hands, voice silent, "You stubborn girl, not good, not tell man what I say. Not fair."

I opened my mouth in pretended speech but emitted no sound.

I did not explain my own shame at being misunderstood.

"Come"—she pulled my sleeve—"we shop other vegetable store."

"Momma," I signed, "wait, it is our turn soon. He not understand all I say."

"Why he not understand you, you hearing child, you speak hearing language."

"Not perfect, Momma, sometimes I make mistake when I speak in out-loud words."

Her eyes dropped to the ground. When she raised them they were blue soft, and she said what she said so often when thwarted by hearing cruelty. "Never mind, we wait, we wait until store empty and vegetable man have time to understand your hearing words."

Encouraged by my mother's tenderness, I spoke up: "Mister, our turn now. We in hurry."

He turned to my mother, patted my head and said, "Sorry, it's been so busy. Now, what do you want?"

"One lib domadoes!" I enunciated each word carefully in my mother's shrill pitch.

He hesitated, not quite understanding me. I caught his pause and pointed once again to the tomatoes. He took my hand and placed a tomato in it. "This is a tomato, and you want one pound, not one 'lib.' 'Lib' is short for 'pound.' Tell your mother to pick her own tomatoes, but not to squeeze them."

I signed his instructions to my mother and she reciprocated with her radiant smile as she leaned over the tomato bin to make her selection.

He led me into the store laden with fall produce and named everything we passed, correcting my pronunciation and pitch, repeating the word, waiting for me to repeat and repeat each vegetable he named until my repetition was correct.

"Now ask your mother what else she wants."

"Potatoes, three libs, and parsley, good fresh green, no spoiled brown nice lettuce, cumbers, onion . . ." Her list went on. And I said the words as I had just been taught, disregarding my mother's speech.

"What's your name, girlie?"

"I am Rathee, what is your name?"

"I am Max, and the next time you come, wait for me, I will take care of you and your mother."

"Thank you."

"How old are you?" he asked, grinning at me.

"I am five, next year I am six."

Max asked, "Tell me your name again. 'Rathee' is a new name for me."

I stopped, embarrassed. I had given him my mother's name for me.

"Rathee" is pronounced like the word "rather" with a double "ee" rising at the end. It was my mother's call. My own name, my private identity, deaf said.

"Max, my name is Ruth, my mother calls me Rathee; it is hard for me to say Ruth in the right way."

The word *rather,* spoken in casual conversation, still elicits a turn of my head, a response to the person who unwittingly almost calls me by my childhood name. It is a hearing misuse of my mother's voice. The name Ruth was not my name, not the name that connected me to my mother. It was a second name, a renaming into the hearing world, my passage to school.

My mother's promises that "teacher will teach you talk perfect English" enchanted me. She assured me that school was the place where I would learn what she couldn't teach me, "many new words," where I would learn "hearing" language. In time I did learn, but the vibrant language of her hands was not matched by oral speech—not ever, not then, not now.

That summer, on Sunday mornings, deep in the bedroom of warm sleep, my father sat on my bed filling me with the wonder of language.

"Watch me!" he said as he rose to his feet. "I show you hearing sounds."

He raised his arms above his head, and with his hands

plucking sound from the air, as a harpist plucks music from strings, he poured melody into his ears. And as he poured song into his head, he told me with a grand smile that school was where I would drink in what he couldn't give me, the sound that he could not hear. Again and again, he played with imagined sounds from the air with his hands. Each motion that touched sound for him was a gift to be opened on my first day of school.

He signed, "School big present, has big blue ribbon, open ribbon, learn to speak!"

It was not to be. I was placed in a class for mentally retarded children. My mother and father's promise of joyous learning was broken. I was apparently a stupid girl, and I was so ashamed that I told no one about the boring days of repetitive teaching, about the vacant stares around me as the teacher pressed on. I shrank, never uttering a word, joining the others in their slowness.

Each morning my mother hurried with excitement. My dress was still warm from the iron as she slid it over my head. She combed my hair and stroked my head with pleasure.

"I go school myself, Momma. Big girl. I careful in street." I signed these words with my lips tightly closed.

I did not want her to see my classmates. I was determined to go to public school alone. I was not afraid of the streets, or of the roaring elevated train that passed over my head as I walked to school. I could do that alone. But I knew that I couldn't fool my mother. Something had gone awry at school. There was no magic.

My mother was deaf, not stupid, not "deaf and dumb." Just deaf. On that first Thursday afternoon after school, my mother, with her well-honed intuitive sense, asked me in the language of hands, "Why you not happy at school?"

Instead of telling her how much I loved school, my hands blurted, "The children in my class are stupid. I learn nothing, just cut paper, play with crayon. Teacher speaks silly baby words, over, over again. Dull time at school."

On Friday morning, my mother and I left for school together. My pleas to go alone were ignored. We walked slowly in Brooklyn's September light to the brick school-house. I clung to my mother's hand, the hand that promised me wondrous schooldays. She would make it right. She would tell the teacher that I wasn't stupid; she would tell the teacher that I could sign when I was eleven months old.

"Come Momma," I said, "take you to meet teacher."

"No," she said, "we see a principal."

"But Momma," I protested, "we see teacher first."

"No," she insisted, "I see only principal." Her hands were firm.

We walked through the cafeteria that smelled of yester-day's free lunch. When we got to the principal's office, I came prepared with a timid speech for the school clerk. My mother did not wait for me to translate her words. She took me by the hand like any hearing mother. She opened the only closed door in the labyrinth of desks and secretaries scattered behind the oak counter, separating students and staff from the adminis-trative arm.

Miss Nathanson, the principal, calmly lifted her round face to us. She had straight chestnut brown bangs, cut flapper style; horn-rimmed spectacles like mine, halfway down her nose; and the hint of a smile. Her voice asked, "Can I help you?"

"Yes," I stammered.

My mother was still.

"What is your name, child?" Miss Nathanson's open smile touched me.

I told her, "My name is Ruthie."

My mother took charge. "Tell principal I must speak with her about your class."

Miss Nathanson was quick. I did not have to explain to her as I had done so many times in the past with the "others." She grasped my mother's deafness. She reached for the pen and pad on her desk; she wanted direct contact with my mother through the written word.

My mother shook her head vehemently. With all her concentration, she breathed four words very clearly. "Ruthie talk for me." Her hands were at her sides as she lowered herself to her knees and signed to me the words and thoughts that I was to interpret. I was proud of her spoken words, proud of her beautiful signs.

"Tell her," she signed, "I not write notes. We talk together with your voice, Ruthie. Not change mind."

As the sentences flowed back and forth, from my mother's hands to my voice, from Miss Nathanson's voice to my five-year-old hands, I was my mother's interpreter, as I had been so many times before, but this time she was pleading for me. Miss Nathanson understood the words I spoke, the words that sounded like a deaf child speaking, and the words that sounded like a normal child. They were mixed together and her keen intuitive sense listened, separating deaf sound from hearing sound, never asking me to repeat a word.

At the end of our three-way conversation, Miss Nathanson said, "Ruthie, child, tell your mother to buy you a radio!"

"A radio? We are too poor," I answered.

She was adamant. "Tell your mother."

"Momma," I signed, trembling, "principal say buy me a radio. I will learn talk better."

These sensitive women looked at each other eye to eye, wordless. My mother shook her head with pleasure at this simple way to teach me to listen and to talk.

So it was that a radio came into my life. It was a dome-shaped walnut box that had a dial. When I turned that dial, a miracle occurred. Normal adult voices came into my home, voices that were warm to the touch, voices that etched themselves into my head. I connected to hearing voices. I heard the news and programs for children. I heard music for the first time. The music made me uncomfortable. I didn't feel that I should listen to music's magnificence. My parents would never hear it. I moved the dial.

On Monday, my class was changed. The children were laughing and bright. And then without warning, my new teacher called my name and asked me to come to her desk. I obeyed, timorously.

"This is Ruth Sidransky, everybody. She is new. And she knows something we do not!"

My body faced the class. My eyes were cast to the floor.

This nameless teacher bent her large teeth to me and said in a piercing voice, "You know another language. You know sign language. Class, little Ruth's parents are deaf and dumb."

I felt the heat rise from my ankles to the backs of my knees, up my back, crawl into my skull until my ears were red with shame. I stood there motionless.

She continued to chirp, "Now, show us how you sign, how you speak with your parents."

I did not move. Teacher, without name, pressed on, "Tell the class, 'I am happy to meet you all.' "

Exposed, my arms dangled at my sides, speechless. Her voice strident, she commanded once more, "Say something for the class."

My fingers were limp. She put her hand on my shoulder, a demand to sign-speak. My arms lifted, my fingers fumbled incoherent letters.

"That's a good girl. Now tell us, what did you say?"

I whispered, "Good morning, all." I looked at this young woman and begged, "Sit down, please?"

This teacher, I presume, spoke in ordered sentences all the

rest of the morning. I only heard the hiss of syllables, meaningless sounds, spitting from the open slit in her face. I turned my head from her mouth, turned my ears from her soundings and sucked on the pain—my lollipop. Her callousness held me captive. I had nowhere to hide from her open gaping, from her fascination with freaks. She was no different from the staring passerby from whom I could escape, at whom I could stick out my tongue, but I was powerless before this master of spoken language.

Slowly, in the passage of days and weeks, I began to see this teacher, whose name has disappeared from memory, as a friend. I watched her mouth, heard her syllables and formed them into spools of meaning; sentences wound one on the other—language tunes, arias, andante, pianissimo. And after that, school was as promised by my father and by my mother, wonderful.

I fingered the sound of sound into my hands. I spelled the letters of the word into myself, into my body. When spelling was too difficult for me to discern instantly, I made up a sign for the new word, signing and saying, saying and signing until the word was mine, an immutable possession.

I searched for an oral-speaking mother, any mother would do. Beguiled by the prospect, I flirted with the girls in my class, charming them, wheedling an invitation for milk and cookies "on the way home." I chose my friends on one pretext and one pretext alone. Would their mothers sit and talk, *oral* talk with me? Would they sit at the kitchen table with me and ask me about my school day? Would they respond to my vocal speech? Could I pretend for the moment that this woman was my mother, pretend just for a little? But I could not abandon my mother, Mary, and left abruptly each afternoon, running home, all the way home to Momma. Mothers with speaking mouths painted in different shades of scarlet slipped into my dreams . . .

I lay in bed at night, waiting for someone to come,

someone to hear my cry. "I am lonely, my tooth hurts. I am afraid. I have to go to the bathroom. Does no one hear me cry?" I had a nightmare, the monsters came and I screamed. And still, no one came.

I left the warm wetness of my bed, left the security of my sheets and went with cold feet to my mother's bed. I touched her and woke her. Without a sound, she raised the covers and pulled me into her bed, surrounding me with her sleeping body. She held me but she didn't hear me. I didn't speak my urgent fear. She was asleep. And I slept with her, safe from the silent darkness.

Silence struck me broadside. It was my secret catastrophe. I was the unmarked child of affliction. I was neither deaf nor blind nor lame. I was imprisoned within myself, within the shroud of silent days and nights, within the sense that no one responded to me. I found human response in fantasy, with word games and sound games; it was my refuge.

I pigeonholed sound, forcing it into a square shape. It didn't fit. I rolled sound in my hand, rolled it into a ball as I rolled wadded gum that had lost its sweetness. I rubbed my hands together as I rolled clay, shaping sound into a cylinder. It was unshapable, amorphous. It eluded me. Sound was an illusion. It had no substance.

I had a voicebox that could accurately speak sounds that I heard. But there were stumbling blocks. I looked at objects, and when I couldn't name them, I chose creation. I structured my own words. I called crunched paper "gribble balls." Mashed potatoes were "shalamus potatoes," a washcloth was a "wepp" (my vocal translation of *wipe*). My vocabulary was studded with words that suited me.

I was a child inventing a child's language, cutting paper dolls out of ten-cent paper doll books, giving names, speaking words that were mine alone. I shared them with no one after my futile attempts to teach my hearing friends the new words.

They looked away from the strange combination of sounds.

I collided with sound; I whispered to its thunder and asked, "Why do you crash from the sky?"

"Bertuple!" was God's answer.

It was a serious word, and no one understood it but me.

I returned to my paper dolls, looking for my childhood; I gave my imaginary companions names that rang with mystery. I created "Perchanane" for the paper lady of the Civil War era, delicate and sweet in her white hooped skirt. "Bredadamo" was the handsome male, in soldier blue, off to fight for the Union army. This was my language, mine. It had its own hum, its own resonance.

I had a blue dress I treasured as a child. I did not know its specific blueness, so I named it "delicious" blue. When my first-grade teacher said, "Your delphinium-blue dress is lovely," I thought, "Delphinium!" It was a long word, a beautiful word, and so easy to say. I was, as always, ashamed to ask about the word. I wanted to know all about the word, where it came from, who made it up, why it was so lyrical. During recess, when the others went out in the springtime to play, I searched the dictionary and discovered that it was the name of a long, slender flower that grew every year from the same seed, a perennial. There was no picture in the dictionary; frustrated, I imagined an enormous blue daisy. I became more competent as time went on, able to find the meaning of every word I heard and sought. I practiced the words, petted them, cherished them.

Words and sounds lulled me to sleep. My nights were radio nights—the radio my mother bought for me. I awakened in the mornings with the radio voices that I had not turned off enticing me to the new day, boring language into my skull as I slept. I remained in bed, deciphering the words, imprinting them into my memory. Many had no meaning, but, oh, the sounds . . .

"Radio very warm, you forget to turn off again?" my mother asked as she gently pulled the covers from my sleep.

"Yes I leave on all night, I forget turn off."

"Electric bills cost much money. Not forget turn off tonight, okay?"

I had not forgotten, but how could I turn off the sound?

Before I finished the second grade, we moved from the Williamsburg section of Brooklyn to the East Bronx, to a gray tenement facing the Simpson Street police station. My mother, determined to live apart from my father's siblings and parents, wanted her own life away from judgmental eyes. So she exchanged an apartment with windows to the street for three small dark rooms that faced the brick alley adjoining yet another gray-faced tenement. Months later, unable to bear the sunless days, she said to my father, "Ben, I look for other rooms. I cannot see life in a street. Too lonesome. We have no light from the day."

He knew the meaning of blue daylight. He understood that light had its own intelligence. He answered with approval: "You look Mary, but cannot afford lots money for rent."

On weekend mornings, instead of taking me and my brother Freddie to the Metropolitan Museum of Art to feast our eyes on Canaletto's light-filled canvases, we walked the streets of the Bronx in search of our own light. I was caught up in my mother's excitement.

"This look good neighborhood. You speak to super, Ruthie, see if he has empty rooms." I approached superintendent after superintendent without success. My mother remained undaunted.

One summer Saturday morning, my mother and father, my brother and I boarded the Intervale Avenue streetcar. "We go that way," my mother asserted, "get off on nice wide street. Maybe we find street with trees and green grass."

We found Dawson Street. It was a wide street that curved up a steep hill. The modern red-brick building at 891 Dawson Street fanned out over a courtyard flanked with dusty green privet shrubs. All the apartments faced the courtyard or the street. There was one vacant apartment available with three sun-filled rooms.

"Fine," my mother said. "Tell super we take rooms."

"Thirty-nine dollars a month. Too much money," my father balked.

We moved into the apartment on the first day of the new month. My mother and father gave me and my brother the bedroom. They slept in the living room on a cot. My father made the mattress for the cot with his own hands. He sewed each cloth-covered button into the mattress with his curved needle. I watched him do this, needle in, needle out, until it was done. But the mattress, the metal cot, and the buttons soon became a source of disgust. The metal coils that supported the cot's frame were infested with bedbugs. In the evenings before we went to sleep my father removed the bedding and, with a lighted candle in his square hand, he burned the bedbugs from every crevice he could reach. We watched him as he caught them in his bare hands and squashed them. The acid smell was sharp. No one spoke during this ritual.

But the kitchen was the first kitchen I ever saw that had sunbeams on the table.

I was eight years old that summer and longed for school to begin again. My English was fluent. I spoke like other children, but I was not like them. I developed other sensitivities. I listened to the inner voices of people, aware of their unspoken words. I could hear what I could see. And I saw. I saw an eyelid lower fractionally. I saw the unseen tremor of a lie within a cheek. I saw a lip quiver when no one else did. I heard and understood the pause, the search for the right word that would mask the truth. I knew people. But they did not know me; I did not reveal myself.

My mother reminded me often, with a clap of her hands, that the essence of life was to "open eyes wide and to see all, to see language speak," as she laced the sign for *language* through her fingers. She taught me to pay attention to life, to be a mystic.

Summer ended in September, and I was admitted to Miss Chanin's third-grade class for gifted children. She was an old lady with faded yellow, tightly curled hair that dropped clumps of scaly dandruff on her navy crepe dress. Her worn black shoes were tightly laced on her large feet. Although she was slim and short, she waddled. But I loved her and her deep voice that rolled words distinctly from her bright red rouged mouth. At the end of each schoolday I waited eagerly for the fairy tales with the happy endings that she read aloud to us.

I wanted a book of my own to read, a book I could take to my bed and read until my eyes closed with sleep. I longed to know more about Hiawatha and his old grandmother Nokomis, who lived together in a wigwam on the shores of the Gitchee Gumee. I read only the story of Hiawatha's conquest of the wicked magician who brought suffering to the tribe. I asked Miss Chanin if there were any more books about Hiawatha.

She answered, "Yes, there are more books in the library."

"What," I asked, "is a library?"

Patiently she explained that I could join a library where there were hundreds of books, perhaps thousands, and that I could borrow a book whenever I wanted to read.

I sat at my gouged wooden desk, stunned, until I remembered that we were poor and asked, "How much does it cost?"

"It is a free public library. Your mother can take you. Stop at my desk after school, and I will give you the address."

I clutched the paper with the scribbled address all the way

home from P.S. 39. I stopped for nothing and talked to no one. I walked home hoping that my mother would take me to the library that afternoon. I ran up three flights of stairs. I read our apartment number, 3H, on the door, inserted my key and opened the door. I didn't ring the bell, nor did I knock. My mother greeted me only when she saw me.

She put down her knitting needles, put out her arms, and smiled her beautiful smile. She spoke to me with her voice. She was not ashamed of her singsong voice in my presence.

"What have you in hand?"

"Look, Momma, look I have library paper. We go now, not far." I spoke and signed simultaneously. I wanted to be very sure she understood my great excitement.

She shook her head. "Not today, we go Saturday. No time today."

"You know what library is Momma?" I demanded.

"Yes," she surprised me, "I know."

"Why not we go before?" I asked.

"No time. We go Saturday when Daddy Ben no work. I promise you."

My mother's promises were golden, but it was only Wednesday. I had to wait three more days, three more days and nights. I dreamed of touching paper with words that formed sentences. My hands caressed pages in the air, pages that were smooth and those that were textured with slivers of wood embedded in the print, and pages that were thick and creamy. Best of all, there were pages that had words that would join me to other people's thoughts.

I could read anything. I read hands and words with complete ease. Sign language is spoken with symbols for most words. But many words that I signed to my parents had no specific sign. These words were spelled out, letter by letter, in the manual alphabet of the deaf. My mother and I sat on many rainy afternoons, writing the letters of the alphabet that I already knew how to sign on the backs of stained brown paper bags. We practiced writing capital letters, lowercase letters and letters in script. My association with the signed letter of the alphabet and the written letter was immediate. For me, reading hands and reading the printed word were the same process. It was all language that connected me to the human mind.

At first light on Saturday morning, I crept into my parents' small bed and shook my mother awake.

"What is wrong?" she asked. "You not feel well?"

"Saturday morning now, you promise take me to library!"

She laughed with delight at my anticipation.

"Too early, go back to sleep. Open later, we go at ten o'clock."

I washed and dressed myself. I carefully pulled my red dotted Swiss dress over my head. I buckled my black patent leather shoes. And I sat on my bed waiting for the hours to pass.

We walked together, my mother and I, past the open fields enclosed with barbed wire, away from Dawson Street, past Kelly Street and Beck Street filled with Saturday-morning shoppers whom I ignored. I was elated. I was going to the library and I would bring home a book.

When we arrived at the imposing site, I ran up the pitted concrete steps into the librarian's feet. "We're not open yet, just a moment."

I could not wait. I blurted, "I want a book, a book I can take home."

This tight-bunned librarian relaxed her face as she peered down over her glasses at me. She invited us in to see her magnificent library before the scheduled opening hour. After she issued me a temporary card, which I clutched as a passport to life, she directed me to the children's section. On my knees, I moved up and down the two-tiered rows of shelves not quite knowing where to put my hands. I stroked the thick hardcover bindings, sensing the gold letters that named each book. I ran my hands over the odd-shaped books, some thick, others slim, all filled with treasure. I reached for a thin horizontal book and sat down flat on the floor. The title page read, *The Coconut Man.* I flipped the pages quickly. There was no color to distract me from the continuing flow of big black words printed in a single line under each drawing.

It was a simple story. A lonely little boy wanted to make a man to be his friend. He constructed a large rag body, but his man had no head. So the boy scoured the beach on his tropical island and found a coconut that had been washed ashore. He perched it on his man. The coconut man had no eyes, no ears, no mouth, no nose, but he could feel with his well-made hands. He could sign with his hands. His signs made him human. He left the boy, his creator, and went in search of someone who could carve out the rest of his senses.

I wanted to finish this book at home, in secret. Holding the book tightly under my arm, I approached the librarian with a timorous question: "May I take this book home?"

"Yes, and you may keep it for two weeks."

I read the book again and again, before lunch and after lunch. As my brother napped, I read the book to my mother, signing each word for her. When he awakened, I asked my mother to take me back to the library to get another book. My mother, with good humor, agreed. We set out again. This time Fred came with us.

The same librarian was there when I returned the book. With her yellow pencil fitted with a dated rubber stamp, she checked in my first borrowed book.

"I want another book please."

"I am sorry, but you cannot have another. You may not take out books, return them, and take out another on the same day with a temporary card. You will have your permanent card next week."

My eyes pleaded with her.

She shook her head. "Rules are rules."

Not wanting her to see my tears, I turned and rushed down the steps to my mother.

"Don't worry," my mother said, "I buy you a funny comic book."

On Monday morning I walked sadly into Miss Chanin's classroom. Thirty eager voices didn't ease the library loss. I sat down at the back of the room.

"Ruth," Miss Chanin called, "that is not your seat. You belong in the front of the room. You wear glasses and need to sit where you can see the blackboard."

I returned to my seat and sat quietly all morning.

As my class filed out for lunch in an orderly line, Miss Chanin stopped me and asked, "Would you like to have your lunch with me? I need a monitor to help me sort out some books."

I looked at her gratefully. We sat together in the classroom filled with the empty wooden seats and desks. I faced my beloved teacher and, glowing with conversation, ate my egg salad sandwich. At home we ate in silence. Our hands could not talk and eat at the same time. When I finished my meal, I crumpled the red milk carton into my paper bag with the crusts of bread I loathed, and dropped the mess into the waste basket under the teacher's desk.

"I am ready to help you now, Miss Chanin."

She opened the locked closet door in the back of the room. The books were piled in complete disarray. Some fell out of the closet onto the floor.

She instructed me. "We have to separate the books that are torn and that have pages missing from those that can still be used. You will put the books in good condition on the desks and the others you will leave on the floor."

I worked methodically, touching each book I held, wishing that it were mine. I found the book from which Miss

Chanin read us my favorite fairy tales. In it was the story of the singing maid Romaine, who enchanted the king of the realm with her lyrical voice. This kindly ruler invited Romaine to come to the palace to sing. Although she missed her poor old aunt and her thatched cottage, she was filled with joy. The raven-haired child sang at the palace every day. But after a month she grew listless because she wanted to be just like the king's fair daughter, Altheda. One day her fairy godmother appeared and granted her wish. Romaine lifted her voice in song, so great was her happiness. She couldn't sing. Horrible sounds came from her throat. After three days, Romaine summoned her fairy godmother with a bell and pleaded to be herself again.

The dainty fairy said, "The princess cannot sing, Romaine, and if you wish to be like her, you will not sing."

"Ruth!" Miss Chanin said sharply. "This is no time to read."

I looked up at her from the floor, still holding the torn book in my hand.

"I have to go to the office for a moment. You keep working until I get back."

When she walked out of the room, I took the tattered text to my desk and slid the book into my blue and green plaid canvas bag. I wanted that book to be mine. All afternoon I sat nervously in my seat, hoping that she would not discover the missing book.

At three o'clock I walked, white with fear, from the classroom. No one followed me home. I put the stolen book in my drawer and touched it lovingly. It had no front cover. It had no title page. That night, in bed, I took out the book and arranged the pages in order. I tied the loose pages together with white string. Each night for weeks I read the words on every page until I memorized the entire book.

I have the book, still, hidden in a drawer.

Part Two

THE WORLD OF
MY PARENTS

Three

SCHOOL FOR
BENNY AND
MARY

Thou shalt not curse the deaf,
nor put a stumbling block before the blind. . . .
—Leviticus 19:14

"You like school now?" my father asked.

"Yes, I love school now. You love school when you were a little boy?" my hands asked.

"No, I not like school, not learn enough. I not always deaf, my father put me in school, I was afraid."

"You not always deaf? I not know. How you become deaf?"

"I was sick, long time, better you ask Grandma, she tell you story. She tell you I was blind too."

I pressed my father to tell me what happened. He was

silent for a moment and then repeated with his hands, "Wait until Grandmother visits here, next time. She explain you all."

When my Grandma Lizzie came to our apartment I rushed to her, demanding an answer to my father's riddle. She sat me on the sofa and I touched her hands, expecting her to sign, but she couldn't. She never learned her son's language. I looked into her face and her deep brown eyes clouded.

She said two words: "Spinal meningitis."

"What is that?"

"Your daddy is the oldest of my seven children. When he was two years old, just a little boy, he was very, very sick. He had a fever that went up and up, he was so hot. The doctor came and no one believed he would live. But I prayed and prayed, I washed your father with cold water and his fever came down. I talked to him and then I saw he could not see me. He was blind. I called the doctor, I went to his house and knocked on his door, I told him to come and see my only little child. He came home with me and told me what I already knew, your Daddy Benny was blind and he would always be blind.

"I did not believe him. Every Friday night I lit the Sabbath candles near his small bed. He was still weak, his eyes did not move, they did not see the light. On the sixth week, the sixth Friday, I lighted the candles once more near his bed and he moved, his eyes moved; they followed the light. I moved my hand across his eyes and those black eyes followed my hand. I ran into the street crying, 'My baby can see, he can see.' The neighbors opened their windows; they thought I was crazy. I did not know that he was deaf."

My father watched my eyes as my grandmother recalled the days of my father's illness in 1905. He took my hand and asked, "You understand now, my story? How I am to be deaf?"

"Yes, I understand."

"I was not all deaf, but sound grow less and less. I not remember all, but I remember school, first day."

My father and I each entered school with a grave handicap. He had no language. I had some. I went to school with hope; he was deposited there like a dumb animal, taken from his mother's side by his father, with whom he barely communicated, and left in a strange place. There were no promises for him as there were for me.

As my father approached school age his hearing diminished until there was none, not even the memory of sound. He remembers turning his head in response to a loud sound but he was never able to distinguish conversation. Any speech that he had acquired as a two-year-old was gone.

On the first day of school in September 1909, my grandfather Morris Sidransky took his deaf son to a big, dark brown brick building on East 23rd Street in Manhattan. It was P.S. 47, a school for the "hard of hearing." My father did not know it was a school, did not recognize the principal's office. He remembers sitting in a hard straight-backed wooden chair, watching his father and the principal, Miss Kearns, speak. A teacher came into the room as they spoke and led my father, a small deaf boy, into a classroom full of children who stared directly at him.

He sat where the teacher put him and wailed in terror. "I cried all the day long. I am frightened and scream, 'Where is father?'"

"Did you know the words?" I asked my father.

"No, I was dumb. I only scream loud noise from my throat with tears until my father came to get me, to bring me to my home once again."

"Did you know any words when you were in school?"

"No, I only know signs my mother make for me, we have private language." He smiled as he signed this sentence hinting at our own private language.

My grandmother created a symbolic sign language to reach her son. She flapped her arms like a flying bird to describe a chicken; she tore an imaginary hunk of meat across her mouth to tell him they were having meat for dinner; she closed her eyes and rested her face on her hands to tell him it was time to sleep; she braided bread in the air to ask him if he wanted a slice. The signs were rudimentary, common to those who do not share a language. And there were not many of them. Language existed only between mother and child. His father rarely attempted to invent a sign to reach his son.

"What happened when your father came for you?" I asked.

"My father did not talk to me until the next day. He made the sign for writing in his hand and took me back to school. Little by little I learned to say the alphabet and read and write some. But I was stupid. The teachers hit us hard with a ruler if we try to talk with our hands."

The teachers' moving mouths mimicked the words of normal people. The young children who had great hearing loss looked at those mouths and generally understood but a few words. Lip reading is an art, and is not given to all the deaf. Lip talking can be taught and the deaf child can learn to mime the mouth to form a letter of the alphabet, a word or a sentence. But lip reading demands concentration and great leaps of the imagination to grasp not only the words but the meaning and intonation of words unheard by the deaf child. Staring hard, with all one's might, as a child does, does not create either conversation or human contact with all the color of language. Instead it creates frustration, and at times it induces rage that can last a lifetime.

It is natural for a person who cannot hear to tap another on the shoulder or catch his eye when he wants to share a word or a thought. It is natural for a deaf child to use his face and hands to express himself. Language without face is flat and toneless. The spontaneous use of the body, the hands and face was rigorously routed from my father's life by incessantly striking hands that would speak with a long wooden ruler.

For many of the children, school was a hateful, tedious place where they stared at the mouths of their teachers learning to name life uncertain of the verbal connection. There were many failures along the way: language was massively misunderstood. Children were denied the most humanizing aspect of life: they were unable to completely communicate with other humans.

In desperation they secretly created signs and spoke to one another in hidden corners. Some of the older students had access to deaf friends who went to other schools where sign language was permitted, and they learned their own language in spite of the harsh dictates of early-twentieth-century educators who insisted on oral speech in the classroom.

Slowly the process of learning language began for my father. First he was taught the letters of the alphabet. Enunciation was difficult.

My father told me, "I remember the first letter *p* and how I learned to say it. The teacher took a piece of paper and made me to blow air on it. She closed her lips together and open her mouth to make the paper move. When the paper moved away from her mouth I was happy. I said the letter *p*. I know it was right for teacher smile at me." He signed and spoke, directing his words at his teacher now long gone.

The letters of the alphabet were learned one at a time in this painstaking fashion. Deaf children learned to vocalize sound by touch. This was paradoxically permitted. An index finger was placed on the nose, pressing down on one nostril to teach the letter *n*. Mouths were opened and the curvature of the teacher's mouth was imitated to create vowel sounds.

Little hands were placed on young throats to feel the sound emanating from the voicebox.

The door to language was opened and then finally shut. How simple it would have been to teach the children the signed manual letters of the alphabet; to grant the sense of touch. The spoken letter and the printed letter would have been indelibly reinforced by adding one more learning tool, the tool of hands. This was denied.

My father was bitter about this.

He was nearly eighty when he signed, "My teacher taught me to name a ball, to name a flower, but she did not teach me what kind of flower was in her hand. I learned that later, much later. They gave to us children small wooden sticks of different colors, and we learned to say the names of colors. But all words were separate. Sentences did not bring the words together for thinking."

His anger continued.

"The teacher put my hand under running water to teach me to say *water,* to know what water is. When I was used to the teacher's mouth and her way, they changed my teacher. Every six months I had a new teacher. I was not stupid, but I was left back two times."

"Why?" I asked.

"I did not learn enough to say things to people. I did not always understand my teacher. I only learned to talk in the world."

My father looked at my questioning eyes sadly. He went on. "When I was twelve years old, I met deaf boys and girls from Fanwood School. In that school, both teachers and pupils use sign language. I learned to say *boat* and *train*. I learned to talk through them. It was late, I was a big boy to just learn to talk back and forth with people."

My father was a bright child, but his intelligence was locked away. Without normal speech at the age when children begin to play with syllables and sounds emanating from their vocal cords, tongues and lips, my father was separated from his own wit. His other senses did become more acute with time. But he never in his lifetime recovered from early verbal neglect compounded by a school system that tried to create an incomplete language system in imitation of normal human sound for deaf children.

My father saw my anger. He reached across the sofa to touch me. "Don't worry," he said, "I improve my mind every day. I learn new words and you Ruth are my teacher."

I hugged him.

He continued. "One thing I will tell you. My father, your grandfather was a stupid man. If he sense had, he would hire for me when I was five years old a private teacher to speak perfect English with my hands. It is too late now." He shrugged his own hands into what might have been.

I looked at him as he raised his hands for one more thought: "You and your brother both graduate from college. This is good for me. You are my dictionary to help me with English language."

When he said, "I try my life, all my life, to understand hearing people. It is hard." He banged the sign for the word *hard* on his tightly clenched left fist.

Language came into his life too late. He never read a book page by page, nor did my mother. The continuing flowing language, line after line, paragraph after paragraph, chapter after chapter is too difficult to sustain. Language denied in childhood is impossible to resurrect in adulthood.

School for my mother was a travesty. Her memories have little to do with language; they are locked in her attempts to leave school, to escape from the disciplined drudgery of "open mouth," "close mouth," "feel throat," "pick up tongue," a meaningless drone without the clarity of hands to reinforce or to enrich learning. So great was the stress on oral speech that educators did not educate, did not flatter the fluency that early speech provides for thinking, for inclusion in the world of the written word, in life's literature. It was in retrospect absurd, a waste of fine young minds denied their very own language with the slap of a yardstick by a well-trained oralist teacher. Most of the children at the Lexington School for the Deaf, in New York, were congenitally deaf. They would never, like my mother, experience sound.

My mother permanently abandoned language growth and used only the few hundred words she learned at school. New words were put aside. Her language was in her face. She face talked. She body talked. She hand talked. I discerned instantly what each pressure of her hand meant on my arm when she called me by touch. I knew whether she was displeased or happy or just wanted to ask me a question. But her curiosity about language was forever stilled.

"I hate school!" My mother flicked her hands in vehement memory.

We were at the kitchen table again, watching the October rain spatter the yellow-curtained window. A stew was bubbling on the gas stove. She stirred the stew and sat down again to her favorite pastime, storytelling. I sat without moving, wondering which story I would hear this time.

"I was mischievous little girl and hate to be away from home. Look at my words and I tell you all."

The stories always began with a loving description of her parents. My grandfather Abraham Bromberg and grandmother Fanny lived near the East River on Brooklyn's bulging shoreline. They crossed the Atlantic Ocean from London, England, in the summer of 1908 on the S.S. *Philadelphia*. On its return voyage to Europe, the *Philadelphia* sank. Their trek to America began three years earlier, when my grandfather fled conscription into the Russian army. "Jews," he said, "do not fight for the Russians against the Japanese." The young couple settled in London, where Nathan, my mother's oldest brother, and my mother were born. They lived in the East End ghetto that housed as many as ten people to a room.

My pious, handsome redheaded grandfather was a skilled cabinetmaker who turned his deft hands to the construction of wooden steamer trunks for those who had enough money to emigrate to America. With his master hands he built a synagogue in London's Whitechapel district. After three years he accumulated enough money to book passage to New York. My infant mother was swaddled in a large fruit basket. Three year old Nathan walked onto the ship's gangplank holding his mother's hand. They made the difficult voyage and at Ellis Island each family was inspected and sent on into the waiting city.

"Lucky for me I was so small a baby. I looked fine. If government man know I am deaf, I would be in Europe today. Not let me in U.S. of America." My mother giggled at the thought.

Her first three years are gone from memory. Perhaps there is no memory without language.

Yet her sharpest memory relates to the word *kindness.* Her mother and father were kind to their first deaf child. They had no experience with deafness; no one in either of their families was deaf. Instinctively they found a way to reach their daughter.

My mother was convinced that her own mother barely spoke English, that her mother carried only the Yiddish language of the *shtetl* with her to America. How then did they understand one another? As I watched my mother's stories over the years, I looked for a clue in her hands. Within the hands

I found the answer. They communicated by touch. It was incessant and tender; it was the same sense of warm touch that was given me as a child.

"My mother," said my own mother to me, "was a busy woman. She cut and sewed shirts for all the sons, she cooked everything herself; with seven children she had no time to care for herself. She never comb her hair in the morning, just roll it up and put pins in it on top of her head. So I take a comb to her kitchen and make her to sit down. I do this every day for her."

My mother stopped, stroked my hair, and said, "You have same hair as my mother—her hair was shiny black like silk threads. I comb her long hair and then I make a bun neatly on her head. She was beautiful woman with big, big blue eyes."

Years later, my mother's brother Sam told me that my grandmother spoke English very well. I never told my mother. For she believed in the mystery and magic of the unique language created by a mother who spoke no English and a child who did not speak at all.

My maternal grandparents had seven children who survived infancy, four sons and three daughters. They were Nathan, my mother Miriam, Sam, Anna, Jack, Louis, and Rose. Anna died of diphtheria when she was two years old. She could hear. My mother, Jack, and Rose were born deaf.

My mother's greatest refuge was within the walls of her own home, where she was understood and loved. When she was separated from her family, she began a lifelong career of hiding. After her first week's exposure at boarding school, she hid in closets and under beds on Monday mornings until her father found her crouched into a ball, trembling. He lifted her gently from her hiding place and took her to school. Even as an old woman, she was reluctant to face a new group of people, and would put one hand over her nose and with the other, say, "I will go hide myself in a corner."

In time she became accustomed to school, but did everything to avoid going, including playing hooky when she was a teenager.

Her education was absurd. *Absurd* is a word derived from Latin and it means "deaf, dulled." And the education was dull. Language and trades were taught. Where was the food for these souls, for these bright young minds?

In the years prior to World War I, the education my parents received was considered advanced. In retrospect, it seems primitive. Yet it was not as barbaric as the nineteenth-century practice of institutionalizing deaf children in insane asylums. Great strides have been made in educating soundless children but these came too late for Mary and Ben.

So their memories are memories of indignation, memories that sear the soul with frustration.

When my mother was six years old, a ringworm epidemic broke out at the school, and her scalp was infected. The little girls were lined up and taken to Bellevue Hospital. "There," my mother said, "we each waited our turn to see the doctor. I was afraid. When my turn came, I kick and scream, but the nurse pulled me into a room and strapped me to a table. Then I remember nothing."

She looked at me and softly stroked the back of her scalp. "They burned away the worms." She believed that there were worms burrowed beneath the skin.

Only once did she show me her gouged scalp. The scar reached from just below the crown of her head to the nape of her neck. It was the size of a woman's palm. The doctors permanently mutilated her. Her hair was long and she covered her baldness with her remaining hair, clutching it to her head with a round tortoiseshell comb.

"Now you understand why I hate school, they spoil my hair for life." There was resignation in her anger.

"I always want to run away from school. And if not run away, I like to play, be devil girl. One night when I was asleep with all the nine-year-old girls in my class, one classmate woke us all up. She tapped us on a shoulder, one by one. We woke up still sleepy."

The girls, still warm in their narrow beds, rubbed their eyes awake. Standing in front of them was their counselor, the woman in charge of their daily lives away from the classroom. Her sleeping quarters adjoined the girls' dormitory. She was furious with them. As they cowered before her rage, she demanded to know which one of them had entered her room and eaten all the cookies on her nightstand. No one would tell.

"All right," she said, "if you will not tell me the name of the thief, I will punish you all."

When the counselor was away, my mother had led the girls into her room to see what they could find. They had all had a hand in ripping up the cookie box, and in their exuberance had left the evidence of their crime, crumbs and torn wrappings, on her bed.

"I will give you all one more chance to tell me who stole the cookies!"

Silence.

"You are punished. All of you. You are not allowed to dress tomorrow or to go to class. You will remain in your beds for the entire day!"

In the morning the girls reveled in their freedom. They played and played in their pajamas, jumping from bed to bed, tossing pillows, laughing, signing their thoughts. "We talk all day with hands, no one slap us on hand, no one punish us. Best schoolday." My mother's hands opened wide as she signed these words.

I asked my mother when she was seventy-four years old if she remembered the first word she ever learned to vocalize.

"Yes," she signed with a deep smile. "My father came to school every Friday to take me home for a weekend. I was so happy to see him, I hate school and I hate to sleep in big dormitory with all the other deaf girls. He took me to the corner at Lexington Avenue and 67th Street, and we walked to 68th Street to take a subway, but we did not go to my home first. He took me to Coney Island to visit his cousin who had a big cafeteria restaurant on Surf Avenue. On trip, he signed to me and I signed to him with words that we made at home. I understand him, he understand me. Not many words, few."

"Momma," I said, "tell me about your first word, not a subway ride."

"Be patient," she admonished, "I must tell you all story."

"My father and his cousin were glad to see each other. They talked lots. I was little girl five years old and I want to go home. I was standing near all the forks and spoons made of tin in big baskets. I was not comfortable. I want to go home so I pull my father's pants leg. He did not turn around. I did not want to use my voice loudly. I know my voice is not normal. I pulled him again by his pants. He still did not turn around. I was angry."

She paused, savoring the moment, with her hands ajar on her lap.

"I put my hand in basket and took out a fork and a spoon. I went between my father and his cousin's legs. My father looked down to me. I held the fork up to his face and said with my mouth and with my voice the word *fork*. The two men stared at me. I held up the spoon in other hand and said word *spoon*. My father picked me up in his arms and cried. He carried me around the whole restaurant. He said many words that I could see but could not hear."

My mother stopped her tale and asked me if I remembered my first word. I did not.

She continued, "On the way home it was a long subway ride. My father Abraham touched many things and said many words with his mouth. I said them too. He was proud on me. Every weekend and every holiday I learn words at home. I learned words in school but home words were best. I learned table and chair, chicken, milk, bread, butter, sister, brother, mother, father, love, kiss, sad, happy, cry, laugh. My father was good teacher, he taught me to say better and I taught him to sign better."

She put her hands down and glistened with her language triumph.

I got up from my chair and my mother took my hand motioning me to sit down. "Wait, now I tell you your first word."

"You were eleven months old in a crib bed when you say your first words to me. You told me someone was ringing a doorbell!"

"Momma," I challenged, "babies don't say whole sentences."

"You did. Your left hand was closed and your thumb was out. You push the air with your thumb over and over again. You look at me strong, shake your head and push the air some more. Your smart eyes so big and black look at me. I went to the door and the laundry man was there. I forget to leave the door open for him on Monday morning like always."

She smiled at me as she often did and said, "You speak at eleven months."

I did not speak, I signed.

My own memory focused as Momma talked. I was nine years old, flushed with the pleasure of being back in school after the long summer. It was Friday and my classmates and I were dressed for the morning assembly, the girls in white starched middy blouses and red scarves, the boys in white shirts and ties. The entire community of children and teachers sang "The Star-Spangled Banner." We remained at stiff attention as the color guard moved down the auditorium to the stage, carrying the American flag. My attention was rapt. Each time I heard the chorus of children singing I shuddered with the musical power of sound.

When the assembly period was over we returned to our room for the tests we took every Friday morning. I was a quick student and remembered my work in sharp detail.

The classroom was quiet, as nine-year-old minds struggled with arithmetic problems. Some children squinted to remember, others curled the tips of their tongues into the corners of their mouths, some chewed the erasers off the tops of their pencils. I gazed directly ahead of me in a visionary state, seeing the answer. At times, I signed to myself to reinforce my memory.

I heard my teacher's voice demand, "Ruth Sidransky!"

I focused my vision and saw her nostrils quiver.

"Yes," I answered, frightened.

"Come up here and bring your paper with you!"

I did as I was told. I frowned as I lay my paper on her desk.

She took a thick red pencil and slashed my work with a cross, wrote a large zero across the top and defaced my good work with another obscenity as she scrawled the word CHEATING in large letters across the entire page.

I protested and she stopped me. "I saw you signaling someone with your hands. I don't wish to hear another word. You are a cheat. Sit down!"

My eyes welled with tears and I sat down, humiliated, at my desk. All the others were writing; I had no work to do.

I dropped my head, but I didn't cry at the mockery. The morning passed into eternity, and I decided to tell my teacher about my parents, something I was reluctant to do. I stiffened at eyes of pity.

The lunch bell rang. As we left the room, I paused at the desk and said with great courtesy, "Miss Luloff, may I speak to you?"

She was indignant. "So you have come to apologize."

"No," I said quietly, "I've come to tell you that my parents are deaf, that we speak sign language at home, that I think with my hands sometimes. And I did not cheat."

I did not wait for her answer. I left with all the dignity my young body could gather into itself.

As the years passed, my mother, now in the seventh grade, found ways to play hooky from school. Her infatuation with the movies and Rudolph Valentino was her undoing. The exaggerated emotive quality of the silent screen flooded her imagination. She related to the broad pantomime. The dialogue that flashed on the screen in simple sentences made the story line as clear to her as to the rest of the audience.

She did not need me to sit beside her in the movies on Saturday afternoons as I did throughout my girlhood, interpreting the role of each character. When she went to the movies without me, she often asked me to see the movie and explain it to her. At times she told me the plot as she understood it, and when I saw the movie, her fantasy about the screen images bore no relation to the script. Frustrated when I told her the correct story line, she often signed, "I like my story better."

She was an excellent film critic. If a film wasn't cinematic, if it had no motion, she said to me in warning, "This is not good movie. It belongs to a theater where actress and actor talk to each other on a stage, not on moving screen."

In 1921, when she was thirteen, a new Valentino film opened in her neighborhood. By this time she was able to take the subway to school by herself. On Monday mornings she took her younger deaf brother, Jack, with her to school. But on this day she decided to play hooky and included Jack in her plans. She did not dare ask her mother for the nickel that was the price of admission at the local movie house.

Instead, she marched to the local butcher at the corner and asked for a job. There was a sign in the window that read, HELP WANTED, EXPERIENCED CHICKEN PLUCKER. My mother entered the kosher shop with purpose. The counter was laden with freshly killed chickens, chickens with brown feathers, with black feathers, with speckled white feathers. Each chicken's throat had been slit and dried blood caked the feathers. The chicken heads lay limp with half-open eyes. The stench was strong. The floor was covered with sprinkled clumps of sawdust.

My mother sucked in her breath and squeezed her nostrils to protect her senses from the overpowering smells.

The bearded butcher in his blood-soaked apron asked, "Do you know how to pluck a chicken?"

"Yes, yes, I show you. I pull feathers. Do a good job."

He led her to a room in the back of the store, pointed to a three-legged stool surrounded by more slaughtered chickens, picked up one and threw it at her. She caught it by the feet. She loathed the feeling of the nails on her hands. For that entire morning she held the chickens by the breastbone and pulled the feathers from their bodies as fast as her hands would fly. She wanted to be on time for the matinee. Jack played among the fallen feathers as he waited for her to finish.

She grinned at me and said, "I did bum job. I make so many big holes in the chicken skin. With my fingers and spit from my mouth, I pinch holes together."

Her skill at mending chicken skin did not hold, and the butcher was angry at her inept plucking. She insisted on payment and he reluctantly gave her five cents for the morning's work, telling her never to return.

She fled with the nickel clenched in her fist, plunked it down at the movie theater and sat through three performances of Rudolph Valentino's love scenes.

"I sat in movies with Jack and scratch and scratch myself all afternoon. My new purple sweater that my mother just knit for me was full of chicken feathers. My hands smell bad. Never mind it was a wonderful day."

The next day her teacher requested a note for her absence. She had none and would provide none.

"So," said her teacher, "you played hooky again. You will be punished this time. You may not go to recess outside after lunch for the rest of the school year. You will go to the sewing room and sew."

This story pleased my mother. "I did not mind sewing. I sew good. And it was worth it."

In 1922, my mother had another reason to work. Her youngest brother, Louis, had diphtheria and her home was quarantined. Except for the doctor who came daily to tend Louis, there was neither entry nor exit. My mother was pleased that she at last had a bona fide excuse to stay home from school. But her pleasure was diminished by my grandmother's worry over her three-year-old son's capacity to survive the disease. She worried too about the coming doctor bills. As the weeks passed my mother grew restless, disregarded the large quarantine notice clumsily tacked to the front door, and sneaked out to find a job.

She wandered downtown Brooklyn until she saw the Brooklyn Eagle Electric plant. In she marched to answer the large sign that read, GIRLS WANTED. GOOD PAY.

She told me, "I was tall for my age, very skinny and tall. I was smart, too. I asked the secretary lady for a job that was on the door. The boss came to see me. I lied to him and wrote on paper, 'I am sixteen years old deaf girl.' I was fourteen, but I fool him. He gave to me a job."

She worked every day from eight to five soldering light bulb filaments, with the tips of her fingers putting the final touch to each light bulb she handled. At the end of each week she received nine dollars in her pay envelope, which she handed to her mother.

Initially, my grandmother was angry that my mother had broken the quarantine, but she was relieved to have the money to pay the doctor. She exacted a promise from my mother. My mother solemnly agreed to return to school once the quarantine was lifted.

When it was lifted and Louis was well, my mother ostensibly left for school each morning. Instead, she went to the factory and joined the assembly line of working women. A truant officer arrived at my grandmother's home and wanted to know why Mary Bromberg was still away from school. My grandmother was nonplussed.

That evening my mother returned to face her scowling mother.

"Where do you go every day?" she demanded.

My mother confessed her truancy and affirmed that she would not go back to school. "I not learn anything important there."

My grandmother told her stubborn young daughter,

"The truant officer says we must pay twenty-five-dollar fine if you do not return to school."

My mother was adamant. "I not go back there again. I work help support family and pay bills."

She went to her bed and withdrew three pay envelopes from under her mattress and handed them to her mother saying, "Pay fine!" Each week thereafter she gave her earnings intact to my grandmother. And she never returned to school.

When I asked my mother if she was sorry she had left school in the eighth grade, she said as my father did, "No, not sorry. I learn more in the outside world, away from school. It was too strict. Better to be free."

Four

A DEAF WORLD

The hearing ear, and the seeing eye,
The Lord hath made even both of them.
                                    —*Proverbs 20:12*

And the Lord said to him, "Who gives man speech?
Who makes him dumb or deaf, seeing or blind?
Is it not I, the Lord?"
                                    —*Exodus 4:11*

*M*y mother and father knew almost everyone in the deaf community. Their exclusive society was created in the schools they hated, in the schools that barely educated them. The Deaf, as they called themselves, entered deeply into the lives of one another. They formed a protected world, shutting out all those who could hear in their quest for human connection. They accepted neither parents nor children, siblings nor grandparents into their silence. The knowing look that passed between deaf people was akin to the intimate sexual glance shared by lovers. It was a look that excluded the hearing person.

I saw them describe each other. "Is he a Deaf?" The answer to the question determined the newcomer's role in their closed society. My father could be cruel; when he did not like a deaf person, he referred to him as a "shut ear, no-hear stupid." His signs were vigorous and made me shudder. I saw them quarrel with arms and faces flaring in anger. I saw them play with each other as children do, without inhibition, touching each other's shoulders to express their fun. I saw them tell stories of their frequent misunderstandings with the local merchants who cheated them. I saw their faces when they told each other how difficult it was to know their hearing children. I saw the expression of ultimate horror when one of them gave birth to a deaf child.

I saw them bonded, sealed together in lifetime friendships. Their bonding stronger than family ties, the bonding of silence.

When my father clasped his hands together and said, "Louis K. my best school chum!", when he almost touched the floor with his open palm, raising it reverently to eyebrow level, describing the passage from childhood to adulthood, and said, "We close pals from little boys to grown men," I felt the power of deaf connection, of deaf family.

Louis Kazansky and my father quit the 23rd Street school after the fifth grade and together they roamed New York's Lower East Side, exploring the narrow streets where my father was born. Water Street, Cherry Street, and South Street were lined with wooden houses. There was a stable behind my father's house for the horses and buggies that still clomped through Manhattan.

My father said, "This just before World War I. Man who own stable gave to us each a penny to shovel horseshit from the yard. It was good times."

His eyes smiled in memory. "In summer Louis K. and me, we went to the East River and swim nude with hearing boys.

The East River before was green, clear water. Now it is black filthy."

I laughed, waiting for him to tell me his East River story once again.

"I was little boy, maybe eleven, twelve years old. We went with large group of young boys, some Christians, some Jews. At the river, we took off all clothes and went swimming and diving into the big river. Sometimes we catch rat. Such fun time for all boys."

He paused for dramatic effect, squinted his eyes and continued. "Some Christian boys left sooner than me and stole all my clothes, shoes, socks, pants, underwear and a shirt. I was only a little boy, but Louis K. who is small did not have clothes to fit me. We decide. He will walk first and I will walk behind him following very close. We begin to walk a long way home. After one block policeman arrest me. I try to explain to him about bad boys who steal my clothes. Of course, he did not understand my voice. So I take this big cop by the hand and lead him to my home and my mother. I know she will explain it all to him."

"What did she tell him, Daddy?"

"She told him that I am deaf and dumb boy and that she will watch me next time."

This story angered Louis K. And through the years, each time my father told this tale Louis finished it with the same sentence, his fingers taut with fury: "Stupid hearing people, not understand deaf ways."

I understood the "deaf ways." I understood their speech patterns. I learned never to look away from a deaf person's attempt at oral speech. I needed both their hands and eyes to understand the words of their lips, to understand the confusing rhythms of their oral language.

Each deaf friend said my name with a different sound. And yet I knew the sound of my name, and whose voice was calling me. When Louis K. shouted "Ruth," I turned to him immediately. His face was sharp with surprise each time I responded accurately to his cry. I opened my eyes wide to communicate that I had heard him. I raised my head, put out my hands and signed, "Yes, I hear you call my name."

"Did I say any other word?"

"No," I reassured him, "only my name."

Louis's sign was rapid. "Turn around, turn your face away, and tell me what I say in voice."

I always played this game of "pretend." Without changing my expression I pretended that his thick raucous voice sounded normal. I had no problem catching the sound flawlessly if the sentence was short. If there were too many sentences the sound blurred and became unintelligible even to my ears. Nonetheless, I became skillful at repeating Louis's words. He forgave my six-year-old hands for the words I missed. He was delighted to speak and have someone understand him.

My reward was a quick heave up on his sturdy five-foot frame and a piggyback ride around the living room. He jiggled me up and down until I could no longer bear the continual laughing and bouncing. I poked him again and again, signaling, begging that I was ready to be put down. Most times he ignored me. He loved parading me about on his shoulders. I pummeled him with one clenched fist, grabbed his sandy wiry hair with my other hand and banged away at him. I screamed. I yelled louder and louder, thinking my yells would magically restore sound to Louis. It never did.

And so one day I stopped yelling; in anger, in pleasure. I, too, became still.

When Louis sensed my quiet frustration, he dropped me to the floor. Instantly he semi-squatted and rocked on his ankles like a bantam cock inviting me to aggression. I stood there with my arms limp at my sides. He waved his curled fists at my face and teased me with his amber eyes. He stuck his head at me like a fighting fowl, daring me to catch him and bite him. I chased him furiously around the room until he let me grab him and bite away my tension. His soft palm tasted of nicotine.

When I spent my anger, he cradled me in his arms and signed compassionately, "Better?"

I hugged him. "Yes, better."

My mother said he was a bum; he had no job. He sponged meals from his friends. He was an outrageous human flirt, grinning his eyes at everyone he touched.

My father was loyal. "He is not a bum!" he protested to my mother.

"Look at his clothes, all worn out, ready to split."

His clothes were frayed. His white shirt was yellowed with age. The points of his collar stood up. His one tie was rumpled. He wore it around his neck like a treasured winter scarf. And he did reek of tobacco.

"Don't worry Ben," my mother assured my father, "I cook dinner for him. Children love him. I love him too."

Louis told my mother that she was the best cook in the world. His flattery earned him at least two hot kosher dinners at our home every week. I know now that Louis went from friend to friend, praising the kitchen skills of each wife. The women responded with gratitude and an excellent meal; Louis never went hungry.

When I was older, I asked my father if Louis ever had a job.

"You know, we were both prize fighters."

They sparred together as young men, at the Monroe Street Gymnasium. In 1921 they met regularly to fight, to bathe and to swim. The gymnasium served as a public bathhouse for the neighborhood men. The women went to another bathhouse, the *mikvah,* to be steamed and scrubbed before the Friday night Sabbath dinner.

"The stink of men sweat was strong. We swim after and be clean." My father cleared an arc around himself in the air, swimming the breast stroke, signifying not only the sign for swimming but his memory of youthful pleasure.

I persisted. "Tell me about Louis."

"Well," he began again, "he was first class amateur boxer. Not like me—I never fight in the ring."

"Didn't he learn a trade to support himself like you?"

"He worked at newspaper, *Herald Tribune.*"

I assumed that, like so many of the deaf, whom noise did not disturb, Louis was a trained linotypist, part of the cadre of men who put New York's daily newspapers to bed every night. The roaring clack of hot metal slugs falling into machines fell on deaf ears. Louis, however, was not a trained pressman. He was hired by the *Tribune* along with the others because he was deaf. He worked for less than two years as a copy boy.

He made a practice of picking pockets. As the men worked he went to the long row of hooks on which their coats and jackets hung, and slipped his deft fingers into pockets, filching pennies and gum, dollar bills—a pocket watch if he was lucky. When he was caught by his hearing foreman, Louis was dismissed at once, given severance pay of five hundred and thirty-five dollars and never worked a day again for a wage in his life.

"How does he eat?" I asked my father. I knew the Depression deprived us of second helpings at dinner. I wanted to know how Louis ate when he was not with us.

"He eats here, with us, with friends, with family. We are friends—family friends."

"He does not eat here every night," I insisted.

My father was ashamed to tell me that Louis was a peddler. He sold the watches he earned as an amateur boxer in the street to any passerby he could collar. When I was young I did not understand my father's shame. But the first time I saw a deaf peddler in the street with a sign hanging from his neck that read, "I am deaf. Please buy a pencil," I went up to him in rage, in full view of anyone who could read my screeching hands in the midst of a winter Lexington Avenue noonday crowd and signed, "How dare you? Have you no shame? You have a body and a mind. Go work. Do not beg. You are disgusting!" I was then a freshman at Hunter College.

So my beloved Louis was a beggar. I never did see him beg on the street.

Deaf hands were wonderful. They could touch, and the touch was soft, real. When my mother's closest friends touched me, whether it was Sadie or Rose, they touched me in the same way. An open hand smoothed my dark hair and said wordlessly, "I know who you are. You are one of us, you are not one of us." It was comforting to be known, disquieting to be unknown, to be locked in paradox.

They were kind people. When the poverty of the Depression permitted kindness with money or food they were generous to one another.

Rose Merlis was the only deaf woman I knew who was fatter than my mother. She was married to a man called Solomon who looked like my father, dark and mustached, but had none of his happy humor. They had a brood of children who were all plump and beautiful. They were round during the Great Depression while my brother, father, and I were thin. Their son Morris and I played together by the hour. He was my favorite of all the hearing children of the deaf.

Rose's father was a kosher butcher. That family had meat every night. From time to time Rose would bring meat and hand it to my mother.

Each time the conversation was identical. Rose said, "Mary, it's for the children."

And my mother would say to Rose, "Thank you for the

children," as she laid the package on top of the slab of ice in the wooden icebox.

When I was five years old I needed a new winter coat. I had outgrown the long woolen coat my mother knitted. My mother took me down to Division Street on the Lower East Side, to the shops laden with clothing and warm coats for children. I saw a blazing red coat with a small leopard-skin collar. I wanted it more than I had ever wanted anything. Later, I learned to stamp out my own needs, to stop wanting. This time, I was able to clutch to my childhood wish and I cried for the unattainable coat.

My mother looked at me sadly when I told her the English military red coat was nine dollars. Her hands moved slowly, saying, "Too much money, I cannot afford." I wept and wept. On the BMT subway trip home back to Brooklyn, she was gentle with my tears and signed openly, "I am sorry, but we are poor." She never signed in the subway—she hated the staring strangers—but she broke her rule to comfort me.

Rose Merlis visited us that cold winter afternoon. She brought Morris to play with me but I was too sad to play with Morris, whom I adored. We were kin. We understood how different our mothers were. But not even Morris could lift my spirits.

When they left in the first moments of nightfall my mother grabbed me by the shoulders, shouting with her hands, "I have wonderful surprise for you!"

I was too morose to share my mother's joy.

"Listen to me," she said, "I have good news." I heard her spoken words and knew that she wanted me to look at her hands.

Indifferently, I lifted my head and saw her words. "My fat friend Rose gave me ten dollars for your new coat. Tomorrow we buy you coat and hat to match with fur."

In our family album there is a rare photograph of me standing proudly with my plump two-year-old brother dressed in my magnificent coat and a broad smile. Most of the pictures of my childhood were without a smile; my eyes were sad, my mouth sullen, shut tight. But this picture stands alone illustrating my rapture.

My mother's dearest friend was Sadie, Sadie with the beautiful hands, Sadie who never washed a dish without wearing protective rubber gloves. Her hands were slim, her fingers long and her fingernails coated with fire red polish. In all the years I knew Sadie I never saw a single chipped fingernail. I once said to her, when I was fifteen, "Sadie, how do you keep your hands so beautiful?"

"My hands are my language, they must be perfect."

It went beyond that. It went with her powdered vanity, her tightly curled chestnut hair, her red red lipstick and her profound silence.

I never heard Sadie's voice say an accurate word. I knew her sound for my name, but I didn't know her other sounds. Some deaf people feel free to challenge their voiceboxes to sound they will never hear, but those who see the continual frown on the faces of the hearing people who attempt conversation and comprehension finally give up in frustration. They know that they, who cannot hear, cannot imitate the sounds they are taught, no matter how they struggle with consonants and vowels, with breath and vocal pressure. They give up and resort to pencil and paper notes with the hearing and take final refuge in their own speech, the speech of their hands.

Sadie kept her language locked in her impeccably manicured fingers. She wore no rings, save a thick gold wedding band, to distract the eye from the beauty of her handed speech. Her hands danced as she spoke. They could move with trained delicacy or with frantic passion. At times I watched her without listening. She scolded when she caught me and signed exquisitely, "Watch what I say, listen to me, forget hands, understand my meaning."

"Sorry," I signed back, "but your hands are lovely."

And she would smile and sign, "I am your true aunt."

Sadie and my mother met when they were five, and remained friends all their lives. It was Sadie who introduced my mother to my father at a party in Brooklyn, when my mother was fifteen and my father was twenty.

My mother and Sadie looked at each other, preparing to tell me once again the story of that romantic evening. I sat back to listen and watch these women become girls for a moment, moving their chipped teacups, waiting for each other to fill me with their youth and begin the afternoon's entertainment.

My mother's family left New York and moved to a farm in New Jersey when she was seven years old. When their farmhouse burned down and they could no longer live at the farm that my grandfather had renovated into a makeshift home, they moved back to Brooklyn. It was then that my mother, almost fifteen years old, remembered her friend Sadie. Clutching Sadie's address in her hand, she went to search for her alone. She wandered the streets of Sadie's neighborhood, not quite sure where she was until she saw a friendly young blond man sitting on a stoop.

She asked in the best oral speech she could manage, "Do you know Sadie Weisbart?"

He recognized the deaf voice at once. He signed painstakingly, spelling out each word, "Sadie is my sister!"

"I want to see Sadie now, take me."

"Sadie is not at home." He took out a pad and a pencil and wrote, "Give me your address and I will bring Sadie to you tonight after supper."

My mother scribbled her South Third Street address on the pad. That evening the fifteen-year-old girls were reunited after years of physical separation. Their only connection had been the penny postcards they exchanged weekly. The limited written language of the young deaf girls expressed simple words and could not convey the eye-to-eye nuance of teenage conversation.

Their first meeting was tinged with strangeness. They had not seen each other for eight years and did not recognize each other's gangly adolescent bodies. That feeling was soon dispelled and Sadie invited my mother to a deaf girlfriend's sixteenth birthday party. The party was set for November 28, 1923. When Sadie left, my mother rushed into the bedroom to tell her father the wondrous news. She was going to a party. She asked for a new dress and wanted an evening gown. My grandfather took her to Delancey Street and in one of the shops, my mother selected her first ball gown. It was black chiffon. The hem was flounced and trimmed in gold. The scooped neckline had a small gold rose sewn at the right shoulder.

On the appointed day, the youngest of her hearing brothers, Louis, took her on the streetcar over the Williamsburg Bridge to Manhattan. He was able to ask for the directions to Clinton Street and Avenue D. There they found the apartment house.

My mother told me, "I feel foolish. I think it was a party in a ballroom. It was an apartment. And I was the only girl in a long gown. We had to walk up five flights to the top floor."

"Didn't you have a good time?" I asked.

"Yes, but everyone talked, talked, talked with their mouths, no signing."

This was a party for the girls and boys who went to the 23rd Street school in Manhattan. Most of the students were hearing impaired rather than profoundly deaf and were more adept at oral speech. Some were born with residual hearing, others had become post-lingually deaf as a result of childhood illness. Meningitis, scarlet fever, and the measles had eradicated sound from some of these young people. If they became deaf after their speech was established they were able to maintain their power to speak orally with continued practice.

"You know," my mother said to me, "that is when Sadie

brought Louis K. to me. He signed to me, his signs were not very good, but he tried hard. When I explained to him where I lived, he marched to his friend Ben and brought him to me, because we were neighbors in Brooklyn."

That night, Mary and Ben returned home together on the trolley car. My father purchased the tickets, "two fares for five cents."

My father was a constant visitor at my mother's house. When my grandmother Lizzie, my father's mother, was convinced that my blond, blue-eyed mother was Jewish, she approved the romance. But when she discovered that my mother had a deaf brother and a deaf sister she tried to stop the young couple. She did not succeed.

Coincidentally, as my mother approached her eighteenth birthday, both her mother and my father's mother wanted to know on the same day if they were contemplating marriage.

My father asked his mother, "Shall I buy Mary an engagement ring?"

"Yes," she said, "do it today."

That evening, my father gave my mother a small diamond ring surrounded by tiny blue sapphires. The engagement party was like a wedding, my mother said. My grandmother Fanny, who was a caterer, cooked marvelous food for the party. The rabbi came and tied a knot in a white linen handkerchief that the young lovers held to seal their troth.

Fanny did not live to see them married. But marry they did on May 19, 1927.

Sadie and my mother looked at me triumphantly when they finished their story. It was one of the few tales they could tell that had a happy ending.

Sadie's marriage to Ruben Tunik did not endure. I remember Ruben as a handsome blond man. He posed with me in my happiness photograph. I have, forever, a picture of him holding me in the red coat that Rose Merlis bought me. After that picture was taken, he handed me a Baby Ruth. Every Saturday he brought me a chocolate bar and one for my brother Freddie. His own poverty did not stop him.

By 1935 he had lost his job. His factory, which made leather handbags, closed down. Sadie nagged him to find work, to buy her pretty things, but Ruben was unable to do so. Sadie took her nimble fingers to an exclusive milliner and made custom hats with a skill so fine that not a stitch could be seen. She continued to nag Ruben to seek employment. In desperation, he turned inside himself and invented a window seat with pulleys so that workmen could wash windows on high buildings with safety.

He took his invention to Washington, D.C., and was able to get a patent for his creative work. Back in New York, he proudly went from office building to office building, attempting to induce someone to buy his window seat. He went to manufacturers who might produce his work; he was not understood and no one bought his invention.

Saddened by his failure, he became depressed and wandered off alone looking for any kind of a job. Then he simply wandered. Months passed and he grew more silent. Early one evening Sadie came to our apartment looking for Ruben. She told my mother that she had prepared dinner after she arrived home from the hat shop and had waited for Ruben.

"You know Mary," she signed to my mother, "deaf are never late."

She was frantic when she left. She had hoped to find Ruben with us.

Hours later, Sadie's neighbor came to get my parents.

My mother signed to me slowly and deliberately. "You be a good girl, watch baby brother Fred, watch the clock and when it is ten-thirty, I will be home. Be brave, you now six years old, you are big girl."

Her hands terrified me. "What happened to Ruben?" I asked.

"Not now, I will tell you later."

When my mother entered Sadie's apartment, Sadie signed, "Mary, I lost my husband. I am widow."

Ruben, crazed by repeated rejection, had walked up to the tar roof of the faded Bronx tenement where he and Sadie lived and jumped off the ledge. Although the police searched for him, they did not find him for hours. He had fallen into the cellar stairwell and his crumpled body was hidden by the concrete wall surrounding the steps to the basement. At his side was an unused gun and in his breast pocket there was a smashed picture frame that sliced his mother's picture in two.

My father came home alone before the hands of the clock reached ten-thirty.

I asked him anxiously, "Where's Momma?"

"She stays with friend Sadie. She comes home later. Now you go sleep, you are good big girl."

I wanted to know what was wrong. No one would tell me. In the morning I asked my mother with my hands, "Momma, why did you come home so late? I saw the time when I heard the door open. It was three o'clock in the morning."

She was quite still when she signed, "Ruben die. I stay with Sadie. I go to funeral and you must stay with your grandfather for all the day. No school tomorrow."

I do not know why but Ruben's coffin was open, and when my mother told me this years later, I wept.

"Ruben's face was all broken from fall to earth, but he was still so handsome, sleeping for always. He was twenty-nine years old." My mother's hands fell slowly to her lap when she finished her eulogy for Ruben.

After a month, Sadie resumed her regular Saturday visits and with her meager milliner's wages continued to bring chocolate bars, one for me and one for my brother. She no longer brought me a Baby Ruth. That was Ruben's gift for me, our little delightful play. She married again and was widowed again.

My mother said often, "Poor Sadie, never had children, never had luck." She did learn to smile again and finally one day I heard her laugh out loud at Louis K.'s antics in our apartment.

No one knew where Louis K. lived—a rooming house somewhere in Brooklyn, a single bed, a single room was probably his home. Was he married? Did he have a wife? The rumor was that he was married to a deaf Cree Indian woman who was a prostitute. I think I saw her once. I remember long, uncombed blue-black hair and the smell of alcohol.

Louis was so delighted with Sadie's first laughter that he repeated his drama and as I entered the room unheard, I watched his delivery. He pulled himself up to his full small height, unfolded his arms and mimed his woman.

"You see," he began, with princely gesture, "my woman, little woman, make lots of money. She has something different that men want." With that he squatted and drew an imaginary line up his open inner left thigh from his knee to his groin.

"You know what this is?" He paused for effect.

"This is a big green snake tattoo on my wife's leg with open mouth and fangs that stop just before pussy-cunt for dinner. That's how we make money."

Everyone howled but me, I was too young to understand.

Louis K. felt my presence. He turned to me and seeing bewilderment on my face did his inimitable farewell speech. On pointed toes he pirouetted slowly around everyone, but his signs accompanied in singing voice were for me alone. He sang, as he always did when he left us, "I will see you tomorrow." It took him a full minute to sing-sign the words. He sounded like a hound dog, baying and crooning his love song for us, full of hope for the morrow.

Louis K. is dead now. He died in a small room squalid with age. His deaf cronies missed his daily appearance at the corner newsstand. One became suspicious and went to his room. Afraid to open the door alone, he asked the landlady to call the police. They came and broke down the door.

Louis lay in days of unrecognized death. The room was neat. The only disarray was the clothes that the police knocked off the back of the door when his jacket and cap fell to the floor. His shoes were neatly tucked under his bed. There were no possessions save his clothes, no books, no papers. The only thing of value in the room was Louis and he was gone from life.

The police searched for an address book, someone to call, a next of kin. They did not find anything until the door was lifted back to its frame. Louis had known he was dying. On the door, on a large piece of cardboard, he had written, "If you find me dead, please call my brother and sister." Their names and addresses were clearly printed. "Tell my friends to come to my funeral. I want to say good-bye to them."

Word travels quickly in the deaf community. The next morning, fifteen people gathered in the chapel to say their final good-byes to Louis. No one knew about Louis's brother and sister, or, if they had known, they had long forgotten their existence. His brother was a dentist or a physician. My father, in the telling, was confused about the exact detail, but he was certain that his name was Dr. Kazansky and that he was a "big rich man." He frowned, shaking his head, that Louis had lived in such poverty.

My father said, "We pray quietly. Louis my best chum was in a coffin box. Poor Louis, he is always alone. I pray to God that his soul have a good rest."

After the brief service, which no one bothered to interpret for the deaf friends who were there, his coffin was put into a hearse. His brother and sister got into a black limousine behind the hearse and the two cars sped off quickly. My father and his friends remained under the funeral parlor's dark green canopy, with their mouths agape. No one told them where Louis was to be buried. No one thought to provide a car for these subway people, to take them to the cemetery.

My father turned to me in anger and said in oral words, "Son-of-a-bitch hearing people. Never caring for the deaf."

My throat constricted and I put my arms around my father. He flung me from his body in rage.

When he quieted, he signed, "Not angry with you, Ruth, just angry with Louis's brother and sister. They have no feeling for us, no feeling for Louis. We can never visit his grave and see his stone. They hear, we not hear, but we not dumb."

When I was a child, when I was seven and eight, nine and ten years old, I often pretended that I was someone else. I didn't pick pockets, steal trinkets and baubles to please the eye as Louis did. I stole parts of hearing mannerisms, hoping in some way that I could be another.

While I was still a child the deaf accepted me. Sometimes fleetingly, they let me step into the circle of cherished childhood. In rare moments they treated me as one of their own, a "deaf." Those were the good times for me: I belonged.

I stepped between the deaf and the hearing worlds never quite fitting into either, never knowing who I was. I was me when I spoke in my native tongue, the tongue of hands. I was comfortably me among the deaf. The sounds of their voices were natural to me. The sound of natural speech was strange. I sat for hours at the radio entranced by the discovery of how a word I knew in "deaf" sound *really* sounded. I was me when I learned to speak normally but I remained apart.

I felt safer among the deaf. And the other children—the

hearing children of the deaf—were another society. There was red-headed Flo, Jack and Anna Bromberg's daughter, my first cousin; Bea and Arthur Rosenberg, children of Frieda and Joe, my parents' friends. We signed shyly to one another, feigning absolute deafness, and broke into gales of laughter at our secret. We could hear.

We were the children of the deaf.

And when we listened to our parents sign speak we knew that we could not fail them. All of us were laden. All of us were bright, some brilliant, and we knew that we had to succeed. Success did not come in laborers' clothing or the lunch pails filled with food to be eaten at the job site. Our mothers, when they worked, were seamstresses, pedaling dresses on old Singer sewing machines in dusty factories; our fathers worked at semiskilled jobs.

We, the children, were the prosperous promise of tomorrow. We were all told, at one time or another, by one parent or another, "If I hearing person like you, I smarter than you." There it was, the anger at deafness. We had to be two people: a little deaf, and a little hearing.

There were those of us who were sucked into a silence we carried with us always. There were those of us defiantly proud of our parents yet secretly ashamed of their garish sounds. There were those of us who, as soon as we were able, left home and abandoned our parents to grow old alone in withering silence. There were those of us who ignored our deaf parents, never quite learning to sign well enough to tell them what was in our hearts and minds. There were those of us who deliberately turned our heads when our parents raised their arms and hands to speak to us. And there were those of us who loved our parents with passion. We were the ones who buried the silence within. We abandoned our dreams and took care of our deaf mothers and fathers. They were our children, and we were their parents. We, the children, were invisible.

* * *

On winter Sundays we sat on my mother's wine-colored linoleum floor, peeling tangerines, listening to the radio, reveling in the sound of the shared airwaves. My mother boiled spaghetti, poured cans of Del Monte tomato sauce on the overcooked pasta, dropped in chunks of sweet butter, and we children ate on the floor, enchanted by the magic of the weekly radio program "Let's Pretend." We entered fairy kingdoms and lived in fantasy for an hour.

And on summer Sundays, our families would gather, when there was enough money for subway fare, on the green grassy picnic grounds in Pelham Park. We traveled the labyrinth tunnels of the city to reach the far corner of the Bronx where we played our Sundays away and learned the meaning of "deaf" dignity.

When I was eight years old, I did not understand the poverty that made elegant Joe Rosenberg sit at the feet of unknown men at the 42nd Street subway corner shining their shoes. I did not understand the slow courage it took for him to move on into the crowd, without words, when the police chased him from the corner that fed his family.

Once at a summer picnic, he showed us how he meandered aimlessly down the street toward Bryant Park, to the massive New York City public library, with his wooden shoeshine shop tucked under his right arm, quietly defying the police. He was a small man with a bulbous nose, one good eye and one bright blue glass eye, and no voice. He never uttered a sound, not even a sound I could attempt to understand. His large glass eye confused me when he signed. I never quite knew where he was looking.

His dark wife, Frieda, was smaller than he and she spoke vocally in clear, grammatically correct sentences. She became deaf after a childhood illness, long after her speech patterns were well established. It took me but a moment to adjust to her slightly atonal speech. But she was totally deaf and never knew that her husband had no capacity to vocalize, nor did he ever know the amazing power of her voice. He was not mute; he would not speak. He was reluctant to expose his voice, this man-shoeshine boy.

Their children were our playmates, our cousins in sound. Arthur was a high-strung boy my own age, who often bit me. His teeth marks clenched my inner arm. He had no Louis K. He was an unruly skinny boy whose eyes softened at the warm sound of the clarinet we heard on my radio. His family could not afford a radio and a visit to our Bronx apartment was a major event.

This ill-clad child had a gorgeous smile that turned down with shame every time his father's shoeshine business was mentioned. His father, Joe, I am sure, even if he had been a hearing man, would have been a quiet man, proud of his small family. And he was especially proud that he did not have to seek financial relief from a government agency clerk who would not understand him. It was easier to shine shoes.

Sometimes, at our picnics, he would take out his strong-smelling shoe polishes, his oxblood cream paste, the thick black polish half gone from the can, the deep browns, the oozing orange viscous liquid, the neutral creams, the shiny rags, the brushes and lay them on the grass. His palette was ready. When he turned to me and signed, "Want me I polish your shoes now?" I was pleased that he chose me.

I placed my small foot on the shoe rest and received his attention with shy pleasure. The other children gathered around to watch him work on his one day off. My father offered him a nickel for his work. Joe looked at him and in his still, emotionless manner signed, "No, Ben, this is Sunday, no one work for money. You save nickel for carfare."

We saved our money for carfare. Forty cents paid my

father's carfare for four days' work; spending it on a single day's outing was a great luxury. My brother and I sneaked under the subway turnstiles long after we were five.

My mother, watching the conversation between my father and Joe Rosenberg, filled a bowl with her chunky, creamy potato salad, flavored with sugar and black pepper, onions and salt, and brought her gift to Joe and Frieda's picnic site. In our enclave at the park, we ate and talked privately. There was no one to observe us, no one to cluck and shake his head at our strange-sounding Sunday community.

"Come, let's play baseball," my mother shouted at everyone. She poked one friend, telling her to poke the next and the next, until all eyes were on my mother Mary.

She stood up and raised her arms full of grace and signed into the summer sun, "We now pick teams. Don't forget must have all children on teams."

No one really knew the rules of the game, or how many should be on each team. It did not matter, there were so many of us.

My father said, "You first Mary, you are Mary at bat."

Yes, Mary was at bat and we followed her laughter around the imaginary baseball diamond. She was strong in those days, with a presence we loved.

As the sun neared the horizon, we gathered up our day and went home, each family to its own tenement apartment, scattered throughout the city, waiting for the next week's work to end so that we could meet once more. For one glorious day we forgot that we were the children of the deaf.

Five

MARY

. . . And the ears of the deaf shall be unstopped . . .
And the tongue of the dumb shall sing. . . .
—Isaiah 35:5–6

SILENT WOMAN

The silence is vast,
The ocean slides to shore on a cat's paw
The silence is fear
The silence strikes dumb with awe
The strange silence estranged
Silence saw
Silence, simple, swift
No refuge in sound
Silence gave sight
Luminous light
Epiphany
We shall observe in silence
We shall have the second sight

We shall have the second sight
The penetration of that alien gift
Given to the few
Denied the sound of the cat mew
Always outside; never inside
Language denied
A face to hide.
In that open human sea
The babble, babble, babble of talk
To whom shall I talk?
With whom can I walk?
Where is it safe?
The face opens
Words on tongues, words of teeth
Words, words, strung together
In a field of billowy human heather
The billow rises, human sounds come
Who can hear them; the humans
With sounded language
Who can know the strangeness
The shutness, the constant reaching
To comprehend the blind sounded words.
What is listen?
Strange, estranged silence.

*M*ary never forgot who she was. She held me to her, weaving me into her life, refusing to allow me to forget who she was, refusing to allow me to be invisible, insisting that I remember her story and her family's story, insisting that my deaf family was not as important as my real family. She slid her pointed index finger under the center of her chin upward, in one long dramatic sweep, emphasizing the word *real*.

"Your life, my life, same, we are one blood. You are true daughter. Must to know, my story, your story. Save for family, it is history."

When I was in college she asked, "Maybe one day you write book on me, on deaf life."

She was her own heroine, and I am her chronicler. The journal that she was not able to write was written in her hands for my eyes and hands to transfer to paper. She cheated the clock and preserved her claim to immortality, savoring the comfort of repetition, clinging to once-lived memories. There was no literary form to her words, yet they struck the chords of poetry. She was her own muse and I was her audience.

Her hand stories were a demand to be known, to be recorded. It was the substance of her life, her stamp upon a world inhabited by hearing men, women, and children whose words formed chaotic sentences confusing her.

Her name confused her once. She sat me down and signed, "My real name is Miriam. I was born on Purim, 1908, in England, London, England. It is the time of year we eat sweet cakes."

I listened to her hands. Her face was marvelous: she never lost the childlike wonder of discovery. When I smiled at her, she waited for my eyes and face to give full attention to her tale.

"My birthday not March 6. You know that. Daddy and I went to England in 1959, alone, brave by ourselves. I want to see my birth certificate. Daddy say we never find it. But I know better. We go to Whitechapel in London to a Hall of Records. There is a clerk man and I write him a note, to tell him I want to find my name certificate. He charge us some English money which I gave to him to pick from my hand. I do not understand pounds and shillings. We went to a room with many shelves, filled with books, all with red leather covers, old and smell beautiful, like big library. I find a book,

1905. I find my brother Nathan's page, with my father Abraham's signed name, and then an *X* for my mother's name. I know she write Yiddish, maybe not write English, so long a time ago. Then I find my name in a book, 1908. I see my name is Miriam and I was born April 10, 1908. Big surprise."

Her eyes questioned me.

"Momma," I signed, "the Jewish holidays fall on a different day each year. In 1913, when you went to school for the first time, Purim, maybe, that year fell on March 6. Who knows?"

"Yes," she agreed, "I think you must be right. This school change my name from Miriam to Mary. My father always called me Miriam when I was small girl. I always see two *m*'s on his lips when he say my name. I did not understand why he say my name this way when I was a small girl. Now I understand."

"My teachers in my first school changed my name to Mary. Maybe they don't like my Jewish name. Terrible. But now, I am Mary and I am used to it. I am born in England and I am Queen Mary." Her hands and eyes twinkled at her joke.

The past was the keystone of my mother's life. It held us together. She repeated and repeated the stories, and they remained the same, verbatim. She told them again and again until they were embedded in me, until they were my own story.

When she was in her late seventies, the cadence of her hands was different, deep into memory, deeper and deeper, down to the place where her spirit remembered unburdened happiness. Gone was the confusion of partially understood language. She was a young girl, safe amid her family. She was joyous, her hands vibrant and young. Her body, slack with age, assumed the energy of girlhood. And I wanted to stretch my arms across to her and say, "Oh, Momma, I see you when you were young!" but I dared not break the rhythm of her memoried hands.

I saw her young face. It was Slavic, rich in beauty, with high cheekbones hinting at the Mongolian intermarriage that spread across Russia in the Middle Ages, but the blue-green of her eyes and her once-chestnut hair denied this as a total heritage. She was probably a descendant of that red-headed tribe of traders that moved across the Russian steppes centuries ago, the tribe that converted to Judiasm. Her father, Abraham, was a redhead. And there are still redheads in Miriam Bromberg's family.

Her stories begin.

"Once my father sign to me and I do not understand what he say to me until I see what he try to explain. It was hard to understand his signs."

She assumed the stance of a small girl as she continued her memory.

"I was playing in a school on the stage with other girls. We were dancing in a happy circle. The theater room was dark. But I look out and I see my father's red mustache standing in the back of seats. I forget the play, I forget the girls and I run off the stage fast to my father calling his name 'Abraham.' Never mind if people hear me, most everyone there is deaf and they cannot hear my voice. I did not care. I was glad to see my father."

Abraham waited quietly until little Mary reached him and then, gently, he motioned her back to the stage to finish her part in the performance. She was six years old and stubborn. She clung to him, refusing to return to the stage. The lights went on, the play stopped, and her teacher marched up to them. Mary watched the conversational exchange between her father and her teacher. The teacher's face softened; she nodded her head, assenting to Abraham's request. And there was no comprehension for the young child watching the mouths talk.

Her father crouched down to his daughter's height and drew the fingers of one hand together so that the fingertips touched and brought this symbol to his cheek and tapped his cheek several times, quickly. This is the sign for *home*. It was a word that they had practiced together, a word that she taught her father. It was a word she knew and it delighted her. Abraham had come to take her home.

On the way to the dormitory to collect her pajamas and weekend clothes he held her by the hand, touching her, willing his message through her young body. She shook her head. She didn't understand his message. They stopped on the stairwell; Abraham faced her and tried to reach her through his own sign language. He pinched his thumb and index finger together and with this invented sign in place, he touched his shoulder and struck his arm all the way down to his fingertips and once again made the sign for *home*. Now there were two words, one that he created and one that she knew. And still she did not understand what he wanted to tell her.

On the journey home, he tried again and again to tell her what she needed to know with his own signs. As they approached their new house in Spring Valley, New York, he had no need for further attempts to reach her mind.

The smell of the charred white house reached her nostrils before she saw the blackened soot marks of the fire that had claimed their home. She understood that her father had been striking a match down the length of his arm; she understood his word for *fire*. Lifting her hands, she turned from the house to her father, spread her fingers upward and out and described flames licking into the air.

She took her father by the hand, pulling him, motioning him to go with her into the burned house. The staircase was seared and the picture at the top of the landing was gone. Drawing a square with her hands, she demanded to know where the picture was. It was a family photograph of my grandparents with their three oldest children, Nathan, my mother and Sam. Abraham struck a match down his arm again and my mother understood this time that the picture had been consumed by the flames. The family portrait connected her to the house; it was what she looked for each time she returned from school and it was gone.

She ran through the house destroyed by fire and smoke looking for her mother. Abraham let little Mary go and waited for her return.

"Where's Fanny?" she mouthed to her father.

"Momma is in barn."

Mary ran across the kitchen garden to the barn, to the temporary home my grandfather had created. Abraham, master carpenter, cabinetmaker, and architect, had fashioned a new home within the walls of the old barn. He built houses and antiqued furniture, he laid parquet floors and made staircases. He carved mahogany banisters and built synagogues. But this time he could not create a permanent home for his family.

My mother said to me, "All was lost. I remember everything about Spring Valley home. It was happy time. I ride horse and play there with my brothers. I ride horse without saddle. I remember everything that happen. I remember where all furniture is, but now no more. Gone. I was so small a child but I know everything that I see in my mind. My mother was sitting in a wagon with a horse, moving goods and sheets, pillows and chairs to our new barn home."

She paused as she always did when her mind clicked to the past.

"Once, we all dress up, we have a new horse with a black

leather buggy, with beautiful cover and fringes. My mother and me, and Jack, who was a baby, went for a ride in the new horse carriage. She gave to me baby Jack to hold in my arms on my lap. And then the three of us ride around the farm. I was four years old, very little girl, I turn around and I drop, by mistake, baby Jack on the ground. Do you think that is why he is deaf?"

"No, Momma," I signed, "Jack is deaf because it is in the family. It is hereditary deafness." I spelled the word *hereditary*; there is no sign I know for this word.

She shrugged at my explanation. "The fire was a bad luck for our family. We move from home to home, to a town to a city. My father always look for work, for money . . . he never find much money. He like to be his own boss. That is one reason why my mother and father fight when I was a girl."

When the makeshift barn was no longer suitable, the Bromberg family began its exodus, shifting my mother from one school for the deaf to another. She lost the continuity of language and never recaptured the flow of minimal language she might have had. Although all the schools and teachers used the oral method, each teacher had a unique mouth, a singular way of forming a word on her lips, and with frequent changes of schools and teachers it was almost impossible for young Mary to learn the words of one mouth. Her visual connection to clear spoken language was continually interrupted.

They moved to Trenton, New Jersey, to yet another white wooden frame house, at 27 Union Street. My grandmother opened a secondhand furniture shop to shore up the sporadic income my grandfather provided.

"In Trenton, I walk to a deaf school every day. I take little Jack with me. That was good, I was with my family every day. But Jack was bad boy."

We both laughed at her memory of Jack. Jack, my mother said, was the most beautiful of all the Bromberg children. He had wavy deep chestnut hair, an impish mouth and the Brombergs' Slavic cheekbones. And a temper. He was strong-willed and shouted his demands shrilly across the room, arresting the attention of anyone who could hear him. Jack was in my mother's charge. They walked together to school most days, yammering at each other in sign language. And when she woke him on school mornings, gruffly, shaking the down quilt over his soft young face, he defiantly refused to go to school. His fingers shot out of the covers and he signed, "You woke me up too hard, for that I do not go to school today." They dressed and went out, but they were truant.

"Mrs. Wrigley, Jack's teacher, told me that my brother Jack is very bright. But why we are two deaf children in one family, Nathan and Sam not deaf?"

She looked at me, still questioning, still wanting to know why she was deaf. I did not answer her eyes. I waited for her to continue.

"So, I tell you again, I ask my father why. I say to my father, 'Abraham, why did God make me to be deaf?'

"And he answered, 'God made you deaf because if you could hear, you would be too smart for the world. So he took something away.' "

My mother partially accepted the answer; she was pleased with her father's wisdom. But she reminded me over and over again, as I was growing up, "If I not be deaf, I be smarter than you. Jack too." Her anger even in age had not quieted. I had heard this before; I would hear it again.

"I have common sense. People call me dumb. No, no, I not dumb, no one fool me. I know." She did know and her knowing was handed to me.

"Forget now why God made us to be deaf. I tell you about wonderful black Jewish man who come to visit my mother in shop. He was peddler of old things. He was good friend to my mother. They talk for hours. They talk in Hebrew. I think he come from old Jewish black tribe in Africa. My mother told me he was from the Lost Jews."

"What was his name?" I asked.

"You know old wall in Jerusalem, you know I think it was Jericho. I think that is his name, same as falling down wall."

When my grandfather Abraham went to Russia to arrange for his brother's emigration to the United States, Jericho was a guest in the house. And when the evenings turned cold and the snow fell, my grandmother Fanny invited him to sleep on the dining room settee. A wooden bench, barely upholstered, and a blanket were his bed for the night.

"My mother Fanny was kind woman, she give everyone food and place to sleep. My house was open door, all welcome. We never lock door. We had no key for a front door. Not like today, so dangerous, with chains on doors. We trust people in a time long ago when I was young girl."

Jericho was at the house the day the World War I ended. He was there to help my grandmother fill deep metal pails with apples when the soldiers came marching victoriously down Union Street. It was November 1918, and as my mother ran among the soldiers handing them rosy apples from Fanny's winter cellar, it was Jericho who watched her, who filled the pail again and again for her until she had distributed five bushels of the fruit.

"I think too that Jericho help my father to build a synagogue for Jews who live in our neighborhood. Maybe he not help him with his hands but he was there. I was ten, eleven years old, but I never forget him."

This old black man touched my mother with his simple wisdom. She was sensitive about her hair and her head. She never allowed anyone to touch her about the head after the crown was permanently scarred and left bald by her first school's attempt to rid the young deaf child of ringworm. Her hair grew long over the crown of her head, and she clutched the hair to the nape of her neck with a round tortoiseshell comb. She did it still, even when her hair was white.

"One day," she signed, "I come home from school with Jack holding my hand. Jack stay with me because I was crying. Jericho was with my mother. Talking. Heads of two bend over. They not see us come in but they hear us. Jericho see my tears and ask me why I cry."

She let go of Jack's hand and showed her mother and Jericho with her hands how her hair had been cut short, too short. She pulled the comb tight to her head, down to the nape of her neck, hiding her disfiguration. Instead of comforting her, Jericho left the room and went into the kitchen. He returned with a salt shaker, held Mary by the hand and began vigorously to shake salt on her hair. She was angry and pulled away from this man who had always been so kind to her.

"I was mad at him. I tell him not to shake salt on my clean hair, just cut so ugly. He smile at me and he say with his big black hands, 'Don't cry, Miriam, shake salt on your hair every night and it will grow back fast, very fast.' We all laugh and he make my tears stop."

She warmed to her memories of this big man. "When my brother Sam was in a hospital, sometimes this black Jewish man take me to hospital on a trolley car. I was twelve years old and Sam was eleven years old when he become sick with the bones in his legs. He was often in hospital, in, out."

Sam had osteomyelitis, and Fanny did not trust the hospital food. She had Abraham catch a pigeon from his pigeon coop, take it to the local rabbi for kosher slaughter. She plucked the feathers and made a rich soup for Sam. She wrapped the small enamel pot with white towels while it was still hot and handed it to my mother to bring to Mercer Hospital for Sam.

"I bring this good soup to Sam for many, many months

to my brother. One time the doctor brought Sam home on a Saturday for a visit. He was wearing crutches. My brother Sam, only one year younger than me, he look so pale, so small. My father faint when he see him. But Jack and me and Sam, we all play all day. Sam learned sign language from me all the time, so we all talk and laugh until doctor come to take him back in small private black car."

My mother's hands moved rapidly. She was unaware of my presence.

"When Sam come home to stay for always, he came still with crutches. Jack was nine years old and he hate wooden crutches. He wait one day, two days and then he tell Sam, 'You walk without crutches.' Sam was afraid that he will fall, but stubborn Jack hide crutches from Sam in a closet. Jack told his brother, 'I am deaf, but still I talk. You have bad legs but you walk; you walk now.' He teach his big brother Sam to walk without help from crutches. We not tell anyone Sam can walk alone."

My mother smiled, remembering the day the secret the three of them shared was exposed in the family dining room.

But she missed Jericho. He had stopped coming to the house. She wanted Sam to parade before him unaided. She asked her mother about him. Fanny had no answer and assumed that he was traveling, selling his secondhand dishes, bricabrac and old clothes. Weeks passed. One Thursday afternoon when my mother came home from school with Jack, Fanny showed her a picture of Jericho in the daily newspaper. Jericho was dead and the article asked for someone to claim the body for burial.

Mary asked, "We bury him? We take the body home and wash him for a grave?"

Fanny answered, "No, we cannot take him, we cannot tell newspaper we know him. He is not our family and we have no money to bury him."

And my mother signed to me sadly, "Jericho never see Sam walk, never see Jack bar mitzvah."

She shifted in her seat and the tone of her story changed.

"We had fun, good times too when all family together. Best times. I tell you we had a big black cat, plenty fur but no tail and fat cat. Every morning he catch a rat, sometimes a mouse from the fields. So ugly." Her hands shuddered with her body.

In the mornings, when my grandmother found the cat's prey with its neck broken, mangled, she summoned Jack to dispose of it. He, with ceremony, removed the flat-faced coal shovel from its stand, tiptoed to the dead rat, scooped it up and waved it under my mother's nose. She ran from him, screaming in mock terror. And then, parading behind him, she followed him as he walked the length of their backyard to the high gray stone wall that separated their home from the seltzer plant next door. With one strong movement he flung the rat onto the factory grounds. He grabbed Mary by the hand and they ran back to the house gloating with their safely executed deed.

On the day of his bar mitzvah, my grandmother did not call Jack to remove the morning mouse. She was busy preparing the table for her guests, for the *minyan* of ten men who were coming to celebrate this ancient rite of Jack's entrance into manhood.

"Why," she asked me, "do you think Jack was bar mitzvah at home and not in a temple that my father build?"

I did not tell her of the rabbinical injunction exempting deaf boys from the ceremony. The minor child, who has not reached his thirteenth birthday, may not be bar mitzvah. The retarded child who never goes beyond the age of twelve mentally cannot be bar mitzvah. He is the child who is called "the fool." And the deaf child may not be bar mitzvah. These children are not valid witnesses. They cannot distinguish between right and wrong. Although they are not excluded from this rite of passage into manhood, it is not mandatory. They do not have to assume the obligations of Judaism. They are forgiven, for they are touched by God.

A deaf boy cannot hear the words of his mother and father. He is the child who cannot hear the words of the Torah as they are read, cannot hear the oral commandments. These words can't enter his heart. But he may be bar mitzvah; he may voluntarily be part of this ancient ritual. This is the paradox.

And so the ceremony was held at home, avoiding the possible frowning of the Orthodox elders.

My mother waited for my answer. I attempted to explain and then I said, "Just tell me about the morning. I want to see the day."

"Many men come to the house. We have a Torah in the house. My father and the men pray, they all wear *tallis*—you know the striped prayer shawl—they move back and forth, they hit their breasts in prayer. Then Jack, it was his turn. My father take him by the hand, so proud together, so beautiful to see. I watch Jack read from Torah, Jack and my father read together. I think so. I see my father's mouth move when Jack talk, you know I can't hear anything. I don't understand the words. But I see my mother standing next to me, cry with tears, quiet, come down her cheeks. She does not wipe them away. But I know she is happy her deaf son Jack, most handsome of all, is a man today in Jewish religion."

The day after the bar mitzvah, Jack, freed from ceremony, in his old clothes, went out to play ball on the street with his hearing friends, his brothers and his sister Mary. Mary was at bat and Jack caught her fly ball, and tossed it to first base. When he turned, wondering where his ball was, he realized that he threw it into a passing garbage truck. Jack ran to the truck and demanded to have his ball, shouting at the driver with his deaf voice. The garbage man could not understand Jack's shrieking voice. He slugged Jack on the head. Abraham, watching his children at play, ran across the street from the porch and punched the man in the mouth. Nathan joined in. Louis, who was only five, flailed his arms, attacking the man who hit his brother Jack. The paddy wagon arrived and they were all taken to the police station.

My mother, hands almost laughing, said, "Nobody went to jail. We had all a wonderful, fun time, long time ago. Now family gone, living all in different places. We were so close a family. I remember good times. Too bad garbage collector not understand Jack."

My grandfather, worried about Sam, decided to open another business, this time in Princeton, New Jersey, where the air was fresh and clean and where Sam could recuperate from months in the hospital, from years of illness. The family stayed in Trenton. Sam and Abraham took up residence behind the ice-cream parlor that Abraham bought with his last dollars.

My mother, who by now was used to traveling alone on trolleys and trains, went on weekends to see Sam and her father. She rubbed her hands together with gustatory pleasure. "I go to store in Princeton and my father always fill up big glass with vanilla ice cream, real whipped cream he make himself and lots of whole walnuts. I ate much ice cream. So delicious."

I shook my head at her.

"I know I am too fat but I love ice cream. My father spoil me, give me to eat what I want, always."

She said, "You know my father, is man with genius hands to make things. He made for us children kites . . . and me and Sam and Jack, we play on lawn park with kites, flying into air. I watch kites go high, higher to sky. It was happy times."

But they had to move again. Abraham couldn't pay the rent on the Trenton house. The landlord refused to allow them to take their furniture unless he received the back rent. Abraham went alone to Brooklyn this time to find work and an apartment for his family and enough money to reclaim his furniture.

"So life in Trenton is over. And we move to New York. I do not like New York, no trees, no grass, no garden for my mother to pick fresh foods for our dinner." There was a slow sadness in her hands as she told me this.

Abraham found an apartment in Brooklyn, on South Third Street. It had six rooms on one floor; it was dark and my mother hated it. She returned to the school where she had begun her talking life. The Lexington School for the Deaf. But she refused to sleep there and each afternoon she returned home from school by subway.

"I walk in a street, past a jail and I see behind the bars my father's red hair. I look again and I see him read the Jewish newspaper. It was the name *Daily Forward*. I know it is my father Abraham. I know sure. I know his neck when he bend down to read a newspaper. I run home, fast, very fast and I tell my mother what I see."

Her hands flew so fast that I stopped her and signed, "Momma, you are too quick, slow down, I cannot see everything you say."

She rushed on, ignoring my request. "I was angry. Why was my father in a jail, like a jailbird? I know he have little money, I know he gamble cards, lots, I know he must be upset now." Her fingers moved so rapidly I could hardly coordinate the speed with meaning.

"He build a synagogue for religious Jews in Brooklyn, near our new home. He working with one man, president, I think, of temple, man who make promise. You understand who I mean, very religious Jews who wear long black silk coats on the Sabbath, with big round hats with fur mink trim."

"You mean the Hasidic Jews."

"Yes, yes," her hands shouted at me, "I tell you now,

don't break my story, I tell you all. My father Abraham, he work hard to finish with his carpenter hands, some things inside small temple. President owe him seven hundred dollars for his labor time and wooden goods. Not good man, he never pay money to my father. Bad man. Not like other good Orthodox Jews. My father work hard, so hard and no money. Maybe he fight him, maybe he hit him. I not know, nobody tell me."

She seethed at the remembered injustice.

"I tell my mother, in Brooklyn house, I see my father in a jail. She confessed to me, yes, that my father was in a jail, just for short time. But she never tell me why."

Her eyes closed. Her hands balled into soft fists. And I waited for her to finish. Slowly she opened her eyes, uncurled her hands, and began again, "My mother say to me, 'Good you know now, you bring kosher dinner to your father tonight.' "

Once again she carried a warm pot of soup wrapped in towels, this time to her father. He was released the next day.

"Momma," I asked, "do you know why your father was in jail?"

"Not sure, maybe he write no-good checks, maybe he hit man who did not pay him for his work. Who knows? Maybe only God remembers now. When my mother and father fight, it was always over money. That is why I true quit a school at fourteen to go to work at Electric Eagle factory. I know I tell you before it was because Louis had diphtheria and I could not go to school, quarantine. But truth was I did not want to go back to school and my family need nine dollars a week I earn for foods and bills.

"We had plenty troubles I tell you. Many stories I never tell you before. Now I am old, I open, I tell all stories about my life.

"My father, good man, but he faint plenty. When he was young man to work on houses, big steel beam hit him on head.

He was unconscious for long time. Always trouble, when he fight with my mother, he faint when he upset. Often. He sweet man, never hit me, never say one cross word to me, in all my life, even when I was mischievous girl. When he see me he say to me, 'Come kiss father Abraham on cheek.' "

One night, shortly after Abraham was released from the local jail, my mother awoke to the smell of gas. She rushed from the bed that she shared with Jack to the kitchen. Abraham was lying on the floor, the gas jets were open and the window closed. She screamed for Nathan and Sam and when they did not come, she opened the window, closed the jets and ran to their beds pulling them from sleep to the kitchen. The three of them moved my grandfather's dead weight to the window and pushed him bodily over the sill until the fresh air revived him. Slowly, gently they helped him back into the kitchen."

"Did he try suicide?" I asked.

"Don't know, nobody tell me, nobody tell me, too hard to tell me in sign language, clear what happened. Maybe nobody want to tell me. They think I am stupid. Not true. I watch. I know."

I sat still and she continued. "I like to think maybe he faint again, maybe long ago steel beam that hit him on head make him to become unconscious. But why gas jets open?"

Six

MARY AND BENNY, A LOVE STORY

> *. . . Let me see thy countenance, let me hear thy voice;*
> *For sweet is thy voice, and thy countenance is comely.*
> —Song of Songs, 2:14

I watched my mother tell me of her mother's sudden illness and death. "She too young to be so sick, to die. She was thirty-nine years old, and me only nineteen years to lose a mother."

And I remember thinking as I had done through my girlhood that mothers were for mourning. My mother mourned her mother all her life.

My mother tapped me on the shoulder, signaling for my attention, recognizing that I had wandered into my own thoughts.

"I went up to a bedroom, early in the morning to wake up my mother Fanny. We needed her to get ready all of us, for work and school. I touched her shoulder to wake her up. She would not get up, stayed still in the bed, a blanket pulling up over her face. I called my father Abraham to come and he could not wake her up. We did not know, but she had a stroke. Her corner of her mouth was pushed over to one side, she could not speak. She could not make a sign to me."

Abraham called for an ambulance and Fanny was rushed to Kings County Hospital in Brooklyn. When the hospital could do no more for my grandmother, when they realized there was no hope my mother said, "They send her to 'crazy house,' a prison for sick people who waved arms and screamed. My father and me, we went into her room, woman nurse open a door with a key. She was locked in. We saw her lying in a bed. She was quiet and smile at us with a twisted face." The asylum decided not to keep her there, and the staff informed my grandfather that she would be sent to a welfare hospital for the incurably ill. Abraham, opposed to this, searched until he found a small private hospital in Brooklyn, the Unity Hospital on Sterling Street. There my grandmother was placed in pleasant surroundings with lace curtains at the window and a pretty pink coverlet for her wasting body. They took turns at her bedside, day and night; someone was always there. During the last week of her life, on that last Wednesday, when it was my mother's turn to sit by Fanny's side, she was so busy with household tasks that she sent Jack in her place.

Jack came back after his vigil and said, "Momma does not wake up!" She had lapsed into a coma. By Saturday she was dead. She never regained consciousness.

My mother paused in her telling and signed slowly, "She died on the Sabbath, same as my father when he die in 1939, when you were ten years old. Shame you never know my mother Fanny, she was good to me, to all people. So kind.

Never said a bad word to me, never punish me, never. I always call her Fanny, she did not turn around when I call her Momma. Only Fanny." Tears slipped down her cheeks as she mourned once more, although more than fifty years had passed.

"There were no funeral chapels, then, like now," my mother said. "They bring Fanny home and we called women to come and make her ready for the grave."

The women washed her, laid her on the floor, wrapped in a white shroud, placed seven candles around her body, and sat with her through the night.

"When at first I see my mother I scream to see her so still, gone for always. So long time ago, I never forget Fanny."

The next day, Sunday, March 13, 1927, they placed her in a simple pine box and draped the coffin in a black cloth with Hebrew lettering. The coffin was placed in a hearse. The chauffeur drove slowly around the Brooklyn block as Fanny's children and her husband followed on foot. A final farewell. She was buried on Staten Island.

"I remember her just like she was here, now with you and me in this room, as I tell you my stories. She never hear me talk with normal voice, but she would be proud to hear my children talk, you and Freddie." At that she smiled.

My mother was drawing me in, really talking to me. Her unlined face, even in age, was the face of a child. Her radiance spilled over me, her smile enigmatic. She still only told me the secrets she wished me to know.

She told me of her eighteenth summer, the summer before her mother's death.

"My father Abraham, he knows Benny Leonard well. In 1925, Benny was world lightweight champion boxer and his friend Charles Atlas was named to be 'the most perfect man in the world.' In 1926, in the wintertime, a man Mr. Epstein, owned lots of land in Sacket Lake, upstate New York, near Monticello. He asked my father to build a camp for children to come, and for Benny Leonard and boxers to practice fighting in the ring. My father accept and he went with other men in spring to build this camp."

Charles Atlas and Benny Leonard were to be drawing cards for this children's camp. My grandfather built the camp, and once again he was not paid for his efforts, nor were Charles Atlas and Benny Leonard paid the large sums of money they were promised.

But before the summer, in the late spring, when the leaves had turned from a soft green to the fullness of summer foliage, when the heat rose early from Brooklyn's paved streets, my grandmother wrote to her husband in Yiddish, asking if the family could join him in the country. Within a week they were there. My mother, delighted to be in the country again, went off into the fields to pick wild blackberries for the first evening meal. My grandmother, who as a caterer in Brooklyn supplemented my grandfather's sporadic income, helped the camp cook prepare the meals.

My mother was joyous in the passing days of summer. "I love the country. It is so good a time with much fresh air, clean, from green leaves and soft brown earth. I was so happy, all family together for a summer. I was young, a free girl. I wear white shorts, white shirt, and white stockings rolled to the knee, like flapper girls. My mother tell me there is a beauty contest, she push me in. I am shy, but I go into the contest. Me, a deaf girl. I did have beautiful legs with thin small feet, delicate."

Without preparation, without knowledge of the unfolding day's event, she allowed her mother to push her up onto the stage that Abraham built. She walked along the wooden platform, not hearing, but following the young contestants in front of her. When they turned, she turned; when they smiled at the judges, she smiled. The girls were given ten minutes to change into bathing suits. And my mother said, eyes smiling, "I wear an ugly tan woolen bathing suit, but my legs and face, everyone see. I wait for the judges to say who win beauty contest. I see everyone in the audience clap; I look around to see who win prize. Then one man, a judge, come to a stage and take my hand and make me to go forward. My face became a red color, I blush so hard, but I am secret proud. I win a first prize. Yes, I win, for most beautiful girl in Monticello, 1926. Best legs."

She turned to me in the fullness of her then seventy years and waited for my response. I clapped my hands, stood up and cheered as I had done each time she told me of her victory over the hearing girls.

"Sit down!" she commanded in a happy voice. "I will finish story about me and people who think I am beautiful girl."

This was one of my favorite memories.

"I was lonesome for my sweetheart Ben, so I write him a letter and invite him to come to Sacket Lake, to swim in cool water and go with me to ride in a canoe boat. He wrote me a letter to say yes, that he will come in one week. I was so happy, I take his letter in my hand to shore of lake to watch the sun play with the water. Nobody there, quiet, peaceful place. I was alone."

As she dreamed of Ben's impending arrival, she sensed movement. Moving closer to the vibration, she saw two lovers partially hidden by a clump of bushes. Moving even closer, she watched them gently kissing, arms and legs around one another. The man looked up and caught my mother's eye. In panic, ashamed of her prying eyes in the moment of their privacy, she dove into the calm lake water. She could not swim.

The water was deep and she screamed, "I drown, I drown!" Her sharp cries drew the boxers from the ring, her father from his hammer and her mother from the kitchen. Benny Leonard went in after her. And within seconds, sputtering, her clothes and shoes heavy with lake water, she was on the shore, facing the crowd that had gathered to watch her rescue. Her mother, relieved, put her arms around her shivering daughter. As they walked up the path, back to the camp, the man whose eye she had caught approached them. My mother, embarrassed, lowered her head as her mother Fanny and the man spoke.

Mary peered at them, straining to understand, to see how angry the man was. He handed Fanny a business card. She lifted her head and looked directly at them, waiting for an explanation. The man was Florenz Ziegfeld's manager and he offered my mother the chance to be part of the famous Ziegfeld chorus line. Flattered, my grandmother, in faltering but firm signs, explained to her daughter who this man was and what he wanted.

My mother shook her head at this offer.

Fanny, understanding, said, "Not need to hear, you can follow the girls on the stage, like the beauty contest."

"I am not chorus girl. I am deaf girl!"

I watched her eyes as she said, "If I not be deaf, I would be famous today. Maybe a movie star."

Her pleasure expanded as her hands continued, "But Ben come from New York one week later. I was happy to be with him, and I forget about Florenz Ziegfeld. I tell Ben about a chorus girl on Broadway, but he not force me, nobody force me. I am me."

My father dismissed the story with a shove of his hands into the air, eager for me to see his words: "Benny Leonard fight with me in a ring. I was good boxer, strong hands, but I think he take it easy with me, not punch too hard. But I punch him good with my fists inside round black leather gloves."

It was a time of life for things that might have been for them; fame as a beauty, fame as a boxer, eluded them in their silences. My father's deep black eyes saw my thoughts and said, "Never mind, we are happy, many years, love Mary best. We have happy life. Deaf not so important."

My eyes did not respond to his acceptance.

He pushed me on the shoulder, forcing my attention to his hands. "Look at me, watch me, I tell you something. You know Charles Atlas, famous perfect man, he think he strongest man in world, always walk around camp with his arms and muscles up for all to see. He big fake, he big fairy man, I give him one little punch and he fell down. Afraid of me, of my strong hands and body. He fall on floor, on earth, without a sidewalk, put his hands in front of his pretty face and wave to me, 'No more, no more.'"

He laughed and I laughed at this nonsense. And things that might have been passed into history. The misunderstandings of their youthful lives, their lives of silence, in old age clarified into acceptance and laughter.

He said, "Ruth, better to fool around than cry." He turned and left the room as silently as he had entered it.

When my father died in 1984, we sat in the sunlight, my mother and I, and she signed to me, "Stay still and I will tell you a story."

I remembered all the stories I had heard before, the reality and the mythology of her life, and wondered which story I was to hear and see again. Then I sensed that this was to be a woman's story. I held my breath at this breach of silence and watched.

"You want to hear my statement about your Daddy Ben; he was a jailbird." She opened the fingers of each hand and gently slapped one over the other to describe my father peering out from behind bars.

I raised my eyebrows in disbelief.

Her words were explicit. "Be patient."

She was about to tell me a secret, to admit me to her private world. I did not move.

"You know when I lost my mother Fanny, when she die on March 12, 1927, I was heartbroken I cry too much. I want to call off wedding to your Daddy Ben."

The first day of April my father came calling on his beloved Mary. In their signed conversation, he inadvertently insulted her dead mother. My mother did not remember the insult, only her feelings of mounting rage and the memory of her shrouded mother on the floor with seven burning candles around her body. My father fell victim to her fury. She took off her small diamond engagement ring studded with sapphires and threw it at my father, demanding that he leave and never return.

I laughed at this moment in the story.

"Not funny!" she retorted in her full soprano voice.

"I want to see Ben, but my father Abraham told me it was over, to forget Ben. It was only two weeks after my mother died. He was too much sad to understand that I was heartbroken twice."

She waited another day and confronted Abraham again. She had been ill, vomiting and crying, filled with physical grief. She decided to tell her father everything about her relationship with Ben. In the days of the promise of marriage, in the days before my grandmother died, in the swell of their declared troth, Mary and Ben went behind the locked doors of my father's bedroom and played in their new love.

"I didn't know about sex. Too bad Daddy's mother not say we not allowed alone in the bedroom. Shame on her. We were so young, nobody explain me anything."

Mary became pregnant at eighteen. When she told her

mother that she had not menstruated that month or the month before, my grandmother knew at once. She tried all the remedies she knew to rid her young deaf daughter of the unwanted pregnancy. She tried the remedies she had learned in the New World and at last resorted to one she had learned in the village of Smargon, Poland, where she was born.

My mother moved her head from side to side and signed, "Your grandmother take me into the bathtub with plenty hot water and add lots of wine that she made herself. She make wine every fall. But that not work. Nothing work. So she find a doctor far away from my house on South Third Street in Brooklyn and there I have abortion."

Late one afternoon, after my mother came home from the factory where she worked, they took the local streetcar to the end of the line and walked slowly to a large wooden house. The doctor took my mother into his office, pulled down the shades and performed the curettage that removed the child from her womb.

"Sad time, yes, it was sad time. My mother understand, was very good to me, told me never to tell anyone. This was woman's secret and now I too was woman, at eighteen. I pay the doctor one hundred dollars, money I save to buy sheets and pillows, blankets and towels for my wedding. It was over."

Hearing this story for the first time, my grandfather, enraged at this violation, had my father arrested for rape. It was not rape; it was the love-play of two innocents who didn't understand the possible consequences of their actions.

Together, my mother and her father went to the local police station and issued a formal complaint. She had merely intended to frighten my father into returning, by charging him with breach of promise. My mother loitered near the corner of the police station and watched as my father arrived, ashen, between two burly policemen wielding billy clubs. When my mother saw his handcuffs, his hands tied by metal rings, his hands unable to speak, she was filled with remorse. She waited for an hour at the corner, thinking, planning, and then made her move. She went into the station house timidly, wrote a note and handed it to the sergeant at the oak desk. The note said, "I want to see my friend, Ben Sidransky."

My mother was beautiful, her smile winsome, and the sergeant succumbed to her charm. He led her to the cell where my father clutched the bars. His handcuffs were off.

She spoke to him contritely. "Ben, I am sorry. Very sorry. Please come back."

He looked straight ahead and ignored her pleading hands. He gave no sign of recognition. He was deeply angry. He had done nothing wrong and wouldn't look at my mother. She tried in vain for some sign from her Ben. He gave none. Despondently, she walked home alone.

The next morning at the Driggs Street courthouse, the case came before the judge. My mother and grandfather entered the courtroom early and sat down in the first row of hard wooden benches. When my father was led before the courtroom by the bailiff, he was disheveled; he had slept in his clothes, refused food, and had neither washed his face nor combed his thick black wavy hair. My mother signaled for his attention with her eyes, with her hands, but he was adamant. He wouldn't look at her.

She was more contrite than ever. Her plea before her father had gone awry.

The case was called. Ben stood before the bench with his mother. My mother Mary watched the proceedings but did not know what was said. No court interpreter was provided. This day my mother sat in her accustomed silence in the midst of oral discourse and waited until the judge freed my father on bail. My father left the courtroom without a glance at my mother. She later learned from her father that Ben was freed on one thousand dollars' bail. My grandmother Lizzie paid the fine. The judge told her that if young Ben did not agree to marry my mother he faced a ten-year jail sentence. When my mother learned this, she was frightened, but undaunted. Her Ben would not go to jail.

That afternoon she didn't go to work, but ventured to Ben's home. She knocked on the door, rang the bell; his mother answered the door. Mary begged for admittance, but my grandmother didn't allow her into the house. She had hurt Benny.

When he had returned from the courtroom he had stormed into his house, picked up a large kitchen knife, rushed into his neat room and slammed the door shut. His sisters and mother banged on the door. "Benny, come out. Benny, open the door!" He didn't answer; he couldn't hear them. And if he could have heard them, I am certain that he would not have opened the door. He wanted his solace. He was stubborn and sat alone in his room until night came. He would see no one, not even his Mary.

Mary mulled over her foolishness; now she not only grieved for her mother but for Ben. She went home and sat in the dining room alone until she came up with a plan and an accomplice.

She explained, "I went to see my friend Tessie, you know she have two deaf sisters, she was deaf too. I know that Ben is friends with that family and visit them often. They were neighbors, they live on Bedford Street, around the corner from South Eighth Street where Ben live. I told her to invite Ben to see her on a special day and to let me know what time, and I would come half hour later."

As she told me this, her face changed; she was animated, delightful, pleased with her own shrewdness.

She patiently waited two weeks before the day was arranged. She dressed for the occasion. She wore clothes that she had been saving for their honeymoon: a pale green angora sweater to set off her green flecked eyes, a navy blue springtime skirt and tiny pearl earrings. She was a warrior and set her strategy meticulously.

When she arrived at Tessie's apartment, she was armed and ready for battle. Tessie's mother answered the doorbell and ushered my mother into the living room. Mary, who was naturally consumed with shyness, marched in with her head high and a glorious smile on her delicate, cameo-like face.

My father turned from his signed conversation with Tessie and saw her. He rose to leave; he could not accept her presence. He had suffered public humiliation and harassment, he had spent the night in jail, and the case was still to come before the judge for the final settlement. His anger rankled. He was stone-faced and did not lift his arms or hands to greet this young woman whom he loved. As he attempted to brush past my mother, on his way out, avoiding her eyes, Tessie intervened. "Please stay, Ben. It is time for me and my family to eat a supper. My father work on the night shift and we must eat early. Wait for me, I want to talk to you. Please." She left the living room; my father was stranded with my mother.

The estranged young lovers were alone. Their eyes touched and then their hands.

Mary said, "Oh, Ben, I am sorry. I was a little crazy. My mother just die, and I say stupid words to you."

Ben was unable to resist. He succumbed to her grace. He said, "Come Mary, we go to the Williamsburg Bridge and we talk more about you and me, about what happen."

Hand in hand, they left Tessie's apartment, walked down the stairs onto the street and made their way to the bridge. In the middle of the majestic span, they paused to circle one another with their arms and to kiss.

My mother turned to me and with a full smile, said, "We made love in the going away sunshine."

Ben turned to his Mary and said, "Let us run away, we can elope, we can marry now, tomorrow."

Mary answered with her hands, "Yes, we will run away.

I not tell my father, and you will not tell your mother. We will do this in a secret."

"How we do this?" asked Ben.

"I will go home soon, we walk together to my house, I will pack small suitcase, you do the same after you go home and we meet tomorrow to marry."

They were gleeful.

When Mary arrived home, Abraham, noticing the difference in her demeanor, asked, "Miriam, you are so happy; when you left here you were sad. What happened to you?"

Unable to keep her secret, she confessed her plans to elope the next day with Ben. He was opposed to the elopement, insisting that the original wedding take place as her mother had wished.

At the same time, Ben was confronted by his mother for the change in his step, in his buoyant mood. When he told his mother of his plans, she said, "It is over, don't marry Mary, there are three deaf in the family. Do you want deaf children too?" Benny was so angry at her rejection of his beloved that he grabbed a knife again, this time threatening to kill himself if she did not agree to their marriage. She relented.

The parents of the bride and bridegroom-to-be met and discussed the wedding plans. My father's mother, Grandma Lizzie, refused to make any plans for the wedding until Ben was cleared in court, until all the charges were dropped. By the end of the first week in May, they were all back in the courtroom on Driggs Street, waiting impatiently for the judge to call their case to the bench. When my father saw his name and my mother's name called, he went before the judge.

The judge asked, "Do you promise to marry Mary Bromberg?"

Ben nodded his head and answered with his own voice, "Yes."

My father understood without an interpreter the judge's

demand: "You must marry in one week. This must be certain."

The wedding was hurriedly arranged to take place on the nineteenth of May, at his mother's house on South Eighth Street.

Mary had won; she was ecstatic. With Abraham, she went to the Lower East Side to rent her wedding dress. She said, "It was a beautiful lace dress, with a long veil and small white flowers, and it cost eighteen dollars to rent for a one-night wedding."

On that Thursday, the morning of the wedding, Mary and Abraham went to the cemetery to pray at Fanny's graveside. It poured on the Staten Island Ferry, it poured at the cemetery. The grave was fresh. There was no tombstone, no sod.

"I do not mind the rain at the grave. I came to see my mother before Ben and I marry. She was invited in her soul to be at my wedding. I was the first of her children to marry."

She paused at the gravesite in memory and signed, "You know my father never have much money, so Nathan work part time as bellboy in hotel in New York for almost one year, he save all money to buy a stone for my mother."

She raised her head and signed after a moment, "My father and I not talk all the way home on the ferry, we both think of my mother who just die."

Weddings are joyous occasions but this one was marred by Fanny's absence. As the marriage vows were recited, both in sound and in sign, my mother and her family wept.

My father glowed. His thick black hair was plastered to his head with Vaseline; my mother's head was covered in a veil that cascaded down her shoulders and over her arms. Her lace wedding dress reached just below her knees and her small feet were adorned with pointed white silk slippers. Ben wore tails and the satin lapels of his jacket reflected the pleasure in his shining black eyes. His mustache was trimmed; it accentuated the smiling curve of his full mouth. In their wedding photograph they stand stiffly, full of promise. Their smiles are slightly contrived for the camera but their happiness is evident in my mother's soft eyes.

She held the wedding picture up for me to see; she had removed it from the dresser.

I said, "It is a happy picture."

She replaced the framed photograph; her hands were abrupt. "No, not too happy. I miss my mother, sad she not there to bless us on wedding day."

She waited for her thoughts to collect. "Wedding day not so good. When we were married under velvet *chuppah* in Ben's mother's living room by a rabbi, and we come to see all people to wish us good luck, I turn around and see my brother Nathan and Ben fight with fists. I not know why. My cousin stop the fight. It was not good, not nice."

She didn't want to remain at the house; she was disappointed at the table my grandmother Lizzie had laid. "Cakes and whiskey. Some herring. A little fruit. That was all."

Her cousin who stopped the fistfight invited everyone back to my mother's apartment. He said they would all have a wedding feast prepared by his wife. My father's family was reluctant to accept the invitation. His sister Anna told Benny to stay at home with his own family, not to go to the wedding party planned by my mother's family. Mary, angered by Anna's request, turned to her. "I look at Anna and tell her, 'What do you want, Ben is my husband now and he go with me.'" Her hands flourished with final conquest.

The estranged families parted, and my father's family stayed at home without the bride and groom. Mary and Ben and her family trooped through the rain-soaked streets to her apartment on South Third Street, five blocks away. This time the living and dining rooms were prepared for a celebration, a wedding instead of the funeral that had taken place two months earlier. The three-piece brown leather living room suite was pushed to the walls, exposing the enormous cabbage roses at each corner of the brown rug. The French doors between the living room and dining room were opened to accommodate the long table my grandfather Abraham made for the occasion. The table was laden with food, hot and cold, sweet and tart. Ben and Nathan shook hands over the food, and peace was restored between the new in-laws.

And when the night was over, Nathan, laden with wedding gifts, accompanied the newlyweds to their new fifth-floor walk-up apartment. The door closed. In the morning Mary awakened, rolled over to touch Ben and he was gone. She looked for him in the small apartment; he was not there. She waited minutes and then an hour, and then some more. At last he opened the door with his key and strode into the living room, sweating, smiling.

Mary asked, "Why are you gone so long a time? I am awake almost two hours."

Ben answered, "I need to run on the Williamsburg Bridge in early morning. You sleep. I cannot wake you up."

My mother recounted these days to me with lucid hands. It was a happy time for them, a time filled with discovery in their new roles, in their love. Six weeks passed and she received a letter from her father.

"I get letter from Abraham in Monticello. I never call him 'Papa' or 'Daddy,' only Abraham, he never answer when I call him 'Pop.'"

I asked, "What did the letter say?"

"My father take three children to Monticello with him to build houses. Rose was five years old, deaf, Louis was seven and Jack was fourteen years old. No one to take good cares of children now that my mother Fanny gone. He ask me to come to the country to take care of children until school begin, only for a summer."

Mary and Ben, barely six weeks after their wedding, put their furniture in storage, and went to Monticello to care for the young children. My mother was happy to be back with her family; she had worried about the young children. Ben, child of the city, grew homesick for the city's vibration and within a week was back in his old room at his mother's house, back to work as an upholsterer. Mary stayed through the summer, but instead of winning a beauty contest, as she had the summer before, she cooked and cleaned and played with the children who were now her own. She cooked in a large community kitchen shared by the families of the working men.

"I never work so hard in my life. We each of the women take turns to clean big stove and very big kitchen floor. Not so bad, I was young. But terrible when we cannot find Jack."

Jack, bored with life in the country, walked to the road, put out his thumb, and hitched a ride to New York. He had no place to go; Abraham had given up the apartment on South Third Street. Jack made his way to my father's house and stayed with him. Neither Jack nor my father returned to the country that summer.

When the summer was over, they all returned, my mother to Ben's house, sleeping on the floor for two months until the young couple were able to find another apartment on Clymer Street and remove their own furniture from storage. Abraham and his young children slept in his car until he found an apartment close by.

With their furniture out of storage, my mother began her cleaning and polishing tasks with zeal. "I was pregnant with my first baby—not you, Ruth—and I sit outside window washing windows, sitting on a sill outside in air, to make glass shine, so I can see. I get stuck when I am finished, I can't open windows to come back into my rooms."

I paused in her story, shook my head at my mother, continually washing windows, ignoring all danger for her window to the world.

"I scream, neighbors hear my deaf voice, call police and firemen. The fireman rescue me with big ladder. I laugh and I cry very hard. I was safe with unborn baby. No problem."

In May, she went to the hospital to deliver her child. She was in labor for nine hours and screamed throughout. No one had told her what to expect. She was twenty years old and frightened. When the baby was born and the doctor held up an infant girl for her to see, with all its toes and fingers, she cried with relief. It was over. This beautiful baby girl was to be named Fanny, for her mother.

"Baby perfect, pink face. I look again and I see baby's left ear a little bent over, but otherwise perfect."

She looked forward to the four-hour nursing schedule. She enjoyed her suckling infant. On the third day, as the nurse brought the babies around, my mother asked the nurse, "Where is my baby?"

"Your baby is not feeling too well. We will bring her tomorrow."

My young mother remained in the hospital bed for nine more days and never saw the baby. Each day, up to the day she left, she wrote notes to the hospital staff asking for her baby. No one gave her an answer. They were evasive and she was suspicious.

On the twelfth day, wobbly from enforced bed rest, she was taken home by my father. That afternoon, Abraham came to visit. Convinced that she was healthy and strong, he answered her question without being asked. "Miriam," he called her by her given childhood name, "your baby died on the third day in the hospital."

"Why?"

"No one knows."

"Did nurse drop her?"

"No one knows, it is better now than later."

Mary wept. "Why nobody tell me before? I am not dumb. Where is my baby now?"

Ben signed gently, "Baby is buried here in Brooklyn. I hold a white coffin box in my arms myself until we put baby in ground to rest for always. She is angel now."

"Did you put baby's name on grave?"

"No, there is no first name, just 'Baby Sidransky.'"

"I know her, she is Fanny for my mother. She is with my mother now."

I was born the following July, in 1929.

I was tended carefully lest I die too. My naming was charged with deep feeling. My mother wanted to name me, once again, for her mother Fanny, but the rabbi wouldn't permit it. I could not be named for a dead child who had never carried the name.

When we left the hospital, my mother and I with my proud father, we went directly by cab to his mother's home. My mother was angry at this; she was tired and she wanted to go home. Ben could not contain his joy; he wanted his mother to be the first to see me. I was named for her mother, Rachel Rosen, according to the custom of using the first letter of my great-grandmother's name to choose mine.

My grandfather Abraham, in his excitement, came straight to my grandmother Lizzie's house. I was his first grandchild and he wanted me to have a middle name, he wanted me to be part of the Jewish naming process. My mother witnessed the angry words that passed between my quarreling grandparents. When my grandfather insisted that I have a middle name, my grandmother scorned, "What for?" And so I have but one name, Ruth.

My mother said, "I never know I have middle name until

I am seventy-seven years old. My brother Nathan write and tell me my middle name is Shifra. All my life I have no middle name, you have no middle name. That is life, funny sometimes."

Frustrated, tired, and hurt, Mary demanded to be taken home. She needed to rest. My father carried me, and my grandfather supported his daughter as they walked the few blocks to their brownstone apartment on Clymer Street.

She turned to me in the fading afternoon light, lifted her arms and said, "Your grandmother should come to my house first. I just had a new baby, you Ruth."

I looked at her as she told me of her anger, the anger she still carried with her, and said, "Momma, it does not matter that I do not have a middle name, I know who I am. I am the daughter of Mary and Ben."

Her face smiled, her expression changed and she signed deliberately, "You have no middle name, but you are Royal Ruth to me always."

Seven

BENNY

*And this is the blessing, wherewith Moses the man of
God blessed the children of Israel before his death. . . .*

*Of Benjamin he said:
The beloved of the Lord shall dwell in safety by Him;
He covereth him all the day,
and He dwelleth between his shoulders.*

—*Deuteronomy 33:12*

No one called him Benjamin. He was Ben, or sometimes
Benny. The hearing called him Benny. I called him Daddy
Ben. He signed his name Benjamin.

And when they called him "Benny the dummy," my ire
rose. Dummies do not make joy. And my father made joy. He
massaged his chest, his right hand over his heart, smiling,
"Come now, we go to enjoy ourselves."

When my face was downcast, he said, "Smile louder." I

laughed and answered, "You know that smiles don't have sound."

"Call Momma," he said. "I will put out the lights and we will have theater show. I will make the show."

The lights were out and it signaled my mother's entrance into our living room. She moved as she always did, as though she were listening to courtly music, effortlessly, to a quiet inner beat.

"Call Momma!" he insisted.

"She is coming, I can hear her."

"I forgot, you are a hearing person." He cupped his hands over his ears, making me laugh with his exaggerated gesturing.

He lit a candle and the glow flickered against the back wall.

"Now, all ready!" he shouted in voice. "We go to the zoo."

He splayed his fingers, arched his elbow and created deer bolting across the sky. He turned to watch us as we sat wide-eyed with the wonder of his magic hands. The shadow of his hands galloped across the horizon and horses moved in an arc up to the ceiling and disappeared. We saw roosters fight, and long-necked giraffes nibbling from treetops. We cheered when we saw the elephant's lumbering trunk slurp imaginary water from his hand. He was wonderful. He blew out the candle and demanded lights.

When the lights were up he said, "Now tell me what animal is this."

Our smiles were loud, vocal. We waited in anticipation for his gorilla act. He crouched down, low, lower, and danced around the room, glaring at us in mock rage, picking insects from his fur, snapping them between his fingers, and then, placated, he sat and calmly peeled a banana, eating it slowly.

My mother said, "Enough fooling around, now we take the children to the real zoo tomorrow."

Not to be upstaged, Ben insisted on taking us out for a walk. My mother protested, the hour was late. He ignored her protests and said, "Come, Ruth, we will go to find the animals in the street."

I put on my coat, my father his jacket and cap, and we went into the lamplit street. I stood at the door waiting for him; he collected the evening garbage in a large brown paper bag and held it to his chest. As we walked down the stairs he said, "Don't tell Momma, I save leftover foods for the dogs, cats and pigeons."

When we got to the alley where the dented metal cans stood, the cats scavenging for scraps scurried away. He grabbed a lid and banged it against a can, creating a loud noise. He sucked his lips together in a welcoming gesture and the cats gathered around, the stray dogs came, and he stood among them, hand-feeding them from our evening meal. The dogs nuzzled against him; the cats arched their backs, ready for attack, fearful of the dogs; yet they all remained. He quieted the cats, throwing scraps to them far from the dogs around his legs. He had no fear of the animals, nor they of him.

He gave me a piece of grizzled liver and said, "Now watch me, how I feed a dog, then you do the same." The liver felt oily in my hand, it smelled of browned onion, but I held it. A large tawny dog with floppy ears came up to my hand and I backed away.

"Do not be afraid, the dog wants the food, do not move, just open hand and put it under his nose. He will come, he will never bite you. He will be your friend."

The dog licked the liver out of my hand, then licked my hand clean.

I giggled and my father patted my head. "See I teach you to be friend to the animals."

I often went down with him after that first experience, and together we fed the neighborhood animals.

One night, still smelling of the upholstery factory, he walked into the kitchen and signed, "I have surprise!" He pulled Momma away from her boiling beef stew, me from my book of fairy tales, Freddie from his metal toy soldiers on the floor, and said, "Follow me to living room."

We gathered to hear his news.

"Everyone sit down now. Supper wait for few minutes."

We were still. He reached into his jacket pocket and pulled out an envelope.

"What you think I have here inside?"

"A letter," I said.

"No, too easy. Think hard. Use brain. You now nine years old."

He was laughing, pleased with himself. "All right, tell you. Inside a small white envelope I have present for all family."

I reached up to grab the envelope from his hand. He was too quick for me. "Not fair. You must tell me what you think."

"I give up, Daddy," I signed. "Tell us now."

"You know big animals come to New York, lions, tigers, elephants, maybe long-neck giraffe, music for children, show for all to see."

"We're going to the zoo again?" I asked, disappointed.

"No zoo, zoo in Bronx, we go to New York, we take subway to Manhattan, we go to Madison Square Garden. We go to circus."

We jumped over him. He scooped me up and signed with his free hand, "You like surprise?"

It was Saturday, time for the circus. It was time for Madison Square Garden. We were excited, and my father Benny was the most elated.

"We can't be late for a circus, much to see, many animals, fat lady, two heads person, smell sweet cotton candy, lots peanuts, see elephant and clowns. Tickets expensive. Hurry, hurry up. We go to subway, we not miss anything." He was electric, charging the air with his body and his signs. We were going to the circus!

The air was sharp as we walked to the subway. My father walked alone, my mother trailed behind him as she always did. I walked with my brother. At the station my father reminded us, "Now remember when man no look, you both go fast under subway, no pay fares, save money." We did as we were told, walking with my mother, while my father distracted the cashier at the booth.

"Hey, kids, you can't do that. You have to pay your nickel. Come back!" he shouted.

I pretended deafness. I raised my hands to sign to my brother, ignoring the man's angry words. I signed to my mother, "Hurry up, we miss train. I hear it coming."

She stopped me. "Do not talk to your brother in sign. You not deaf, you hearing children, speak, with mouth now."

I shrugged my shoulders at her, defiant.

On the trip from the Bronx I never uttered a word, nor did my brother. We signed. My mother and father turned their heads from us, angry that we refused to speak orally. When we were outside, walking to the Garden, my mother said, "Why you sign? Are you ashamed you can hear? Are you deaf, same as your mother and father?"

My father stopped her harangue. "Just children, when get older will understand better. They just play. Forget it. We go to have good time."

The Garden was noisy, smelly, and I darted away from my father. He pulled me to him. "You hold my hand till we sit down. Not get lost, very big place here. Momma hold your brother Freddie hand."

He held me tight with one large hand and with the other pointed at every new sight, teaching me how to look, how to see.

"Touch with hands. Feel shaved wood on floor. You must touch with fingers. Hands will make you understand more."

I touched the trampled sawdust with one hand and clutched my father with the other.

"Now remember, do not touch lion in cage. He bite off hand, maybe then you feel nothing, learn nothing."

The noise stilled, and I listened for the silent spaces, spaces that allowed me to ingest the sights. I discarded the extraneous sounds filtering from the continuing crush of people entering the circus uproar.

My father pushed my shoulder. I looked up at him and he signed, "Remember when we lose you on a Williamsburg Bridge? Not lose you now. Stay close to my hand. Hold my belt, tightly."

I left the circus, lost the smell of the three-ring extravaganza below as we climbed to our seats. I was on the bridge that linked Brooklyn to lower Manhattan.

My father said, "Look at the thick wires that hold the bridge to the land. They are strong strings, metal thread that weave water to the land." He wove the cables through his fingers, awed. And we walked across the bridge, holding hands.

And when he wanted to praise the bridge, he relinquished my small hands and said, "See, see the bridge, look at it, learn it. It is a song made by men, by men who work with their hands like me."

Solemnly he lifted me to his shoulders so that I could be taller than he and said to me in voice, for I could not see his hands, "What more can you see?"

He swung me off his large shoulders and said, "Tell me what you see, Ruth, my baby Ruthie."

I saw the water glisten, the sunlight skipping on the gentle ripples. I saw the birds whose names I didn't know fly high. I was joyfully alone.

"What do you hear? Can you hear the bridge? Does it have a sound?" he signed with one hand.

I heard the bridge sway but did not know how to sign the word *sway*; so my hands danced in lyrical hum to the hum of the bridge over the water.

"Good you hear. I feel what you hear." He lifted me down to the ground from his shoulders.

On the slope downward to Manhattan, my father's hands were animated. "This is my home. This is where I was born." His conversation went on, but I had stopped listening to his hands. I was plotting my solitary walk across the magic bridge.

By now I was out of the circus. Although my eyes saw tigers leap through flaming hoops, clowns pour from small cars, elephants lumber, trapeze artists swing from one to another, I was back in the city with my father—his adored city. I walked alone on the bridge. Unafraid. Walking in the watery wind. There was no rain, just a sense of river wetness. I was young, happy.

Later, when I was a college freshman, he said, "Ruth, come we take subway, we go to see a bridge where you run away, so long time ago."

I had work to do, books to read, papers to write, but his love of the city, his possession of its streets and alleys, its bridges and subways, its filth and fever, separated me from my texts. In the subway, on our way to Manhattan's Lower East Side, the gateway to the Williamsburg Bridge, he struck his breast with his fist and signed, "This is my New York. This is alive city."

He was uncomfortable in the country. He loved the broken asphalt streets and cracked concrete sidewalks. He knew the city's rustle, its motion.

"Listen!" he said. "I feel train coming."

With my mouth I said, "I hear the train coming, Poppa."

When we left the subway, we walked toward the bridge.

He peered into stores, into people's faces, smiling. Before we reached the mighty span, he stopped, pressed his back to a brick wall and said, "I tell you small story I not tell you before."

I was used to my mother's stories, but his were rare and I focused my eyes on his telling hands.

"It is here where I run on the Williamsburg Bridge, before you were born. Momma sleep in the morning, we were married four days only, I know Momma worried when she wake up, but I must run on this wonderful bridge, back and forth two times. It is this bridge that you walk on, you were not four years old. We could not find you. You were gone. We call police. No one found you. But me, Ben, I walk to a bridge and I see you with my eyes, a little girl with a blue dress smiling at river, looking up high to top of great bridge. You love bridge like me. You love beautiful New York City, like me. You are real my daughter. I was not angry with you. I understand why you must go to the bridge."

He gave me a gentle pinch and grinned his mustached grin at me.

I saw a rat, shuddered and turned away, remembering the games my father played with us on cold winter mornings. On Sundays we snuggled under the quilt filled with goose down that he had made for us. One Sunday, when I was six, he was the first out of bed, and with great ceremony he proclaimed, "Wait, I come soon, have interesting surprise for all family." He moved like a cat to the dumbwaiter that hauled the tenants' daily garbage to the basement. I heard him open the door, closed my eyes and slid under the pink comforter. My mother gasped for breath and pulled the comforter from my head.

My father's voice said, "Take off blanket, I have something for children today."

I opened my eyes. He dangled a matted dark gray live

rat over our heads. He laughed as he swung the rat by the tail. I was frightened.

My mother pulled the quilt from our warm bodies, grabbed me with one hand, my brother with the other, and in one movement we fled to the opposite corner of the room. My father chased us around swinging the rat by its tail until my mother demanded, "Ben, throw away rat now!"

He was undaunted. "Wait, look at rat I catch, good work. My hands so fast to grab big mouse." He shone with pride, parading the strength of his hands before us, signing with one hand, holding the rat in the other.

My mother glared at him.

"Okay, I get box and put rat in a box, feed him foods later. I want to show him to people."

The kosher butcher was open on Sundays and my father had a plan. He went to the closet, found an old shoe box, lined it with newspaper, dropped in the rat and tied it with heavy twine.

"Hurry up, get dressed, we have breakfast and then we go out to show a big rat on the street."

It was a cold morning and fresh snow powdered the streets of Williamsburg as we walked to the butcher. I remained behind him, uncertain of his pranks, ready to flee home to my mother, who refused to come with us. It was unusual for me to go to the butcher with my father; I had been there often with my mother, speaking for her, ordering for her. This time I watched my father lift his cap from his head and say in a clear voice, "Good morning, Mr. Roth." I heard laughter in his voice. His mirth went undetected by Mr. Roth's ears, untrained in the nuance of the deaf voice. But I heard it and backed off to the doorway.

Mr. Roth pointed to the shoe box, tilted his head and with his eyes asked to see the contents.

My father turned to me in the doorway, nodded, and

asked with body gesture alone, "Shall I open the box?" his face wide with merriment.

I lifted my shoulders, lowered my head, and shifted my eyes from his, refusing to be an accomplice to my father's prank. He lowered his eyes, telling me without sign or voice to be quiet. With great seriousness he untied the shoe box on the counter. The rat moved. In one motion he lifted the lid, grabbed the rat by the tail, and dangled it before Mr. Roth, who screamed, "Get out, Benny, get out and take that thing with you!"

I stumbled out the door, afraid of the butcher's booming wrath, and slipped and fell in the snow. My father walked out slowly, holding the box in one hand and the rat by the tail in the other. As he approached me, I jumped and rubbed my scraped knee and tried to run. My father dropped the box and held me fast to him with one arm, the rat still dangling in his outstretched right hand.

"You afraid of rat?" He smiled the words at me. His hands were occupied. I shivered, pulling away from the squealing rat.

He crouched lower. "Watch, we free a rat." Clutching its tail with his fingers, Benny set it on the ground, and let go. The rat remained still, staring at its captor, then turned and darted down the street.

I let my breath out into the cold air and punched my father's thigh. I was angry, and frightened by his humor. He had publicly humiliated me. I would never go back to Mr. Roth's and order chicken for my mother.

"No be angry, no shame. We play joke on Mr. Roth. Never mind, he cheat us sometimes, give us less meat weight, too much fat. I teach him lesson!"

I relented and reached for my father's hand. He pulled his hand from mine and signed, "Poor little rat, will die from exposure."

I looked straight at my father and with my own hands repeated the spelling of the word *exposure*.

He repeated the spelling for me, letter separated from letter, and broadly signed, "You not know what mean word *exposure*?"

"No, what does it mean?" I asked in full sign language.

"You not know true?" he asked.

I stared at him blankly.

"I teach you new word I learn just last week. It mean rat, poor rat has no home, no foods, no warm place to hide. Too much cold, no heat, means rat will die."

I stared at him. He was teaching me language.

"Surprise, I know words you not know. Father Ben study every day learn new word."

Summertime is the time of sharpest memory. In winter my father was covered in upholstery cotton and horsehair, worn with his day's work. But in the summer light and on summer weekends when the factory slowed its production of stuffed sofas and chairs, my father had time for us, time to take us on family outings, time to play and time to teach. Playtime meant new language games, new thrills and whooping joy.

In the summer when I was ten, we went to Toms River for days in the country; we took a bus from Manhattan, across to Newark, and down the highway until we reached the Toms River bus station. My father's sister Rose, with her laughing eyes and thick black hair, met us at the station and drove us to her house. It was perfect, set off the road, surrounded by trees and grass; there was no pavement, no sign of the city. The sun warmed my back and I was content.

Rose bustled us into the house and then, without letting a moment pass, bade us all get into our suits for a swim in the river. Hurriedly I pushed my legs into my bathing suit. I remembered my father's tales of his swim in the East River when he was a boy and now I would swim in a river.

I asked my hearing aunt, "Are there any rats in Toms River?"

She laughed. "No, Ruthie, this is a country river that winds through New Jersey. There are no rats in this river, just cool water on an August day for a city girl like you."

Down at the river, I put my foot in the water; the bottom was slimy and I hesitated. My father took my hand and led me into the water until it reached my waist. "Now swim," he signed. "Don't be afraid. I am here to watch daughter Ruth."

I moved slowly off into the water and felt myself pushed forward by a river within the river; the current grabbed me and pushed me to the opposite side of the narrow bend. I was frantic, I had lost control. I called to my aunt. She was no-where in sight. Toms River roiled and I clutched at reeds as I moved through the water. I took a breath and shouted, "Help! The water is fast!" No one heard me. I saw my father standing on the bank, I raised my left hand. He waved back. I signed, "Help me, I drown."

He signed swiftly, broadly, "Stay, hold grass."

And he swam great breaststrokes toward me in the churn-ing current. As he came up for breath after each powerful lunge of his arms, his eyes fastened on me, measuring the distance, warning me calmly not to move. He reached me and in voice he said, "Hold my neck, Ruth."

I flung my arms around his shoulders, locked my fingers around his neck, and piggyback as one body we swam, wet and close, to the riverbank.

"You safe now. Brave girl."

I cried, relieving myself of fear. He cradled me in his arms and crooned in his garrulous voice until I stopped trembling.

We sat motionless in silence.

"Ready now!" he commanded. "We go back to swim in a cool water."

I refused.

Gently he took me by the hand. "We swim together. I teach you not be afraid. You watch me, I teach you swim good."

He pulled me into the water with him, laughing, saying, "Swimming time is good time."

He splashed water over me, held me afloat and then suddenly let me go, pushing me into the deep water away from the current, swimming with me.

He lifted one hand out of the water, signing, "See, you swim easy, water take your body, no work too hard, your body swim by self."

He motioned me to turn back to the shore, and we swam side by side until he could stand; he grabbed me and tossed me into the air. "See no afraid, we make fun, we make good time."

Out of the water, he demanded that we walk along the riverbank to look for treasure. "What we look for?" I asked.

"We look for perfect stones, round, smooth."

We walked with our heads down, searching the soil.

"I found, I found!" he shouted. "I find a new penny."

"That's not a stone, that's money."

"That," he signed, "is people stone. People need money stones."

I found a stone, mottled pink and black, perfect, flat faced, but when I turned it over it was scarred, uneven.

"This is the life, perfect on one side, ugly on the other." He signed this deliberately. "Some like me, perfect outside, but deaf inside."

It was a rare pronouncement. I felt his years and years of silence, the silence of his life.

I like the phrase "stone deaf." They say "profoundly

deaf" now. Gone is the language that says "deaf and dumb." I do prefer "stone deaf"; stones may be mute, but they are warm in the sun, they feel soothing in the palm. It is a piece of the earth, attached to God. I do not know what the pedants mean when they write "profoundly deaf" to describe the person who has never heard a sound. Deaf is deaf and silence is forever.

My father gave me many stones, even pebbles he found in the street, to turn over in my hand. "Stones simple, stones clear," he said.

On the Saturday morning before we left for Toms River, my father sat me at the window and asked me to watch for the "knife sharpener." I was bewildered and asked him for an explanation.

"You wait at window, open window and listen for bell to ring. He come every two or three months to sharpen people's knife. He walk with round wheel, big stone, he push his feet on pedal like Momma's sewing machine. Call me when he come. He is immigrant man from Italy, makes a living."

I saw this man come down the street in rumpled gray trousers, singing, "Knives to sharpen, I sharpen knives!"

I ran to my father, who was reading the paper in the living room, and pulled him to the window, signing, "Hurry, hurry, he is here. He will go away soon."

Patiently my father took the knives from the kitchen drawer. As he collected the knives, he said clearly in sounded words, "Get Momma's scissors from sewing box. Careful. Do not fall."

He put everything in a brown paper bag and signed, "You take all this to man, tell him twenty-five cents to sharpen all things. No more. He understand you. Show him quarter first, then give him knifes."

I walked down the steps slowly, afraid I might fall and stab myself, but even more afraid that the knife sharpener would be gone. He was there, in front of the doorway. I spoke as my father directed. The man did not answer me as I handed him the bag. I watched as he took each knife from the bag and honed it against the sharpening wheel. The sparks fell onto the sidewalk. I moved back, not wanting to be ignited. My skin stood up in goosebumps as the grating sound penetrated my head. I was mesmerized by the moving wheel, by the sound. He handed me the knives and held out his hand for the quarter wordlessly.

I asked, "Can I touch the stone wheel?"

He took my hand and put it gently on the hot stone. I felt the dying friction heat rise into the pads of my talking fingers. I pulled away.

He spoke. "Don't be afraid. Give me your whole hand. Put it on. It will not hurt you. Feel the stone. Beautiful? Yes? It has a life. Warm life, stones have life."

I asked, "Can stones hear?"

He laughed. "Stones, hear? Only God can hear a stone."

Head down, quarter paid, I walked back up the stairs thinking about his words. I thought, only God can hear my father Benny.

I wanted to ask him, when he greeted me at the door and praised me for a task well done, if his silence and the stone's silence were the same. I didn't ask. I had no words to sign my feelings. I was dutiful, without a voice, without parental awareness of me, the hearing child. I found no rest from the silence, yet I clung to it. It was my only solace, my daydreaming place. It was a slender tie to the fantasy that I created. I was Pocahontas, the Indian princess attended to by my tribe; my ladies spoke to me in royal sign, a language reserved for the high born. I was Romaine, the shoemaker's daughter with her glorious singing voice, listened to by an audience. There was no self, no anger at silence, no rage at the inattention to the child that I was. There was no mourning for the caverns of silence, no mourning for the listening that never was.

I didn't dare hear myself. It meant breaking an unforgivable taboo; to hear myself could only diminish my capacity to hear the others who needed me. My mother said, "I am helpless." My father said, "Take care of us." I did not ask, "Who will take care of me?" I was alone, walled in their silence and mine. Incommunicado. Blank.

My mother, ashamed of her silent voice, said, "I hide myself." And I went into hiding. I hid behind the stone. It was the price of survival for both of us.

Benny sensed my mood and refused to allow my distant reverie; he brought me back to the present, to Toms River.

"Come, we go back, find Momma, Rose come soon with car, and we go back to house in country. We play baseball with family on grass. Okay?"

"Okay," I signed the letters as he did, with fun in them.

On the way to my aunt's house we stopped at a bakery. My father shoved me out of the car, signing, "We buy bread, we buy cakes, for family. Tell Rose I pay."

I pressed my nose to the warm smells behind the glass counter.

He pulled me by the arm. "Tell baker man, don't fool me, give me fresh bread. If not I bring back. Tell him my words perfectly, like I tell you."

The baker said, "Can I help you?" to my father.

"Yes," I said, quickly, "I would like a loaf of fresh white bread."

My father eyed me, watching me, trying to read my lips, but I had turned my head and spoken rapidly, softly. He said, in voice, "Tell man I want fresh apple pie, make today, not yesterday."

As we walked out of the door with our purchases, my father asked me, accusingly, "Why you not tell bakery man my words, perfectly?"

"It's not necessary, Daddy, he does not want to cheat you."

"You stupid." He banged his fist on his head softly in the sign for *stupid*. "You not understanding hearing ways, always try to cheat deaf."

I didn't answer him.

I was hearing. Who would trust me?

His senses were sharp. "I trust you Ruth, you not cheat me, you good daughter."

I didn't believe that his anger at the "hearing" excluded me.

On an afternoon when the summer's heat stilled the urban air and the wind sound rushed over the streets breaking the summer silence, I asked my father, "Who makes the wind?"

His hands *whooshed* repeating the wind song and he answered, "God make the wind to broom the streets clean, to tear dead leaves from a tree. Now we watch high summer wind, rain will come to wash the streets. Wait here in a doorway. Rain sure to come anytime soon."

Huddled on the narrow step of a dry-cleaning store, he held me to him, protecting me from the city's August wind. He pointed to the sky. "See black cloud hold water, hold thunder, hold lightning, when rain come we go quick catch one fat raindrop in hands. See how God water earth, one drop, then another drop and we have a wonderful cool rain."

He beamed his smiling light at me.

The rain came, a drop at a time, as he had promised. We stretched our hands out of the doorway, his large and firm, mine young and small, to collect the single raindrops.

We stepped out and in that moment with our hands open the rain sluiced through our fingers, drenching us through. We ran all the way home. We shook our bodies, squeezed the water from our clothes.

I tugged his sodden leather belt and asked with my hands, "Momma angry we very wet?"

"No, never angry, God made us to have a good time, to play in his rain."

He knew the secret of play, of time off and time out. It was not passive play. It was exuberant. He did not complain about his silence. He used it for internal laughter, used it to think, to plan, to prepare his life.

A small part of him, that part born with sound, knew me as a hearing child. Somewhere in the dimmest part of his memory he held sound and offered it to me. As we entered the apartment building, hand in hand, breathing hard from our rain run, he turned to me, releasing his hands for signed speech. "When you grow up, you go alone, like a wind, over everywhere, you make life yourself. You take hearing ears with you.

"Look outside, heavy rain stop. We have more hot weather tonight. Maybe we sleep on roof. Come, we ask Momma Mary."

My mother laughed when she saw us. "You so wet. Are you little boy Ben, why not wait until rain to stop? Take off all clothes. I find dry clothings for you."

"Wait!" My father touched her shoulder. She turned to face his hands. "Wait, I promise to Ruth, if hot tonight, very hot, no air, all family sleep on a roof."

My mother glared at him. "Not private, too many neighbors sleep on roof too. I do not like."

When it was dark, I helped him push the mattresses up one flight of stairs to the roof. He had no need of my strength, but he enjoyed my presence, grunting with a feigned load; his strength was enormous.

The families collected in their spaces. My mother insisted that we move off, far from the doorway leading back down to the stairs. "I not want anyone see us or bother to us when they must go down to use a toilet. We go to a corner, where not one person bother us, see us to sleep the night."

We complied with her wishes, and settled in for the long summer's night of open-air sleep. I could not sleep. I heard my mother snore gently, my brother was asleep beside me. I sat up. My father also sat up and beckoned me, sweeping the air softly with his hands, to rise and join him at the roof's edge.

He pointed to the sky, as if to touch the stellar constellations. "I know stars have names, all stars. I sorry not know names. Look up. See stars like milk in a sky, looks like street when milkman spill silver milk."

I hushed him. "Daddy, not use voice, other people sleep, talk only with hands. I can see you. Light is bright from stars."

As I watched him for words, my ear was not listening. And the vibrating sounds of the night entered my skull. I turned from him, to steal the sounds of the night; I heard a low lion's roar rising from the paved street below. It was the hum of the hot city settling in, its last turn before sleep. Holding my father's hand, I moved one more step to the roof's edge, leaned my head over and saw silence. Black below, illumined by the stars above, the red brick five-story buildings stood facing each other down the long, long Bronx street. Sentinels in the night. We were not all walled inside.

I saw the bodies stretched out in loose bedclothing, on mattresses or piled blankets, finally asleep. Only Benny and I were awake. It was a dream for me to see everyone at rest, to have no one calling my name, to have no one ask, no one make a demand. My father receded from me, allowing me to be alone with myself. I tried to smear the stars together with my hands, tried to create a white night. I was busy with the heavens, happy. It was a night of bliss.

Benny took my hand, led me to my mattress, lay me down, kissed me, covered me and left me to sleep the night.

Summertime was the best time, the time when I had my

father for long stretches, for hours of play. We went to Coney Island. We went to the beach where the deaf collected in circles near the Washington Baths. I could see them as we approached over the hot sand, wending our way, creating a path through the bodies oiled to absorb the sun's rays. No matter what time of the morning we arrived, there were always people, throngs of people laid out on old chenille bedspreads, towels and sandy blankets. It seemed to me that only the deaf remained on their feet, gesticulating broadly, facing one another, speaking to one another. The same hearing people lay on the sand Sunday after Sunday during July and August and still they stared at the standing deaf signing to one another in full animated speech. The circle broke, the choreography shifted as new deaf arrived with their families. The children remained outside the circle. And my father, who loved to talk, to fool with the deaf with his clever hands, enjoined me to play with the other children, signing that soon he would come and take me into the wide ocean with him.

He was my cohort. I made no demand, gave him the time he needed to be with his own people, speaking his own language, without paper and pencil, without struggling to have a hearing person understand his oral words. His silent signals made more sense than most of the inane speech I heard.

I turned to my castle in the sand and made my magnificent structure complete with moat and secret passages to great rooms that shifted in the heat.

Suddenly I was lifted from my crouched position. I recognized the smell of his body and I grinned inwardly. He was going to take me to the sea with him. He pulled us all from our places and raced with me to the water. The foam hit my toes. I protested the cold water. He ignored me and pushed me into the ocean. It was dark; I could not see my feet as I looked down. He splashed me, threw water at my mother, grabbed my brother and tossed him into the water.

He shouted, "I play with family." People turned to identify this strange sound. I put up my hands to shush his oral speech. He was quick. "Never mind if people look at me. They not understand deaf talk. They see we have a good time. They jealous."

I joined his abandon and frolicked in the water. "See," he said, "now you swim, not like last summer when you were ten, when you almost drown in a Toms River."

We grinned at one another. He nodded his head up and down in full approval.

"Come, we swim together, far away, not be afraid, I am with you. I watch you. Daddy Ben, good swim, many miles. Salt water help you." And for the first time I swam with him, my small breaststrokes paralleling his long ones. "You work too hard. Slide in a water. You can do that, can do all you wish." These words he said orally.

I tried. "Put arms around my shoulder. We swim back together. You must kick feet, help me to swim too." When we came into shore, he said, "You good swimmer, brave girl. Later we go for rides on Coney Island Boardwalk. Present to you because you try hard to be a good swimmer, not afraid."

I was afraid, but his courage spilled onto me, leading me beside him, protected.

I fell on our old blanket, happy to be back on dry ground. I looked up at the perimeter of the signed hands dancing language and it had widened, and I looked again and saw a second circle of young unmarried deaf signing words I did not always understand. Each generation refined the language. I strained to understand. I asked my mother, "What they say?"

She answered, "Many words, new words, I not know all new words from a Gallaudet College, I like spelling words best. Then everyone understand."

My father reproved my mother. "Mary must learn new

signs, new language. Make mind grow. We ask what mean new signs." He always asked, always wanted information. He needed language.

And he gave it to me. A gift. I held a perfect thing in my hands: language.

"We go dress now, we go to a Steeplechase ride. We go to Luna Park on Boardwalk. I have money extra, work overtime.

"We go hurry, so we have ride in a daylight, then we go to Nathan's and I buy a hot dog for everyone for a supper. Momma no cook. Today is rest day for everyone."

The great billboard-size mouth full of smiling teeth towering over the entrance to Luna Park lured me with the unknown treats within its portals. Today we would all go. When we passed the park on the Boardwalk I saw the mechanical horses, looking very much like the horses on the merry-go-round, race on the track around the park. I heard the people on the horses screaming with feigned fear, I heard their thrill. And now Benny was taking me, taking all of us.

Although we washed as best we could, I felt the salt cling to my skin, the sand between my toes. "Not important, not all clean from salt, we go have a good time." He would not allow me to ride a horse alone. He sat me in front of him, shielding me with his body; the switch was thrown and we raced over the course. The wind caught my open mouth, and I screamed as I had heard the others shout. I heard my father scream but this time his shouts were mingled with the rest and I paid no attention to what the others might think of his sounds.

I was riding the Steeplechase. I had seen the billboard clown face peer down at me every summer. It was painted with hair parted in the middle, slicked back, and a toothy smile framed with deep red lips. I dreamed about it at times, and I was afraid. I was fascinated, drawn to this wide open mouth.

I forgot the mouth, I forgot the face. I was flying with my father on a wide grassy plain, talking to him, telling him my words. He heard me.

The fantasy was over as we came down off the mighty brown steed. I heard him as he squeezed my waist: "Wonderful trip." He exhaled the words on one deaf breath.

He grabbed my hand, pulling me to the next ride and the next and the next.

"No more money, now we go to eat best hot dog in world. We go Nathan's. Stay close, very, very crowded. All people like best foods to eat there."

I did not want to leave Luna Park, I did not want to leave the mechanical brown steed that Benny and I rode; I lingered. He cajoled, "Come now, you come now, good time finished but you will remember for all your life this day."

I walked beside him holding the day. I did not speak. I moved closer to him lest I lose him in the gathering crowd. The rhythm of the feet as the crowd rushed to the subway at day's end, the smell of grilled hot dogs and hot waterlogged corn on the cob, the scent of frying onions mingled with the sticky sweet pink cotton candy and the colors of the sea pushed me along, away from the speed of the horse, away from the thrill of the Steeplechase, away from my fulfilled fantasy.

We moved into the crowd at Nathan's hot dog stand. The glass-topped counter, five feet from the wall and covered with signs announcing the price of each item, provided a backdrop for the army of countermen shouting, "How many hot dogs over here? Any fries? Seafood over there in the rear. Cokes? Who's next?" Benny took my hand and with his other hand signed, "You order for us, so busy here, so many mans here they not understand me. No patience to listen to deaf voice."

I wriggled through the people lining the counter, chose a face from the men dispensing this pungent food, caught his eye, and softly, distinctly, I demanded, "Four hot dogs please, lots of sauerkraut and mustard. And two sodas with four straws."

The man, wearing a Nathan's white cap, slowed his rapid delivery, slowed the shove of hot dogs across the counter, and one by one handed me the hot dogs as I passed them to my family.

"How much is that?" I asked clearly above the din.

Benny had the money in his hand, counted out, ready to pay before I signed the price of our dinner.

"Give him money, tell him no change necessary. I count correct," he signed.

The man behind the counter looked at me, looked at my father, at my mother, glanced down at my brother, and said, "It's paid for. Get out of here!"

I repeated his words for my father. He nodded his head, tapped us one by one on the shoulder and moved us away from the people shouting their orders.

"Hearing people fool sometimes, he feel sorry for us. So we have a free dinner." He laughed. "So, not so bad we deaf sometimes."

And then he looked at me. "What did you say to that man?"

"I just told him the order, nothing else."

"You have good voice, Ruth, I see people listen you always when you speak. Do you have a magic in your throat?"

"No, Daddy, I just wait to find the eyes. When I have the eyes, when people look at me, I know they ready to listen."

He stroked my head. His hands smelled of sauerkraut and the sea.

He shoved the last morsel of food into his mouth, looked at me once more and asked, "You think man lose his job because he give us free foods?"

"No, Daddy, he is Nathan. I know he is Nathan the boss."

"How you know that?"

"I feel that," I signed.

He did not question my feelings.

"Now, stomach full, we go home on subway, when you tired you sleep on Daddy's lap." I moved close to him, touching him, until we reached the subway station.

That same summer, I talked to my gifted brother Freddie; he answered briefly and turned away, isolated and remote. These were the times when I was immersed in deafness for days on end. And when the days followed one another without relief, when they went on too long, I thought I would go mad. I was wild for spoken sound, for the exchange of contact through my ears. I found myself rubbing my ears. I turned on the radio, and heard words of Nazis marching in Paris. I longed for the summer to be over, for school to begin again, so my mouth and my ears could partake of normal human conversation. I kept this longing close to my chest, so close that my chest bones hurt.

My father insisted, "Go outside and play with other children. Talk to young girls in your language." He always knew.

"It is Sunday, and everyone, all girls are away with their families."

"We go to a park, take walk, we play father Ben and Ruth in summer sun time." He sign-sang these words. His voice resonated and I smiled at his sound.

"Better see smile, school begin next week, September almost arrive, then have plenty to talk."

He opened the door. "Come, we go out, listen to people talk, maybe we meet interesting person?"

We went forth, always hand in hand. Silent. And then, with his eyes pressed to the street, he said, "Remember to look, to find something wonderful."

This time I found a piece of green glass worn smooth by the city and I showed him my treasure.

"Tell me story about green glass. Invent big story."

I didn't need any prodding. My hands were alive with make-believe.

"Long time ago, a rich man had a wine cellar. Inside lots of bottles of wine, down in dark place with spider web threads. Depression come, man lost all his money. He had one bottle wine left. He went into the street, holding his last wine, tight. Somebody try to rob him. He dropped bottle. This French green glass break into many pieces. Man heartbroken, he break into many pieces inside himself. He walk away and leave red wine and broken glass on the sidewalk. People kick this glass everywhere, from Manhattan to Brooklyn, over the bridge. And this is the last piece of glass from his wine cellar. He is dead now but this last piece of green makes us remember his story."

Benny clapped. "Good story. Best!" he said with his voice.

I felt better.

"Come, park is here. I push you on swing, higher, higher, up you go to sky."

I settled into the swing, balancing my eleven-year-old body, and gripped the link chain hard, readying myself for his powerful pushes. I went up higher and higher with each push. I screamed, "No more, enough!" I shook my head. Ben was caught in the rhythm of the push. He couldn't see my face, nor did he notice my head moving from side to side, expressing my fear.

He pushed so forcefully that the swing went over the top. I never let go, although I knew I was upside down. The swing righted itself and my fingers were red, the skin broken from the metal links that I had clutched to prevent my fall. Frightened, but with his wits about him, he decreased the momentum of his pushing to avoid a sudden stop. I held on, white, after the swing came to a full stop. He pried my fingers loose, moved me over on the wooden seat and sat down with me. The swing swayed from side to side and his hands in full calm said, "You very brave girl, use your mind, not fall off. I proud of you."

He was daring and expected me to have his daring.

He signed, "Now we have plenty conversations, we go home and tell Momma swing story."

I was angry with him. He had almost killed me and to him it was just a story.

September came and I was back in school. The summer was over. The days settled into a routine. Monday nights we had spaghetti for dinner. As we ate in silence, I remembered how I had signed the teacher's words under my wooden desk at school, trying to memorize them. In the summers I fell into the habit of signing to myself as I had seen my father do so many times. It was a facile mode of thought for me. I tried to break myself of the habit. I said words aloud, keeping my hands clasped on my lap under the table. I was concentrating, retraining myself, and I heard my father laugh. He sat on the kitchen chair, facing my mother's back as she scrubbed the evening pots, signing and laughing.

I reached across the table, tapped him on the shoulder; he turned and I asked, "Why are you laughing?"

"I think of something funny!"

"Tell me!"

"No, it is not for young girl."

He turned his back to me, and went on signing and laughing. I couldn't see his hands.

He went into the living room, lay down on the rose sofa and fell asleep, signing, dreaming. I watched his dream-hands move, but averted my eyes from the meaning of his words. They were his, in sleep. Then, tempted, I read his words, but the signs were indecipherable. His hands were covered in whimsy and I didn't understand anything but the pleasure in his face.

In the morning I crept to his room, wanting to catch him in sleep, trying to understand his dream words. I watched his hands play. I awakened him and asked, "Daddy, tell me what you dream, what funny?"

He opened one eye. "Do not wake me, not finish my story. You broke my sleep, tomorrow finish dream."

"Will you tell me funny dream when you finish?"

"Not always remember all dream. Maybe tell you if I remember."

"Why you sign Daddy, when you sleep to dream?"

"I sign? Not know that!"

"Yes," I nodded.

"Your Daddy funny man even when sleep?"

I, too, dreamed in sign. I awoke often with my hands formed in the shape of a word. When this happened I paused, warm with sleep, to think. My hands moved and before I uttered the sound in my hand, I hesitated, signing the word again, whispering it, to be sure I could say it. Hands and voice aligned, I spoke the word, my voice clear.

I still think in hands. The movement of silent words is supple. The arm, hand, and wrist swing to language in one graceful motion. I do not allow my tongue to shuffle words without meaning. My hands are as primary for me as they were for Benny in his dreams.

I flattened my nose against my bedroom windowpane and daydreamed with my hands. I was an Indian princess clothed in soft skins the color of bleached bone. I was a

European princess with golden hair plaited in one braid down the length of my slender back.

My father came into the room and said with his voice, "Why you sign to yourself?"

"I sign my dreams, same as you do."

"Remember, you are hearing girl, you cannot be deaf and hearing at same time."

I learned my father's lessons.

There is no emptiness in silence. There are no intrusions, no exceptions to the mind at rest.

And out of that rest came the perceptions of the child, asking questions, urgently demanding discovery of the unknown. I was gifted with the lingering curiosity of a child. It was Benny's blessing.

Benny used his silence well. It was who he was. At times he saw the world as a crooked place, askew. He considered himself as one of the others, yet apart. His arrogance lay in the knowledge that he had not been born deaf, that he had had a chance at greatness, at great hearing and great learning. He did not isolate himself as my mother did, as I did. He lunged into the hearing community wary at first, and then with abandon mimicking himself, permitting the men with whom he worked to approach him without any shame or fear. They admitted him as a man, relieving the monotony of work, sharing their ribaldry with him.

He said, "Never trust all. Sometimes men at work steal. But I like company of men, together we make money, fool around, tell dirty stories."

He spoke of the men with benevolence, smiling at their stupidities, forbearing their disdain of him when they called him "dummy," when they too roughly attacked his shoulder for attention. In a world of fools, of frightened men, his watchful eyes forgave the profanities against his silence. With an unbiased mien, he reserved judgment and turned from their malice. In a world of fools, locked in stillness, he was not the fool. He was pleased with himself.

I was not. The twist in my soul was firm.

My existence overshadowed by deafness was assuaged by Benny's laughter. Without it, I don't believe I would have survived.

He was masterful, captivating. He lived alive, striding almost mystically to the subway, to his daily work. He talked to himself, thought to himself, signed to himself; he created himself. His language was fragmented; he wasn't. He was in possession. He owned himself.

Eight

BENNY AND RUTHIE

Smoother than cream were the speeches of his mouth . . .
—Psalms 55:22

*I*n winter, when the icy air hit my lungs and I gasped for breath, when the air was clean, when the snow fell on my face turning my clear cheeks red, my father took the sled from its corner in the closet and announced, half signing, half speaking, "We go for a ride in snow, before it melt, before it become black, dirty with people overshoes and gas from cars that fart on snow."

"Daddy, don't say that, not nice words."

"But real talk, hurry up. We have a Saturday snow, Ben not work today, we must go now. Early morning best time."

Benny was rushing again, generating excitement, his power unmistakable.

"Mary," he signed, "leave laundry, we go out now, breathe winter sun air."

She smiled at him, touched his shoulder. "Who will make breakfast foods for you and children? You will come up hungry. And I must finish to wash clothes. Go take children, go play in snow. Save a little snow for me when I go out later."

He touched her shoulder in return, chuckled and shouted to me, "Dress up now, we go." It was a command from Benny, a command to savor life.

The snow was locked in absolute whiteness. Nothing moved. There were no footprints scarring the pristine city snow. It was very early in the morning. The cars were tunneled in, their tires invisible. The building superintendents were still in their beds. They hadn't dribbled the residue of ashes left by the night's coal on the sacred white coat covering the street. It lay untouched.

"You want to be first to step in snow, leave small footprint with Daddy's big print from man's shoe?"

I looked at him wordlessly.

"You go alone, you young girl, you make own path, own way in white land!"

I set off to mar the snow, to leave my mark before another entered this pure realm.

I walked the length of the virgin street alone. It was my twelfth winter. The sun lifted from the east. It was a February morning. The Bronx was white. I tromped in the snow; I slid across the crunchy wetness; I listened for the sound of snow under my overshoes. I was too warm, over-sweatered, layered lest I catch cold. The hair clung to the back of my neck, damp with heat. I heard the clang of the ashcans as the first superintendent came out of his basement apartment, tucked away in the alley, dropping the coal's excrement on my snow. I turned and saw my father waiting patiently for me at the end of the street. I ran to him, heart beating hard, slithering across the snow, stumbling in my race to reach him, to feel his love. He carried a piece of my soul in his hands.

When I reached him, he pulled me up into his arms, slobbered a kiss on my warm face and insisted, "Take off hat, take off gloves, too many clothings, not good. Give me hand, touch snow, soft, soft before another man spoils good snow. Taste snow. Stick tongue out."

Mocking him, I refused.

"Open wide mouth!" he said as he swept snow into his hand from the car fender he was leaning on. "This better than candy bars, Baby Ruth!"

I laughed at his play on words and opened wide and I heard the crystalline snow melt in my mouth.

"Now," he said, "now we ready to go for sleigh ride. We go to park, ride down hill. We go fast, faster than Steeplechase horses in Coney Island."

I remembered the winters before and knew my father could be reckless. I was afraid of his speed, but knew if I clung to his neck I would be safe. I said, "You and Freddie go first, I watch you fall down a hill faster." My syntax had become his again. It was easier to speak that way; it conveyed a more direct meaning.

My father handed me the worn rope tied to our old sled and said, "You pull sled, watch tracks it make in a white ground."

My nine-year-old brother sat on the sled and waited for me to pull him along. The sled careened at my first tug and spilled Fred onto the snow. He shook himself off and signed, "You sit Ruth, I pull you." My father, annoyed, shook himself off and signed, "Do not sign, you are hearing children. I want see you talk with mouths to one another."

In my father's presence we automatically signed, including him in our words.

But Benny's anger bounded across the landscape. We succumbed to his wish and spoke to each other, omitting him from our speech once more. It made me uncomfortable but he took pride in watching his offspring speak. For him, it was a mark of success, an entry into another place from which he was permanently excluded.

We reached the park outlined in white. The trees were thick with snow. And as we passed under a laden limb, my father shook the tree and the snow fell on our uncovered heads. He rubbed his hands. "A wonderful snow. God's snow cold good wet. He made us to have a pleasure in His nature." He pushed us onto the ground. "Now we have a ride. Ben lay first on sled, then Freddie, then you Ruth on top. You are lightest person." We piled onto the sled, and instantly we were off down the hill screaming with glee. He maneuvered the sled around the bushes skillfully. When we got to the bottom of the hill, he rolled us off his back, rolling our bodies in the snow, wetting our faces and hands in the solid whiteness. The temperature kept the snow from thawing, and we played for hours.

People collected in the park, gathering on the hill's crest. But we had already left our mark on the snow; we created the paths that others followed.

"Too many people, spoil our fun, New York too crowded. We go home now, we have breakfast Momma wait for us."

It was noon. We had not recognized the passage of time. We walked home swiftly in the soiled snow, pulling the sled behind us. My mother's arms were out the window, pulling in her frozen laundry, each piece stiff as she lifted the clothespins from the line stretched across the alley. I touched my pajamas, still cold, and my hand left its print, softening the icy flannel fabric. My mother sensed human presence, turned around and asked, "Why you so long time away? Miss breakfast, now time for lunch. What is matter with you Ben, not think of hungry children?"

"Children not hungry before, we have good time in beautiful snow, all quiet."

"Help me finish laundry, you Ben fold towels, make

warm with hands, not so stiff. Then we have a lunch for all family.

"Spaghetti lunch ready, I will warm up, put plates on table."

My father turned to me, black eyes shining. "Snow is better than spaghetti, right Ruth?"

"I am hungry now."

"Well, hurry up to help me fold clothes and sheets and we eat so soon as finish our work."

I trailed behind him, putting my mother's laundry in the drawers, pushing him with my hands. "Hurry up!"

"Be a patient, work before eat!"

It was a happy time, a cocooned time. The winter of 1941.

The snow came again, heavy, coating the windows in sheets of white, one flake overlapping another. I rubbed the windowpane with my hand, breathed my warm breath against the open spot, wanting to see the sky above, the street below. The wind pushed the whiteness in small hills against the windowsill. I couldn't see outside.

My father came to help me see into the air. He rubbed the glass with his hands and still we could not see outside.

"Winter special time, time to stay inside and tell stories."

"You do Charlie Chaplin again, make show."

"No, not now. Now I tell you real story of real people. You always listen stories Momma tell you her family. I tell you my story. You listen. You watch what I say. Interesting story." His fingers elongated the signs.

"My family very smart in Russia, long ago. My mother's father, he was doctor to the Tsar. Had big family, rich man."

I imagined the court, splendid, with jewel-bedecked men and women sliding across cavernous rooms, paying homage to the Tsar and Tsarina. I saw my great-grandfather advising the nobles, I saw him care for the ills of the courtiers.

My father shoved my shoulder. "Stop to dream, listen what I say. Maybe he not a doctor, maybe he was man who make medicines for sick people, pharmacist, like drugstore man on a corner store. Maybe he was secretary to big Tsar. But sure, he was with the Tsar, big important man."

Did he never get a story straight? I wanted to know why the stories he told me were incomplete, fuzzy, why I had to fill in the blank spaces; I was confused and he was clear. The specific detail was absorbed in the drama of his hands. He manufactured what he did not know. And I never quite knew what was true, or how he embellished the truth.

"All story true!" his hands insisted.

"In Russia, like all places in world, people hate Jews." His hands opened at the thumb and forefinger, he placed them against his waist and banged his waist twice to make the sign for *Russia*. He did it once more, forcefully. "Russia not good for Jewish people, but my grandfather friend of the Tsar. He help him to escape to America. Big pogrom coming."

"That's not true, why would the Tsar help a Jew?"

"I have proof. Listen me. I tell you at end of story."

I waited in disbelief for him to continue. He didn't use his voice, only his body, his hands.

"The Tsar give to my grandfather many horses, I think forty horses, and he take a big boat, with his family, and horses in bottom of old wooden ship for many days, weeks, maybe months, took with him all his ten children, boys and girls, and boat went across ocean, over wavy water, till at last they reach Texas and my grandfather have horse ranch. But my grandfather stupid with horses, not know how use hands for horses and big farm work, only know how use his mind."

He had me believing him. His hands were convincing. I asked, "I thought your family lived in Canada? What is this about Texas?"

"Be a patient. I tell you."

"My grandfather, he lose everything, all horses. But he still rich man, he take his family by a boat, once more, this time to New York City. There he need to make money. Some smart people, they sell him Newark, New Jersey."

"Newark, New Jersey?"

"Yes, I tell you true story about my grandfather. He still stupid man, he buy all swamp land. He disgusted, again people fool him."

"Did you ever see a picture of him? Did you know him?"

"No, I never see him, he leave for Winnipeg, Canada, to be near friends from his town. His name Moshe Katz, his wife name Rachel. You, Ruth, are name for her, for my mother Lizzie's mother."

"Why didn't you see him?" I wanted to know.

"Wait, wait, you mix up my story. He go north country, cold like Russia, and take with him all family, but not my mother. But he take with him pearls that Tsar give to him."

"What pearls?"

"The Tsar, he like Moshe Katz, and gave to him a reward for his work, pearls and horses. Horses now dead many years pearls still in my family in Winnipeg. I know this true, we talk of pearls often. Maybe one day family break up pearls and you get two pearls, one for each ear. I wish this. For earrings, for pretty ears. Your ears and my ears look the same; stick out from head, but your ears smaller and hearing ears. Yes, I shall write a letter to family in Canada and ask to give you two pearls from Tsar's necklace. You named for Rachel, and you shall have Rachel pearls from my grandmother."

My father's letters are famous. The family has saved them. He wrote as he spoke, not in the language of spoken English, but in the language of the deaf transposed to written words. It was awkward. At times his language was incomprehensible to the hearing reader unaccustomed to his deaf thought process, but it was his language, striking at the essence of meaning.

"Don't worry on me, I write a letter! My cousin who has pearls will understand what I say, what I mean. Be sure, I write correct letter."

"Why," I asked, "not your mother have pearls?"

"This is other long story. Some in family say my mother only eleven years old when she marry my father, some say she thirteen years old. My father Morris, he was thirty-four years old, with two children, Dora and Sam, when he marry my mother. His first wife, she die when she have third baby, baby die too.

"My mother Lizzie, she work for my father Morris in his cork factory. She was young girl, maybe they love, maybe he need her, nobody knows. But my grandfather, Moshe Katz, angry, very angry, take his daughter to a courtroom. He tell judge she too young to marry, under age, not allowed to marry so old a widow man. My mother, she lie, she say she is old enough, she is fifteen years old, ready to marry. Court judge believe her so she marry my father.

"Her family leave her, go away to Winnipeg, she never see her father again, he never let her in his house, to death."

My father paused. His hands stopped. And he said to me in voice, "You understand my family history?"

"Yes, it is a sad story."

"Not finished story. I tell you more. My mother alone in New York, all family gone and she have two big children as stepmother. I think Dora was eight years old and brother Sam twelve years old, and my mother maybe only thirteen, most fourteen years old. Maybe really eleven years old. Who knows truth? My mother and father have their own baby, a boy, Bernard. He die. Then I born, I become sick at two years old, my health dropped down and I am blind with meningitis. Nobody know I have only weak eyes, don't believe I was blind, just poor eyes, not follow people with eyes. But nobody know I am deaf for long, long time. My mother leave me on a bed on big oak table in kitchen room to watch me all the day while she work to cook foods for big family. My mother tell me, 'God punish me because I marry your father.' You think God punish my mother because not obey her own father? Make baby Bernard die, make me deaf?"

"No, Daddy, I don't believe, life sometimes run that way."

We are speaking deaf words, one to the other.

"Once I see a picture of me, I was little boy, I sit on my mother's lap. She told to me that it was a snap photo of us in Winnipeg. I think my grandfather must be in grave, dead. I know my mother miss her family. She lonely long time, so she have big family, many children. She had ten children: Bernard born before me first; then me, deaf son; and many sisters, Anna, Bessie, Rose, Sylvia, Frieda, twin girls Mildred and Pearl, twins die as babies, diphtheria, and last baby brother Irving. Only seven live whole life."

His eyes focused away from me. He was remembering without me, his thoughts concealed.

"Never mind past, it is all gone, sometimes I think it is better to forget, then I tell you no. Better to remember, every person on earth has story. I tell story to my daughter, you Ruth tell to your children, then no life is lost and all remember all people. This is the life. Past must be to know. Help life to live, important to children who come in family later, maybe hundred years later. My father never tell me about his family. I know nothing. He is absent man on earth. I remember little of him, only he not sign much, not talk to me, but he help me to find job when I leave school. And he love your Momma Mary better than his own daughters. He sign to me all his girls stinky, but not Mary. You remember my father?"

I remembered him, tall, hollow cheeked, gray; I remember him as a disheveled, dirty, wordless man. When I was five he took me by the hand to his apartment on the main floor of the brownstone we shared. He put his index finger over his lips admonishing my silence, my vow of secrecy. He led me to a large oak closet, pulled a huge ring of keys from his bulging pocket and opened the door. I stood before his treasures. Each shelf was jammed. Jars of food, Oriental enamel vases, brass bowls and stale rye bread wrapped in newspaper littered the top shelf. Half a dry salami, herring in cream sauce with onions floating in a chipped crock, and a small keg of sour pickles and sour green tomatoes and garlic buds shared the next shelf with open boxes full of buttons in all colors. And on the bottom shelf, next to open boxes of needles and thread, were squares of glossy cardboard on which he sewed buttons for my grandmother's pushcart and a pair of used roller skates. I was awed by his stored wealth.

He handed me the skates and a skate key. I didn't move. Was this for me, from a man who never spoke to me? In silence, he motioned me to sit down on a kitchen chair; he bent over and put the skates on my shoes, took the rusted skate key from my hand and tightened the skates. He lifted me out of the chair, held me, balancing me on wheels. He pushed me gently and I slid across the uneven wooden floor, stunned by my sudden speed. He grabbed me as I fell, pulled me up and walked me to the door. He held my hand down the steps, put my free hand on the iron railing leading to the street. In the street, he walked me on the skates. Then he let go, pressed the skate key into my hand and shoved me off. His face turned into a small smile as he walked away.

We never spoke. I never said thank you. Did he think I was deaf too? I recounted this memory for my father. He signed, "Strange man, Morris my father. He did same to your Momma Mary when we just marry."

"He gave Momma skates?"

"No, he gave Momma herring from same closet when all family go to work, when no one stay at home. Momma say most delicious herring in all world, she taste.

"Before he old and no can work more, he find me a trade. But before that time, when I was young boy I work hard for my family. We live in Water Street and every morning early, before family wake up at five o'clock in mornings, I put wood and coal together in a stove to make fire for family in wintertime. I was good boy.

"I help my mother Lizzie by washing and sweeping floors every day. I think myself a female sister sometimes, probably a fool, no sense. They use me too much? You think I have a fool sense?"

A fool sense? No, not a fool. Not Benny, not my father.

"I like help everybody. I wish give you million dollars. Work hard, too hard not good. Have money, then you free person, do things to enjoy a life."

"When I was a boy need money to go to movies. I look for work with sanitation department men who sweep streets clean from horseshit and dirty papers. The supervisor of sanitation men gave me piece of paper, list of hot meals to buy at grocery store for working men. I get tip, two cents sometimes. So I go look for hearing or deaf boys who had few pennies to share. If a boy had three cents and I had two cents, then we had one nickel, enough for two boys to go to movies. I do this often, to share with other boys so we both have a pleasure afternoon at movies theater.

"When I was older, bigger boy, I had plenty free times. But I grow up. I want earn my own money. I quit a school when I am sixteen. My father tell me to stay at school, he sign writing in his hands, he push hard to tell me to stay at school. I was sixteen years old, I leave a school to learn life outside, to earn my own money, real money, not tips like errand boy for men who sweep garbage.

"Near to our house, few doors down at 110 South Eighth Street, was upholstery shop. My father take me there to arrange to learn a trade for me. I there work for two months, apprentice boy to learn without a pay. Later many years, my sister Anna tell me that my father give to shop owner eight dollars a week to pay me salary. I never receive. My father kind like me but talk to me little. I sorry that. Not know who is my father.

"I go to work in funny clothes for today. I wear knickers and high leather shoes. I wear lisle stockings, black stockings, girl stockings belong to one of my sisters. But no one laugh, no one know. In this time I strong, smart. I enjoy to work, learn trade, learn fast. In third month, owner pay me himself ten dollars a week. In fourth month I make twenty-one dollars. I work there for one year until union delegate come. I have raise to twenty-six dollars and fifty cents each week. I work good, perfect, never mistake, very neat.

"Still not enough money. Myself, I go to union office, write notes to delegate on pad with pencil, look for better place. Make thirty-one fifty a week, then later forty-five dollars in shop on Broadway and Twelfth Street in Manhattan, New York City. I know how to fight for myself, talk better than my father. I get what I want. Deaf, very smart.

"People tell me big whale stories at work. Want me lend money. I not believe them. Not listen. Let them think what they want. I know real world. I learn more good lessons every day, learn new words, understand language and money."

I was no longer present for him. Like my mother he went on in his own hands, not to tell me his story but to tell himself, to remind himself that he was Benny.

Part Three

GROWING UP
HEARING

Nine

CHILDHOOD LOST

> *Say not: I am a child;*
> *For to whomsoever I shall send thee thou shalt go,*
> *And whatsoever I shall command thee thou shalt speak.*
> *Be not afraid of them . . .*
>
> —*Jeremiah 1:6–8*

One winter's day in 1936 my father Benny rode the bus to Philadelphia. Cornered by the Depression, desperate, he went to his hearing brother Irving to borrow money. Irving, young, without cash reserves, unable to help, turned my father away. Almost fifty years later, Benny bit down, gently, on the nail bed of his index finger to show me how he fought the tears in his brother's presence. My father was thirty-three years old; Irving was not yet twenty. Perhaps Benny believed that sound provided money. His hair white, hands still strong, he signed, "I left Irving's home, love brother Irving, ashamed to ask so young a boy. I cry, each eye cry a tear. Big. I do not know what I must do for family foods. I think of Ruben who jump from roof. Not me. I have family."

He touched me, pausing in memory. "I leave to come to New York again by a bus. I sleep not in the night. Next morning I get up from the bed early, at the milkman's time. You, Freddie, Momma still sleep. I go down, follow milkman, and when he is away from truck, I steal two bottles milk to give my children foods."

My mother's hands gasped, "Ben you never told me before that story."

"I not tell you everything," my father said, dropping his hands into his lap.

"Do you remember," my mother shouted at him, hands flying, "I find five dollars on a street in big pile of snow, same day you come home from Philadelphia?"

"Yes," my father nodded, "we had plenty money for foods all week. Some left over."

Credit fed our family. In those years we were always behind in our payments to the butcher, the grocer; each merchant thumb-licked the frayed pages of the neighborhood's financial status; each merchant determined how much credit to extend, when to withdraw. When our payments to the butcher exceeded the unspoken allotted amount, it was cut off, resumed again when partial payment was made.

When we moved from Brooklyn to the Bronx my father left a debt of four dollars and forty-four cents at the butcher. A year later we visited the old neighborhood and my father saw Mr. Roth, the butcher. He signed, "I am afraid butcher punch me in the nose, so I carry you Ruth, fast down street, the other way." He laughed.

But I didn't. By the time I was seven, I became part of the credit ritual, aware of counted pennies, skilled in food trade. I could speak fluently. There was no need for pointing, no need for handwritten notes. My mother did not know that my short journey to the grocer's was a dangerous one, all for a quarter pound of sweet butter.

Izzy the grocer had a small domain. The store was crammed with food that fed the street in the days before the supermarket. His wife Sara and his two sons ran the Dawson Street store; it was safe to enter when his family was there. When Izzy was there alone I waited outside until another customer arrived, but it didn't always happen. Then I walked in alone, my breath silent.

I had to do my mother's bidding. She flashed her hands at me, cajoling, "You go down and tell him we need butter, tell him mark it down in the owing money book."

My mother reminded me as I opened the door, "Tell him we pay him what we owe, tomorrow or Saturday when Daddy Ben gets a pay."

Was the butter eighteen cents? Our food was purchased daily and the money was doled out daily by my father, the guardian of cash.

I walked into the grocery store. The butter sat creamy rich in the center of the large glass-enclosed refrigerator; there were two tubs, one of salt butter, the other sweet. I could smell it over the dried beans and peas, sitting in rolled burlap sacks on the floor; over the crinkling cellophane of the balloon-dotted Wonder Bread on the counter.

Izzy had receding red hair and dark freckles, and wore a large white apron. I watched those hands lift the side of the apron and then wipe a soiled buttered hand across the face of his abdomen. I stiffened with resolve, with fear, wanting to deny the price he extracted for spooned sweet butter.

Still and solemn, I let Izzy take me to the back of the shop, a small dark area where he kept his accounts, new stock, and fresh eggs. "Let me show you how to candle eggs. I have large ones today."

The store was empty, his wife was not there nor his sons;

not one son for protection from this man. Steeled and quiet, I let him stroke me and find the baby genitalia with adult fingers and hands. Hands were meant to speak, not to hurt.

A voice broke through the curtain. "Izzy, are you there? I need a quarter pound Swiss cheese and two onions. Izzy, where are you?"

He put his hands over my mouth and cautioned silence. I was silent. Frightened.

As Izzy was waiting on his customer, I slipped from behind the curtain and said, "I was here before Mrs. Garabedian, I was just in the bathroom."

I turned to Mrs. Garabedian. "I hope you don't mind, my mother is in a hurry."

Firmly I addressed Izzy: "Don't you have my mother's butter yet?"

The child molester, the grocer, put my mother's package in a small brown bag and sent me off, knowing I would be back before my father's next payday. But I had escaped with the butter and my body for the moment.

Did my mother pay the same price? Did my mother send me instead of going herself? Or was she so ashamed of her deafness and her lack of money that she sent her mouth and her ears, me?

Or was I bad? Had I done something wrong? I was never sure. I turned for solace to my pen, and in another year I wrote a poem that I titled "No Self." When I was young, Freud was unknown to me. He might have helped when I lamented:

> *Cross eyed cross faced little girl*
> *Sad, bad little girl*
> *Eared, heared little girl*
> *Give me your ear*
> *Give me your voice*

Give me your tongue, your mouth
I gave you life
Your life is mine
I did not have ears
I made a pair
Be me, be me, be my dream
Be me, sad bad little girl
You are lost and I am lost
I love you for you are mine
Little girl, little girl.

I found my own path to mourning. When I was alone, I veiled my fear; I had an empty dead face. In public I sparkled. By the time Izzy the grocer made contact with my heart and body, I was cemented into a pose that hardened with each passing year.

I learned the art of pretend and practiced it to near perfection. I read fairy tales and assumed new personalities. I read comics and pranced full-breasted in my imagination. I chose pretentious names for myself. Within a single week I changed my name from Dixie to Russell and back again to Dixie. Ruthie was too plain. Ruthie described someone I wanted to shun.

I converted dreams to reality, reality to dreams. I was a comic-strip figure, a curved blond female named Dixie, with no past, no future, a line drawn into the present, into the daily newspaper, to be discarded into each day's garbage. Exchanged words appeared in carelessly drawn shapes over the heads of the cartooned heroines. I rejected Dixie; she was silly. Perhaps I should be the Dragon Lady with slanted eyes, Chinese silk brocade gowns, hands clasped together, hidden by long sleeves, nostrils arched, dispensing cruel commands. Or a lady detective.

It was safe to sink into another.

I lied openly in the classroom. When asked to tell about our backgrounds, our parents and grandparents, I boldly volunteered to be the first to speak. I was nine years old when I walked to the front of the room and said before thirty children, "I am descended from an American Indian tribe. My great-grandfather came from England and was a pioneer with Daniel Boone, in Kentucky. There he met my great-grandmother and married her. That is why I have such dark hair."

I was delighted with my charade. Although my teacher smirked at my recital, I did not know her kindness. She never mentioned my historical confusion. And no one knew my deaf secret.

I would not see the tragedy of deafness; I would talk of nothing but pretty things. I rejected my soul's longing to be like other children. I believed that there was only one side to a coin, the fair side. I never dared turn the coin over; the dark soundless void, I knew, would make me mad. I couldn't countenance madness. Instead, I grew lovely and gay. Blessed with my father's passion for life and my mother's looks I passed for a whole person. No one entered the withered side of my being. Not even me.

My mother glimpsed my sadness and her remedy was play. She loved fun. Up, up went the arms, the two middle fingers of each hand banded by imaginary thin leather straps, clicked down and she snapped her castanets, tossing her head into flamenco frenzy. "Come play, we are gypsies now. I teach you dance like gypsy girl! We have good time now."

She swirled to Freddie and handed him two tablespoons; she raised a finger to me and said in full voice, "One minute, your turn soon." She lifted a tambourine from the table and shook it in the air. It was the dented lid of her stewing pot.

"We make music now. You, Fred, are boy, you play

drums on table with spoons; you, Ruthie, sing with girl's voice. And I play drum with bells and dance."

She lifted her skirt to her knees in haughty gesture, tossed her head again, shook her tambourine and in one bold strike and voice conducted, "Begin now."

Freddie banged with his spoons. I opened my mouth to sing a tuneless song. I could not sing but did not tell my mother. But Mary, my mother Mary, was the star performer. She strutted and stomped with Spanish gypsy fire in perfect cadence. Her ebullient joyousness erased the nocturnal silences, but not Izzy the grocer's vile hands.

I sensed my mother's solitude at the window. When her day's housework was done she sat framed by the window meditating, in repose, resting her face on her hand, gazing unobserved at the people in the street. She studied their faces, their gait, their clothes with heightened acuity until I came into view. Momma was always at the window waiting for my return from school, waiting for her family life to begin.

"Momma, what do you see in the street every day?"

"I see people, I understand their lives, what they do, why they are happy, when they are sad. I like to see a rush of life in the street."

"It is raining today, no one is in the street."

She looked at me surprised. "There is rain to watch."

I looked at the rain with her, my school books still in one hand, and thought my own thoughts . . .

—It is raining. And the lightning cracks. The thunder comes and no one hears it but me. She does not cower in fear. She loves the sight of the jagged light across the visible sky. I want her to hear it. I want her to feel my shock and momentary fright. Momma has her face up to the sky waiting for one more strike of light. The walls reverberate with overhead thunder. Her lower lip trembles and her eyes light with the sky. She says, "I feel thunder, I hear thunder." She does not hear it; feeling is not hearing. It passes through her as it passes through the walls. Only I hear it, huddled inside myself.

She caught my thoughts. "Don't worry, I see plenty. Never mind I do not hear thunder. It is big thrill to feel heavy noise."

She kept her windows sparkling clean. When I saw her sitting outside the window, five floors up, holding herself to the window frame with one hand, scrubbing away the city's grime with the other, I held my breath in silent prayer:

—Please God, don't let Momma fall.

I rushed up the stairs, anxious not to startle her, yet wanting desperately to hold her knees to the wall inside the apartment. She scolded me when I did this: "I not fall, I know how to hold myself."

She washed the windows with clear vinegar and water, and squeaked them to a shine with a discarded copy of the *Daily News*. When the window shone, she raised the sash and slid from her unsecured perch on the window ledge into the apartment. "See," she said, "I am safe."

"Momma, why do you wash the windows outside? Inside is good enough."

"No, not good enough. Window is my art, my painting to world. To see art, windows must be clean."

On wintry Sundays, she hurried us into our coats and warm gloves, insisting that we wear hats, and took us to the Metropolitan Museum of Art on Fifth Avenue. We feasted on Tintoretto and Canaletto, Rembrandt and Vermeer. She studied the names of the artists and the paintings, forgetting them from one Sunday to the next. She did not know art history but she moved unerringly from masterpiece to masterpiece.

She pulled me by the hand across a room laden with treasure. "Come," she beckoned, "see this painting, see how the artist paint."

My father did not have time for learning in the years when I was young. He worked sixteen hours a day when he could get work, and when there was no work, he scoured the neighborhood and found work here and there that would put money in his pocket. "You look at art with Momma; you tell me beauty later," he signed.

I wanted a telephone but did not ask for one. Whom would I call? Nonetheless, it was my heart's desire. I loathed public telephones. I did not like relaying messages, however urgent, for my mother and father. Early one evening, my mother gave me a nickel and asked me to call my father at a small upholstery shop where he had found temporary work. I went to the corner candy store, where three telephone booths were clustered together in the darkest corner of the shop. As I walked into the shop, past the magazine racks, past the sour smell of unwashed ice cream dishes, the owner of the dank emporium greeted me with his usual remark: "Still don't have a phone?"

I kept on walking, repeating my mother's brief message to myself. "Please tell your father's boss to tell Daddy Ben to come home early tonight, no later than ten P.M."

I hated going into the booth, closing the door and smelling the bodies that had been there before me. The heavy black receiver through which I listened and the mouthpiece through which I spoke were soiled objects. I dialed the number my mother had written on a piece of scrap paper.

After the second ring a man's voice said, "Hello."

"Is this the Westchester Upholstery Shop?"

"Yes, what do you want?"

"Are you the owner?"

"Yes, what do you want?" the voice insisted. "I don't have all day."

"I have a message for Mr. Sidransky, from his wife, my mother."

"I don't know any Mr. Sidransky!" He was annoyed.

"His first name is Ben. He is my father."

"Listen girlie, I don't have time for this. I'm busy."

"He's deaf." I gave my father his worldly definition.

"Oh," he responded with recognition. "You mean Dummy. Just a minute, I'll get him. Why didn't you say so in the first place?"

I don't remember the rest of that conversation. All I remember is the word *dummy*. It reached into my ear, into my skull, through that black phone.

No hearing person had used that word in my presence before. I heard my parents described as "deaf and dumb" all through my childhood. I took great pains to explain to anyone who would listen that although they were deaf, they were not dumb, nor were they mute.

I wanted to shriek into the phone, to that faceless voice, "You are a dummy! You are hearing and dumb!" I did not speak the words. The anger and shame coursing through me at that moment crystallized into resolve. I was determined that no one would ever call me or my father by that name again. I learned whatever was set before me and I taught my father whatever I could, whenever I could. When other girls played house, I played school and I was always the teacher.

I asked my father the next day, "Why do you let your boss call you Dummy?"

He shrugged, his nostrils still full of cotton from the shop. "I tell him my name is Ben. I tell everyone my name is Ben, but they call me Dummy. It is easier for them. They remember me."

I was enraged. "You are not a dummy. You are my father and a smart man. Tell them over and over that your name is Benjamin."

He smiled wanly, tired with the long day's work. "It is all right. I know I am not dummy, that is enough."

It was not enough for me. I became gluttonous. I read the dictionary every night, absorbing language, and taught the language to my father. I discarded my old make-believe words. He was insatiable. He and I had purpose. Our minds melded in study.

"I glad you teach me. I work hard. To learn new things make me happy."

His struggle was not ennobling. There was no advantage to it; there was no joy, no beauty, no fulfillment. It was boring work to keep our mouths fed, our bodies clothed and the rent paid. Yet he was the consummate craftsman, proud of his dexterity.

I stopped hanging my head. I walked with a firm stride, my head high. I was eleven years old.

I put aside my world of pretense, denying my fairy tale existence. I chose another path; the path of academic excellence. The attitude grew quietly within my child's chest, year after year stunting my emotional growth. I prepared to show the world that I was no "dummy." "Sticks and stones may break my bones, but names will never harm me." I repeated the refrain to myself, almost prayerfully, to eradicate the hateful word. When I walked along the streets I traced the word DUMMY on soot-laden cars with my index finger, and then with a swift swipe of my hand I erased the word from my sight. I wrote the word in my notebook in pencil, across the surface of the page, tore it out and crumpled the defamation into a ball. I sat in the classroom after the insult and lost days of learning until my father prodded me with his quest for knowledge.

He reawakened my thirst for language. In our mutual hunger to have words feed us and connect us to the hearing psyche, we resumed study. His primary passion involved clear thinking and comprehension. When I was in doubt about a concept or a word that I was teaching him, he said, "You must ask the teacher again. Must be clear."

The sign for the word *clear* is a revealing one. The fingertips of each hand are closed, forming a small circle, the two circles join as the tips of the fingers touch, and then the hands are opened wide permitting light to enter. It is a sign of illumination. Clarity becomes the epiphany, the moment of knowing. The sign takes but a second to execute.

Knowledge alone was not what my father sought. It was the process, not the product, that thrilled him. He taught me the art of knowing and the art of questioning. If I didn't understand the teacher's response to a question, he assumed that I had asked the wrong question. He said, "You smarter than teacher, you ask another question and another, make sure teacher know what you ask. You teach the teacher."

And so I became a teacher, skilled at communicating. I learned the art of presence from my father; I was present at my own learning and present when I taught him. I questioned my teachers until I understood every facet of their teaching. It made no difference whether the teacher was inept or masterful; each had a gift for me. My teachers were flattered by my rapt attention and they responded with verbal attention.

I loved my teachers. I manipulated my own behavior to achieve their nurturing words. Each woman teacher was a parent, stroking me with audible words of praise. I both loved and loathed the praise; they praised my mask, not me. I had been rubbed raw by pain and had never named it. My elementary school teachers recognized this and tended me carefully.

The jolt came when I went to Junior High School 60. I had so many teachers in one day—one for English, one for French, one for math, one for history—that I was unable to find one single comforting teacher. I was just another face in the incoming seventh grade. There was not enough time in a fifty minute class to develop a relationship with a mother-teacher.

When we changed classrooms, we were ordered to walk the halls in silence or get a demerit for speaking. I was horrified. How could they punish anyone for speaking to people who can hear? My new world was hideous. I traveled the black halls winding in silent roads from room to room, from one aging gray-haired teacher to another, sat locked in classes that had been taught at the turn of the nineteenth century. My English teacher, a tiny, shriveled martinet, sent terror into my soul for a dangling participle or an incorrectly parsed sentence. What did she know about living language?

There was nowhere to breathe and I went into deep emotional hiding. I became ill. In that first month of school, I retreated to my bed and spent a week in lethargy. The pressure had become too great for me to bear. I stepped back into my abandoned fantasy, fondling my childhood in fairy-tale sustenance. I was reaching for someone to understand me as I understood the young princess who was banished because the king, her father, did not understand her innate goodness. After years of exile the princess and the king were reconciled. There was a happy ending, as there was in every fairy tale filled with trial, and I wanted a happy ending for my own life.

The wounds of the week healed and I returned to school; I forged my path once again. I centered all my energy into my intellectual life. It was a gargantuan effort that hid me from me by day. Carefully tucking away my fear of the unknown, I entered the cloistered life of the dedicated student, absorbing the words of others, denying my own. My mind was rapacious and grew rampantly, but there was a part of me that remained isolated.

My family treated me like a prodigy. I heard them say

in whispered corners, "Isn't Ruthie remarkable?" They patted me on the head like a smart dog who performs faultless tricks. I said nothing. I was incapable of publicly identifying myself. My hearing aunts and uncles only saw my passive smile.

I continued to hoard words as a miser hoards gold. I collected books and saved them, saved the words that would make me full, that would make me like the rest.

At times I went hungry as a child. My father said, "Do not eat all dinner, we must save some for tomorrow." We always had food but Benny lived in dread of the day when there would not be enough to feed us. Once food was consumed it was gone. I couldn't consume the words on a printed page. The words could be saved, read and reread. My hunger transferred to my books and as an adult I transported books, across the Atlantic Ocean, across the American continent, several times, never rereading them. I put my books on a shelf, dusted them, and sighed in safety. I had my words with me. They were the reflection of my childhood. They dispelled my grotesque nickname: Dumbo. I recoiled when I heard that word. I made every effort to ignore it, until the taunting became worse than the sound of the word. My skin crawled and I turned to the enemy and said in even distinct tones, "My name is Ruthie."

And the words came, "Fly away Dumbo, take your dumb floppy ears and lift off into the sky."

My ears were small, shaped like tiny flat teacups. I wanted them out of sight and out of range of the verbal abuse that struck me. I hid my ears behind my long dark hair, hoping that one day they would be perfect.

Even more, I wanted a telephone of my own, I wanted to call my friends and have them call me. I asked my mother for one, and she said, "Ask your father." And he said, "What for, you don't need telephone, go down to candy store and make calls to your friends. I give you five cents." I explained that people could call me at any time, that I could be part of the world, connected to everyone. He was adamant and closed the conversation. "Not need phone. Too much money."

I felt stripped, unable to make him understand what I needed, unable to make the hearing understand what I needed. In the stillness of denial I repressed my urgent need and waited for a telephone until I was fifteen.

I lied about my age and got a part-time job selling books at Macy's at 34th Street on Broadway at Herald Square. I passed their version of a literacy test and was surrounded by books on Thursday nights and Saturdays. I earned seven dollars a week before taxes and saved the money to pay for my telephone.

When the phone was installed in our living room my father asked, "Does it work? Call someone!"

I called the operator and asked for the time of day.

My mother laughed, "Can't you call a real person?"

"I don't have anyone's phone number, but I will get them and call everyone."

We sat down and wrote postcards to everyone we knew, announcing the birth of our new phone. And I thought of Alexander Graham Bell, who had invented the phone to help the deaf hear. Only Freddie and I could hear it ring. I gently rubbed the phone with my hand and felt its connective power. I could speak through it and receive messages through it. It was a miraculous instrument. My mother reveled in its strength.

If she happened to be dusting the phone when I was out and it rang, she picked it up and said, "Ruthie not here, call back tonight." When I got home she excitedly told me that there was a telephone call.

"Show me how you answered the phone," I said.

She put the speaker to her ear and the receiver to her mouth. We practiced until she got it right. Delighted with her new skill, she said, "See, I use phone like hearing people."

She was never able to use the phone and receive messages until the advent of the TTY. The TTY is a telecommunicator that uses both a typewriter terminal, which looks like a toy, on which messages can be typed and read in the space above the keyboard, and the telephone handset, which is cradled onto the top portion of the typewriter. Each time a letter is pressed the impulse flashes the letter on both screens simultaneously. About six words can fit on the screen at one time. It is a simple machine to use once the keyboard is mastered.

I pleaded with my parents for years after I left home to install a TTY in their apartment. They argued that they had been deaf all their lives and had done quite well without a phone. I argued that they were getting older and could not go out in the middle of the night and collar a stranger to make a call for them in case of an emergency. I told them that they could call me and their friends who already had TTYs. They agreed reluctantly.

Our first phone call, many years later in 1978, was momentous. They stumbled over the letters on the keyboard, taking turns talking to me. Their typing was slow and inaccurate but they were using the telephone. I received their words in flashing green letters. My mother finger pecked the words, "Ruthie, I love you."

I typed back quickly, "Pick up the phone and say the same words to me so that I can hear your voice."

She repeated, "Ruthie, I love you." And I heard three distinct kisses on the phone. My father took the phone from her and said, "Here is Daddy Ben, I love you lots." He, too, sent kisses into my ear.

I put the handset back on the typewriter and typed, "Your voices are clear, I understand your words and I love your kisses."

My mother typed back, "I am surprised. Did not know you can hear a kiss."

My fingers raced. "Yes, you can hear a kiss, the sound of a kiss is soft and sweet, but the sweetest sound of all is to hear my mother and father call my name."

My mother typed, "Why you not tell me get phone before?"

Long before that time, before the time of electronic connection, I was the disconnected child. By day I was in command, but at night, wrapped in silence, I had the heart of a frightened child.

The book I had taken from Miss Chanin's class was peopled with fairies and elves who granted wishes to wounded children. I took an elf from the book and made him my own. He wore pointed cloth shoes and had a tiny brown peaked cap no bigger than a thimble on his head. He fit into the palm of my hand. He appeared to me only once and bade me look for a wishing stone. It had certain requirements. It had to be flat, perfectly oval and pure white. It was to be a stone to fit into the warm center of my palm. It could not be given to me. I had to find it.

I looked for that stone, kept my eyes to the ground; it was not on the asphalt streets. I searched for it in nature's silence, hoping to find a chunk of earth carved to my dimensions, a flat stone to hold to me in secret, to be my talisman, to be my talking stone.

I found the elf's stone lying on the sand and asked as I held it tightly, not noticing the brown scar on its underbelly, "Do you have speech? Can you be attentive to me?" I talked to the sea in a whisper, "O mighty sea, can you talk to me?" I went into the park and asked the trees, "Will you talk to me?" The leaves hummed in the wind, the birds sang their song and the insect life moved unseen. But God's earth had no voice for me.

My stone was as mute as the Stonehenge monoliths. I stood encircled by the pillars at Stonehenge erected by unknown men in an English field and knew the mystery of silent stones. My dream of Stonehenge was a recurrent one.

The stones were stones and they were towering people, close, close to one another, tightly bound with their heads bent, peering down at me. They stared at me with wide rock eyes. They stared at me, Ruthie, the child in the middle. In unison they said, "No, no," with their stone mouths. Bewildered, I looked for one kindly stone face to take my hand and say, "I will do it for you. You don't have to do it yourself, all alone."

I stood within the sculpted ring of human stones with my mouth open, saying, "Don't say no, say yes!"

The stone heads didn't answer.

I shouted, "I will say yes."

The stones did not hear me; they were deaf. They gazed at me. My words had no meaning; they did not hear my plea, nor could they hear my cry or my sound, my wail or my laugh.

Again I shouted, my small fist waving in the air, "How can you be human if you are stone? You are deformed and ugly. Why did you make me human, with sound and feeling, to walk around alone in stone?"

I waited in my dream for a response. None came.

I continued my tirade: "You are faceless and formless. I will not water the weeds that grow around you in the poor scratched soil, nor will I clean your stones, nor will I listen for the intruder who can break your ring of stones. Stones you are, stones you be. I did not make you, you made me. And you did not make me of stone, so I must leave you, I bid you adieu."

I awakened angry, time and again. I pushed the anger away, mindful of its destructive power, rose from my bed and said to myself, "It is only a dream." I couldn't leave the ring of silent stones; they were deaf. I had nowhere to go but further into fantasy.

I fingered my almost perfect white, flat oval stone hoping it would reveal happiness with each magic caress. I froze into illusion, shutting out any possibility of thaw that would restore me to me. I was a hushed nomad wandering in search of sound. I knew peace in the green earth of summer. I sucked the soft sweet end of new grass and knew the word *promise*. In time, I became one with nature's mute earth, finding solace in grand silence. God, too, is silent.

Ten

WHEN OTHER
CHILDREN DIE

I exist as I am, that is enough. . . .
—*Walt Whitman,* Song of Myself

Death was remote and forbidden, yet it entered my life at moments when I was most open to wounding. We didn't talk of death at home, except on rare occasions. But when it came into our lives, we saw it and then brushed it aside until the next time.

My mother spoke of her firstborn child, Fanny, named for my grandmother who had died prematurely. She shook her head and said, "Nobody tell me why my baby die. Such a beautiful baby."

I was born thirteen months later. As I grew, my mother's fear that I would die diminished but her concern for my health was always present. When I had scarlet fever, she hovered at my bedside and told me that my friend Morris Merlis had scarlet fever too.

"You will get better and Morris will get better," she assured me.

Morris and I were bonded by parental deafness. He was dark and handsome, with a round face, soft brown eyes and a dark forelock that he continually pushed from his forehead with his delicate hand. We played hide-and-seek, crouching in the neighborhood's dusty privet hedges. My mother and his mother Rose guarded us with their eyes across the trolley tracks as they leisurely signed their afternoons away deep in animated conversation.

The street drunk lurched down toward us at play, and my mother shouted, "Be careful, bad drunk man comes." We responded instantly to the shrill voice and pretended not to hear. His mother shouted another warning and we stopped our play. For a moment our eyes touched and the silent sadness was there. We disregarded the glance immediately and Morris grabbed my hand, dragging me to the soil beneath the hedge out of the wobbling drunk's path.

Morris whispered, "Drunk is worse than deaf."

We didn't like people who were out of control. And the sounds our mothers made were out of control to the hearing person. Their sounds disturbed us only when we were in public; at home we were comfortable with the oral utterings that imitated normal speech. We instinctively understood that our parents were in control, that it was the rest of the world that did not understand us or our parents.

We grinned at each other, sharing our mighty insight, and played together. I was six and Morris was eight years old. It was 1935.

I remembered Morris as I was lying in bed recuperating from scarlet fever. I said to my mother as she sat on my bed reciting nursery rhymes for me with her hands, "I want to see Morris when I am better."

"Yes," she promised, "you and Morris will play together."

One week later, when I was well but still weak, she laid out my favorite red dress and said, "Today you wear happy dress. Morris like red color. We go out."

Excited, I dressed quickly and collected my sickbed presents to show Morris. Louis K. brought me a small sack of shiny colored marbles to roll around on my blanket. I wanted Morris to see them and shoot marbles with me at the curbside. I raced toward the door down the long corridor of our apartment and when I got to the kitchen my mother pulled me by the arm and scolded, "Wait! You must drink orange juice and cod liver oil before we go, make you strong."

My stomach retched at the thought of swallowing the thick spoonful of fishy oil, washed down by acid orange juice. I stepped gingerly into the kitchen and watched my mother open the brown wooden icebox, take out the vitamin D–fortified cod liver oil, pour it into a teaspoon, and push it toward my mouth. I kept my lips shut. She insisted and I opened wide, swallowed, drank the juice, asked for water and pleaded to leave without any more food.

It was a short walk to Morris's apartment. The warm sun touched the back of my neck. I was happy to be outside away from my bedroom, happy that I was going to see my friend Morris. My mother held my hand and said nothing to me. But she walked more slowly than usual.

We turned the corner to Morris's street and I pulled my mother, rushing her on. She paused, began to speak to me, then dropped her hands and said nothing. I ran from her side when her voice stopped me. It was sharp and I turned at her words: "Ruthie, do not go without me." I waited until she reached me and together, hand in hand, we walked slowly, deliberately to the Merlis home. We were standing on the opposite side of the street, part of the crowd that had gathered to watch four men carry a small mahogany coffin down the stone steps.

Rose Merlis, her husband Solomon and their children walked behind the coffin, crying softly. I was bewildered.

I pushed my mother. "Momma, where is Morris?"

"Not now," she shushed, "I will tell you later."

I watched as the men hoisted the coffin into the waiting hearse. The family members seated themselves in the black limousines and the small entourage drove off to the synagogue. The crowd drifted off, and my mother and I stood alone on the street.

"Momma, what is wrong? Why is everyone so sad?"

"Morris is no more. He die. He goes with God now."

I didn't understand that a child had died. I knew that we stepped on the cockroaches that scurried around the kitchen floor when we put the light on in the evenings, that we stomped on them until they were no more and threw them into the garbage, glad to be rid of the pests. I could not imagine that Morris would be thrown into the garbage. I could not imagine my life without Morris, splashing in rain-filled puddles, chasing each other down the street, waiting for the trolley car's clang on the streetcorner, counting the passengers who stepped down into the street. Where did Morris go?

"Momma," I begged, "why is Morris no more?"

"He was sick."

"Is he dead like the roaches? Did God step on him?"

"Nobody step on him. He very sick with scarlet fever. He was born with a bad heart. Too much sickness for little boy. Only eight years old."

"I had scarlet fever. I did not die. Why not?"

She held me in her arms and then freed her hands to tell me, "You not die, not your time to die. You healthy girl now."

I hid my fear of death, grabbed my mother's hand tightly and with my left hand asked, "Who will I play with now?"

She smoothed my hair with her hand and said, "You will find other children. You play with brother Freddie."

"Freddie is too little to play. He is three years old. I want a friend like Morris."

I never did find another Morris.

I only found my mother's tears. On gray November afternoons and on sun-filled May days when I came home from school, I found her stretched out on her bed, wracked by murmured sobs. Her stockinged feet faced me, her body heaved in labored rhythm; there were no audible words, only painful moans crushed in her throat.

I shrank.

She was not dead, she was in mourning.

"Momma," I said to her feet, "Momma, don't cry."

My mother, deep in her loss, was unaware of my presence. I spoke those words for me, to calm myself, hoping she would not die in her own tears. I couldn't face her swollen eyes, wet with unrequited grief. I turned from her privacy and hid in the kitchen until her sobs stopped.

On other afternoons, when I was stronger and found her alone and anguished, lamenting her mother's premature death, I sat on her bed and introduced my presence abruptly. She raised herself quickly and swung around, pivoting on her elbows, ashamed to have me find her so bereft. She took me into her arms and stroked my face. I had no tears on my face, nevertheless she dried them.

"Momma," I asked, "why didn't you watch for me at the window?"

"I watch for you always, I watch the hands on the clock. I know Ruthie come soon. And I begin to think of my first baby. Then I think of my mother. Too much death."

"Momma, it was a long time ago. Why do you cry so many afternoons?"

She stared beyond my head into the unknowable reaches of her mind and slowly signed, "I miss my mother. So kind a woman. She die too young."

"Momma," I asked, "how old are you?"

She sensed my fear and said in her shrill lilt, "Don't worry, I not die. I will not leave you alone."

She left the past and returned to me. She took my hands in hers and eased me from the bed. Her face changed. She was my mother Mary again.

"Come, I need you. We go shopping."

I refused. "No, I have homework to do."

"Too much homework. We go buy ice cream cone."

She relished ice cream but I did not like the sugary taste. I asked for tea, rye bread and butter.

"After, we have tea. Now we go outside, breathe fresh air and walk. We walk away crying tears. We laugh. We kiss life."

I laughed at her poetry, unable to resist her charm.

In 1939, her father Abraham lay dying. His impending death was accepted by my mother with greater peace than was her mother's death.

"We go visit my father today. He not live long and he want to see you and Freddie."

Freddie was seven and I was ten years old when we encountered the living face of death. We had little comprehension of the meaning of death. Life, as it is for the young, was forever. I could not perceive my grandfather, gray-faced with his eyes hollowed with lung cancer as I saw him. I imagined him propped up by ceremonial pillows at the Passover seder table, reigning over his family, praying and reciting the story of the Exodus from Egypt endlessly, until my mother caught my eye and surreptitiously signed, "Grandpa finish soon. Be patient. We eat soon."

I approached his bed. He lay, barely alive, like a faded wooden carving under the voluminous down comforter. I thought, how warm he must be. It is August and hot outside. His bright red hair was now the color of sand but his navy blue eyes were the same laughing ones I remembered from the festival table.

I went closer as he slid one hand slowly across the bed and strained to touch me. I gave him my hand but didn't speak.

"Come, Ruchal, come closer to me." He gave me my Yiddish name.

I moved closer, but was careful to keep my distance from death.

His tones were soft. He reminded me to take care of my mother and father as I had always done, to be a good girl, and then he said, "You must learn to eat olives. Do not spit them out." There were other words but I remained stuck on his olive sentence; I did not understand what he meant.

My mother led me out of the room, saying, "Grandfather tired now, he sleep. You play in living room with Freddie, I come soon."

I pondered over his cryptic sentence for years and only when I was an adult did I realize that he knew the bittersweet portion of my life. He knew I was loved, he knew of my pain in deaf parenting; he was the father of three deaf children.

When he died that September, my mother mourned but her grief was contained. I never found her crying for her father as she did for her mother.

I had mourned for my little friend Morris, but I didn't mourn my grandfather or the grandmother who died before I was born. Instead, I mourned my cousin Ruthie Babroff.

Ruthie was my father's sister Bessie's only child. Bessie had had other children, blue babies who were either stillborn or died immediately after birth. But Ruthie, the last of her children, survived infancy.

On the Sundays when my father and mother took us to the Lower East Side, we stopped at Bessie and her husband Sam's shop on a Rivington Street corner. It was a bigger, dirtier spinoff of my grandmother Lizzie's pushcart. The store tumbled with unkempt cardboard bins of razor blades, shaving cream, unbranded bottles of after-shave lotion, cheap slippers, needles and thread, hangers and belts, buttons and jobbers' close-outs of toys and assorted junk unsalable in the better stores. Sam stayed outside the store fondling a stack of one-dollar bills, snapping the rubber band that held his wealth while Bessie waited on customers and took cash.

In the lull between customers, Bessie often invited me to visit my cousin Ruthie and spend the night. I always refused. I didn't want to be with Ruthie. I was jealous of her treasured status and her pretty clothes. I was jealous of her hearing parents and her father's wad of cash.

I avoided the overnight visit until I was twelve. My mother finally prevailed upon my sense of courtesy: "Not nice you not visit Ruthie. She has the same name as you, for great-grandmother Rachel. Shame on you, you must go to Brooklyn to visit. You know how to go by subway alone. You big girl now."

So I went.

I was in awe of Ruthie's social skills; she wore lipstick when her mother was not in sight, and kissed the neighborhood boys. In the early evening, while Bessie was still in the store, we waited on the street corner for the young males to arrive. I watched Ruthie move off into the shadow of a doorway and kiss a boy. I stood there, not quite knowing what to do with my prepubescent body. A nameless boy rescued me and led me to a vacant darkened doorway. With my back pressed to the wall and our bodies wide apart, he graced my mouth with a slobbery wet kiss. It repelled me, but did not erase my admiration for my cousin Ruthie, who thrived on inept doorway romances. She was, after all, older than I; she was thirteen.

When our fumbling touching was done, we returned to her apartment to wait for Aunt Bessie's arrival from work.

She came in alone, exhausted, complaining that her feet hurt in spite of her heavy black laced shoes. She sat down, untied the laces and gently eased off her shoes, rubbing each foot. She smelled sour after her hard day's labor and the subway ride home. She sighed with relief.

I asked, "Where is Uncle Sam?"

I did not receive an answer to my question. No one, not even my mother, told me that Sam was in jail for a white-collar crime. Perhaps he failed to pay a debt; perhaps he embezzled some money; perhaps no one but Bessie knew the answer.

Bessie looked up and asked a mother's question: "Did you girls eat?"

"No," my cousin shouted. "We're hungry. Go down to the deli and get me and Ruthie hot pastrami sandwiches!"

Bessie cried with weariness.

"Cry blood!" Ruthie screamed at her mother.

I hated my cousin for those words. My envy and awe gave way to deep anger. I wished her dead for her cruelty.

I went home and put Ruthie and Ruthie's words out of my mind. Weeks passed and I had settled into the routine of my junior high school days—morning classes, home for lunch, back to school for the afternoon. On one bright June day, I came home for my favorite lunch.

My mother prepared a single pan-fried lamb chop, fresh boiled spinach, a baked potato and hot chocolate pudding. I always saved the baked potato and chocolate pudding for dessert, spooning the hot pudding over the potato. When I had the last delicious mouthful on my tongue, my mother said, "Take off your glasses and look at me. I have a bad news for you."

I looked up from lunch startled by her oral words.

"Your first cousin Ruthie, Bessie's daughter drowned and is dead."

I sat in horror, a lump of hot chocolate pudding on my tongue.

"How?" I asked.

Quietly, without using her voice once to clarify the words of her hands, my mother told me, "Ruthie's friends telephone to her and invite her to go rowing in Gravesend Bay. Ruthie did not want to go, but her mother Bessie told her to go and have a good time with friends, five people all together. Boat turned over, some swim to shore safely, but Ruthie drowned. They find her body and one other after two days in water."

I did not go back to school that afternoon, frightened of my power. I had wished her dead.

Years later I visited my father and mother unannounced. I walked into their apartment in mid-afternoon with my key as I had done as a child. My father, who was seventy, was sitting in a chair with his back to the door, dressed in a navy blue kimono. He turned to me, dazed, his arm in a sling, unaware that I was present.

"What happened to your hand?" I asked.

"My sister Bessie die in motel room. Poor Bessie had so hard life."

I pressed him. "What happened to your hand?"

"I think of my sister Bessie and poor daughter Ruthie all dead now. I think of them and not watch my work, and machine take off my finger."

He was then a mailer at *The New York Times*. As he had lifted a stack of newspapers from the assembly line to prepare them for the delivery trucks, the top joint of his right index finger was sliced off. Part of his voice was amputated. It took time for him to adjust to the stump; a link in his capacity to communicate had been damaged. When his finger finally healed, I had to pay close attention to his stubby finger, never telling him that I struggled to understand some of his signs.

His rage at deafness had quieted. Instead he feared death.

He saw my face and said, "My finger cut off, in grave I will have no finger."

I said nothing.

And he said, with a wide-eyed grin, "Never mind, I have new name. I am Nine-and-a-Half-Finger Ben." We both laughed.

"Don't worry, your father Ben, me, I will be all right. Just a big shock; Bessie die, Ruthie die and I lose my talking finger."

We sat quietly. He looked at me and signed awkwardly with his left hand, "I not afraid hearing people no more, I only afraid to die."

When my cousin Ruthie died, a part of me was buried, for I rejected a part of my own being. I slipped further into the pattern of nothingness. I didn't attend her funeral; my mother would not allow it. She told me that the funeral was a sad one. "To bury a child is worse than death."

I asked, "Did her father come to the funeral?"

"Yes," she answered, "he came with two detectives and after the funeral they took him back to jail. Terrible to watch Sam walk to grave on his knees."

The first time I saw my Aunt Bessie after that was at a family gathering months later. I looked at her blood red manicured fingernails as I spoke to her. She would not hear me; she moved off and spoke to someone else. She peered through me as though I were invisible. I could not bear to face her, nor did I wish her to utter the sound of my name. She averted her eyes from my presence, and I wondered if my five hearing aunts would look at me with aversion forever. My grandmother wept when she touched me but did not say my name. I wanted to know why my cousin had died and I lived, but I did not dare ask the question.

I moved over to my Aunt Sylvia for comfort. She smiled

and asked politely as though I were a stranger, "How are you today?" I answered tonelessly, "I am fine."

People moved back and forth across the room in a blur, babbling words to each other, ignoring me. I sat alone, a stranger in the room. And I was angry. I had been estranged by silence, and now I was estranged by my own name, a name that no one could say.

I was no stranger to pain. I recognized it in every wounded psyche that I met. I understood intuitively when people were denied touch, when they were lonely, when they were frightened of the unknown. In return I gave these people my smile, afraid that their pain would snake into my young heart. For a brief moment we touched, these nameless people and I, and we took solace in my smile.

But the silence my family lavished on my unwelcome presence was unbearable. I couldn't bear the pain of the wild silence, feigned a headache, and persuaded my mother to take me home.

I wasn't able to disgorge the enormity of that pain, nor was I able to mourn my cousin's death, until a year had passed. It was the weekend of my thirteenth birthday and my parents planned an outing to the beach. I laid my own plans, and bought a flower to lay on Ruthie's Atlantic grave. Coney Island and Gravesend Bay are waters of the Atlantic Ocean. I had decided that a beach funeral was appropriate, for I too needed to lay to rest this child who haunted me, so that I could be free.

I waited until my mother set up her domain on the beach, blanket pulled out, corners held fast by the family's shoes, sandwiches and drinks in everyone's hand, so that I could slip away, undisturbed and alone, to the shoreline. In my hand I had a small white box tied with a pale blue grosgrain ribbon that I bought the day before at the local five and dime store. In it I placed the single red rose, which had withered in my room during the night. I placed the rose on the florist's crumbling fern and wrote a note bidding Ruthie farewell.

I recited a prayer as I laid the box on the shore, waiting for the incoming waves to wash my gift to Ruthie out to sea. The waves pushed the box back on my toes. I picked it up, waded out waist deep and laid it once more on the sea. The Atlantic Ocean received the tribute and I watched my box bob on the crests of the waves until I could see it no more.

Little did I understand that I was throwing a flower for me, washing my childhood away, burying myself at sea. I attended the funeral rites alone, my young cousin's and mine.

I took a new name and a new identity. I no longer permitted anyone to call me Ruthie. I was Ruth—adult, hatched, full-grown.

Eleven

PRAYER

There is no mediator between God's children and God.
—*Talmud J*
Berakoth, 9:1

God requires no synagogue—except in the heart.
—*Hasidic saying*

I remember the men chanting. I hear them. I see them rocking back and forth, gently striking their breasts. I see the children run around them, the little ones between their legs. The *davening* goes on, the children are noticed, but not admonished. They run out of the storefront *shul,* press their bodies to the glass, grab a mother's hem, laugh and chase each other on this High Holy Day. I do not run and play with the little ones; I am older, almost twelve. I remain, still, off to the side, staring with my ears. The noise rises. I listen for the harmony, for the unified song of prayer. I listen. And I hear singsong gabble;

the sounds are not clear. I strain to hear these men robed in blue-threaded *talaysim.*

I focus on two men bobbing side by side and in my cone of vision, I concentrate on their lips, expecting to see them speak in unison, expecting to make sense of the Hebrew melody. The lips speak, they move, and the words that issue forth are distinct, different in each mouth. Each man prays alone, each man prays in community; they chant their common chorus of prayer.

My mother catches my eye with her hands as she walks in the door. Her hands, struck by sunlight, say, "Why you stand with open mouth in front of all men who pray? Enough to watch, come outside."

I am fifty feet from her language. I pretend not to see.

She signs again, "Come soon, we go home, eat lunch."

I avert my eyes and this time I do not strain. I allow the melody to pour into my heart and ask, "God, is this the language you speak; is this the sound that created the world, that made me?"

The chanting stops. An old graybeard catches my lips and asks in English, "You pray?"

Embarrassed, I answer, "I have to eat lunch now."

The men, no longer bent in rapt prayer, talk to one another. Their eyes follow me out the door. The women and children gather in clusters on the sidewalk, in groups of three and six and ten, blocking my mother from view.

I do not see her. I cannot call out to her; she cannot hear me. I think, Momma, if God can hear me, why can't you? And I know in that instant that she does hear me. It is a different hearing. We speak and hear another sacred language. With our eyes.

The language I heard in the windowpaned *shul,* sharing its walls with a grocer on one side and a tailor on the other, remains a deep and mysterious memory. Hebrew. It was Hebrew. So powerful did I believe language to be that I willed myself to absorb God's original voice. I sensed the haunting melody of prayer, unsynchronized, chanted in the separate voice of every man bent over the Book. I sensed that it was a language apart, holy, not in daily use. I asked myself how could I learn a language I did not hear every day, I did not see every day?

Written Hebrew, with its rounded forms and strange black letters, written from right to left and read from back to front, was another form of sign, an ancient calligraphy. I believed if I rubbed my fingers over the letters I would learn; learn the same way I learned the language of sign, deep and mysterious too, in its fingered nuance. I needed a teacher. I needed practice, repetition, explanation.

Afraid to ask, I kept this longing hidden, this need to learn God's voice, close to my chest, where I kept my other unrequited longings.

"Momma?" I asked, in very small signs, when the High Holy Days were over, "I want study Hebrew. I want go to Hebrew school."

"What for? Not important girls learn Hebrew, it is for boys. Your brother Fred will go, you not necessary go."

Shut down by her casual reply, I slipped into stillness.

I asked my father the question the next morning before he left for work. He saw my longing and answered, "You go to Hebrew school, around corner, ask rabbi-teacher how much cost each lesson—maybe not too expensive, you go."

Once a week I went to Hebrew school and learned enough to write my grandmother Lizzie a letter in Hebrew. The letters are gone from my hand today; there is no teacher to help me form the letters, create the script to write a simple message.

My grandmother wrote back in her Yiddish scrawl, letters squiggled on the page, that I could not decipher without the aid of my teacher. But I put my confusion aside when two one-dollar bills fell out of the envelope.

I waved them at my father, full of pride when he came through the door.

"What do you do with money my mother send you?"

"I buy something that live forever, I buy flowers."

"Flowers not live forever, better buy plant. Hold money till weekend, then we go buy together."

He took me as he always did, by the hand, preventing speech, filling me with his strength, to a florist shop.

"I want to buy a plant that will live always!" I said, pointing to a vase filled with fragrant blood red roses.

"These will die within the week."

I walked out of the shop and in my hands was an ugly tropical snake plant; the pointed stalks poked into my nose with every step.

My father signed, "Happy buy plant now?"

"Yes happy!" I signed with one hand, holding the plant close to me with the other. "This plant not make flowers every year, but live long, long time."

The plant lived in my room for years. The earth dried, the stalks shriveled in the winter's steam heat as it hissed through our apartment. I watered the plant and miraculously it took life one more time. And one day when I was in high school, after my grandmother died, it was gone.

"Momma, where is my plant?"

"I drop, break, I throw out, enough old plant. We buy new one, with soft running leaves, pretty shape, this plant have leaves like knifes."

And there went my Hebrew plant. I had not yet learned the language.

The meaning of meaning, present somewhere in the stories signed year after year on the anniversary of a holiday, sent my mother Mary careening, eyes refocused, into the past—not her past this time but the fragmented telling of her father's observance of Jewish law.

"You not understand Jewish ways," she admonished. "You know not allow to blow out Sabbath candles each Friday night, must leave to burn down, alone, all out."

"Yes, Momma, I remember, you tell me many times."

"I tell you how Cossack come with long legging pants, like long wool bloomers, high leather boots, big fur hats come into temple in Kiev where my father pray Friday night Sabbath with heavy whips, whip heads of old Jewish men, young men and whip out light burning on candles. One candle fall to floor, burn small synagogue to ground, burn Torah, books, all burn."

Through her fingers I had a vision of the *shtetl* synagogue, of the flames consuming Abraham's house of prayer, of the Cossacks' savagery as they rode their horses through the synagogue, as they picked off the men's skullcaps, as they flung the *talaysim* on their whips, as the Jewish men ran from their proscribed Sabbath welcome.

I shuddered and my mother touched my shoulder with her hands, saying, "Remember do not blow out Sabbath candles on Friday night. Never."

It was a trilling of hands, a continuing song repeated each spring at the Passover table. Grandfather Abraham's crowded Bronx apartment became a festival hall, a gala room celebrating the Exodus with gleaming silver candlesticks, white dishes, starched white linen, rich with the smells of the seder meal that came long after hunger had abated, long after I could keep my head up.

The hours of Hebrew prayer intoned by Abraham, propped up by huge white bed pillows, the master of his house surrounded by his family, were interrupted by my mother's reminder not to lick my wine-coated finger after we dipped to commemorate the ten plagues visited upon Pharaoh's people for his refusal to release the Jewish slaves from bondage.

"We eat soon, now listen to my father Abraham."

I understood none of the Hebrew chanting, only those portions he explained in English, and I did not interpret this for my parents. It would only lengthen the service. I was young, I was tired, and I wanted my dinner.

I was ten when my grandfather died. And each Passover thereafter I conducted the seder service myself, with my father Ben, as always, gently commanding, "You do it self, Ruth, you pray for us, you are oldest child."

On Sabbath eves we returned home to the smells of my mother's cooking and cleaning. And to her words. "We are Jews. This is Friday night . . . we light candles and pray. After dinner we tell stories about family."

The soot-covered trees on the street were bursting with hidden green and the Passover season was near. And my mother spoke of another Passover.

In the springtime of renewal, in the biblical time when the Angel of Death passed over the homes of the firstborn Jewish males, saving them for life, my mother remembered the birth of yet another child to her mother. It was April 10, 1922, three days before the seder, celebrating not only life but the Jewish Exodus from Egypt.

Angry at this seventh birth, my mother pushed her way into the bedroom and demanded of her mother, still weak from the midwife's delivery of her last child, "Why you have another baby? What for? To work more hard?"

My grandmother Fanny smiled and said, "Look, a girl. Shall I throw her out with the rubbish?"

"No, no, don't throw away baby. Does baby have a name?"

"She is Rose. She is sister."

This pleased my mother; she would not be the only girl in a family of boys.

Three days later Abraham lifted the carp swimming in the family bathtub and killed it. My mother took the wooden chopping bowl to her mother's bedroom and said-signed, "Teach me make gefilte fish for seder. Abraham tells me I must do it."

With the infant Rose in the crib, her mother still in bed, my mother at the age of fourteen had her first formal cooking lesson. The smell of lake carp and whitefish, onions, eggs, matzoh meal, salt and pepper was pungent. But my mother sat in the room chopping the ingredients together until the fish was smooth and ready for the pot. And as the fish cooked, unwatched, the carefully prepared patties disintegrated.

At the seder, Abraham and his four sons, Nathan, Sam, Louis, Jack, and my mother ate the fish. On the table was a cup for the prophet Elijah, and a tiny beer stein for the newborn child, Rose. The service was long and my grandfather washed his hands again and again as my mother brought him pitcher after pitcher for the cleansing ritual before prayer. When the service was over, the feasting began as each one ate a salted hard-boiled egg signifying the beginning of life.

My mother brought each course to her mother in the bedroom. She served her wine, in a fine cut crystal goblet. When my teenage mother shamefacedly brought the fish dissolved in aspic, my grandmother praised her first cooking attempt.

After the seder was over, my grandmother, recovering from the birth of her last child, remembered her own mother, Itkeh Milkovsky, in Smargon, Poland, and asked my mother to bring her ink and paper. Carefully she poured ink over the paper and asked my mother to lift her infant sister from the bassinet, put the baby's tiny feet on the wet ink-stained paper and place them firmly on a clean sheet to mark her footprints.

The footprints were sent off to Poland in lieu of a photograph. My grandmother Fanny never told her own mother that she had had two deaf children, my mother Mary and her brother Jack. Rose's three-day-old footprint did not reveal her last secret. Rose, too, was born deaf.

My mother's memory of her own mother is tied to the kitchen and the marvel of hands that cooked for Sabbath after Sabbath without a written recipe. On Thursdays my grandmother prepared for the Sabbath. She kneaded flour, water and eggs together to make noodles for her clear chicken soup. She lifted the sheets of dough, rolled and ready, to her own bedroom and laid them out on the clean white cotton pillowcases to harden, and when they were the right texture she brought them back to the kitchen, rolled the dough once more, placed a knife between her deft fingers and swiftly sliced the dough in slivers to form the slim golden noodles that would float in her soup.

On Friday mornings, disregarding the unmade beds, she made six loaves of challah for her family. And when the bread, kneaded and braided, was placed in black pans, she took a chicken feather, dipped it in egg white, and coated the bread so that each loaf shone when it came steaming from the oven fired by coal. She made strudel dough, laying out long, thin sheets on the tablecloth, and filled it with sweet dried fruits, nuts, cinnamon, and sugar. She flipped the tablecloth over and over, placed her rolls in pans, and once again the house was filled with a sweet aroma. When the strudel was baked, she sliced the long rolls, readying them for dessert served with glasses of hot tea, lemon, and cubed sugar.

After the summer harvest, she made barrels of sauerkraut from her garden. She weighted down the raw salted cabbage in her wooden crocks with heavy stones that she had gathered from the fields over the years. In the early fall she crushed grapes with her bare feet in the bathtub and made exquisite wine for the following Passover seder.

Rose was four years old in February 1927, when her mother had a stroke. On month later, on March 12, my grandmother was dead. And three days later at the Passover festival my mother, now nineteen years old, prepared the food, made the gefilte fish, which did not disintegrate this time, and served the wine that her mother had made in the fall of 1926.

"No one can drink wine my mother make. We cry." My mother's hands spoke slowly.

"Did you not drink the wine?" I asked.

"Abraham, he make us all to drink Fanny's wine."

Years later, when I had a seder at my own home, with my own children, I asked my mother to explain the seder to my children. I watched her hands unfold. "Yes, it is spring-time. It is time to thank God for new life."

"Momma, tell the children about the Egyptians."

"Oh, Egypt people, they gave to us Jews a home."

I stopped her signs and her voice. I signed with my face still. "Momma, we were slaves in Egypt."

"Slaves? Jewish people were slaves in Egypt?" Her hands were incredulous.

She loved the Passover ritual, but never knew its story. No one, not Fanny, not Abraham, had explained to this deaf child, to this deaf woman, why we Jews tell the story of Passover to each generation with ceremony, why the seder nights are different from all other nights. She was seventy years old when I sat in my own dining room, far from the memory of her mother's sweet kitchen, and told my mother the Passover story.

"I not know much Jewish history, but I know Abraham. I know what he do. He build synagogue with his own hands in London, before I am born. In Whitechapel. He build synagogue in Brooklyn too with other men. He is carpenter. I see him do this with my eyes. I see him carve lions for a new synagogue. He carve all Hebrew letters himself. He bring Torah to temple. He write my name in Torah, write Jack's name."

My grandfather sculpted each letter of the commandments, carved the Lions of Judah, symbol of strength for the Ark, for the Holy Closet that housed the Torah. My grandmother made a blue velvet covering, trimmed in gold for the Torah scroll.

It is written that every man and woman should write his own Torah during his lifetime. Custom and time have altered this precept. It takes an artist a year to hand-print the Hebrew letters on parchment with a quill. Neither plastic nor metal object may be used to write the sacred text; metal objects may be used as instruments of war.

The scribe writes the last paragraph with just the outlines of the letters. During the dedication of the synagogue that Abraham built, both my mother and her brother Jack had their hands guided by the scribe as they filled in the letters, each holding the quill. In this way they participated in the blessing of writing their own Torah, a Torah they could not read.

I asked my mother in the excitement of her telling, "Who wrote your name, your father or you?"

"I remember now, somebody hold my hand. I write, father tell me I write my name for always."

When the dedication ceremony was done, the celebration began. "It was parade, just like a wedding, in street."

The Torah, held high by two congregants and canopied by a *chuppah* held by four men, was taken into the street. The congregation followed their Torah singing joyous Hebrew melodies.

My mother said, "I remember everybody sing, happy face, almost dancing."

My grandfather led the crowd behind the Torah with his deaf children. He held them, one in each hand, and marched with a firm step around the Brooklyn street. People lined the street to watch the ancient ceremony and my grandfather's step never faltered.

My mother signed, "He was not ashamed on us because we are deaf. He was proud. He told me that we are also God's children, not important we cannot hear."

And somewhere in Brooklyn today, in some small synagogue, there is a Torah that has my mother's and Jack's names inscribed on it. As long as the Torah survives, their names will survive on the parchment. When the Torah is old and frayed it will be buried in full religious ceremony.

I remember another temple, another time. My mother and father returned from the cemetery on Staten Island where they had gone to place stones on their parents' graves. It was the time before Rosh Hashana, before Yom Kippur, the High Holy Days. It was 1943. I was fourteen, my brother eleven.

My mother, as usual, bustled with joy at the approaching holiday eve that held the promise of a new year, of a slate wiped clean. The red linoleum in our living room was scrubbed clean and waxed, all the linen on the beds and in the bathroom clean and white, the windows spotless. It was a prodigious feat of cleaning and cooking all in one day.

As I walked back from school, I looked up at the window as I did every day to see my mother's face and hand waving to me. This day she sat outside the window, high up on the fifth floor, holding on to the window sash with her right hand, washing the window with her left.

"Momma," I signed, as I entered her bedroom, "don't do that. It is dangerous, you can fall five stories down."

She opened the window, slid onto the bedroom floor,

and signed quickly, "God watch over me, don't worry, I never fall. You tell me always! I tell you stop to worry on me."

"You say that! And I always worry about you."

"I finished now. I go for a bath and a rest."

My father came home early that afternoon, his arms covered as usual with bits of cotton and sweet horsehair, smelling of the upholstery factory.

He kissed me. "Where's Momma?" No signs. Just words formed on his dark-mustached lips.

"In the bath," I mouthed.

"I bathe next, very dirty, you wait."

He looked so tired, so relieved to be home before nightfall.

"Momma, cooking best in world. Kitchen smell good."

The kitchen was rich with the smells of the holiday meal. Chicken soup, roasting chicken covered with golden onions and chicken fat, and sweet carrots with honey simmered on the stove. My mother's hands were part of that meal and she made the same meal every Sabbath eve.

When we were all bathed and changed to welcome the New Year, I helped my mother lay the white tablecloth. I always set the table myself. The dishes were cracked, chipped, the silver was tin alloy, the candlesticks were wrought iron, the napkins were paper and it was our festival table. I reached for the candles to be placed into the candlesticks and my mother stopped me.

"Do you know I buy this candlesticks in Woolworth's in 1927 for one dollar?" The country no longer suffered the Depression, yet the memory lingered in our household.

"You pray," my father said to me as we gathered round the table. "Momma lights the candles, you pray, Ruthie."

"Yes, Daddy." I didn't know the Hebrew prayer, but I had watched others. My mother handed me a white cotton scarf for my head. I put my hands over the flickering flames, closed my eyes and whispered, "Thank you God, for my family, for our food, and bless us all this New Year." I looked up, opened my eyes and signed the words.

My father touched me on the shoulder, softly, and then, with a swift downstroke of his palm against his chest, he signed the word *good.* He smiled his approval of my simple prayer.

"Now eat!" he commanded. "Momma make good cooking dinner for this night."

There was no conversation at the table. We ate in silence, unless we put down our knives and forks. Language wasn't possible except between courses. We praised the food, we praised my mother and she glowed. Before she served stewed prunes for dessert, which I loathed, she said, "I have to say something. Long time we not go to temple."

We looked at her expectantly, waiting for her pronouncement.

Her hands were deliberate, slow. "Tomorrow we go to temple to pray."

My father answered her, "We have no ticket."

Momma was adamant. "Tomorrow morning we go, children must go to Temple."

He said nothing. It had been so long since I had been to a synagogue. My grandfather Abraham, synagogue builder, had spoken of the joy of prayer. And I wanted to enter a house of prayer once again.

In the morning we dressed for our trip to the synagogue. My mother hurried us along, reminding, "Not nice if we late to God's house."

We climbed the steep hill up to the Grand Concourse. The synagogue was on the corner, gray granite, austere in its square architecture. It was September, that time between summer and autumn, the morning cool, promising a warm sunny afternoon. We mingled with the arriving worshipers. They were dressed for the High Holy Days. My mother noted this dress and that pair of shoes, making her remarks with her hands discreetly at her side. She was happiness.

My father said, "Ruth you go talk for me, tell man at door we want to come in and to pray with others on this New Year Day."

We had no tickets. How would I approach this man, I thought, this nameless stranger waiting to receive admission slips? I had no doubt that I would be able to accomplish this task; I had succeeded so many times before. My parents were not in view. He couldn't see them signing their words.

I said, "We have no tickets, my mother, my father and my brother. We would like to attend the services this morning with all of you. May we come in? May we join you?"

He was soft spoken. "I am very sorry, Miss. You may not enter without tickets."

I remained there motionless, my breath caught in my throat.

"You must move along, Miss, there are people standing behind you waiting to get in before the services begin."

I felt like a Jewish orphan, a fringe Jew, hanging at the bottom of the fringed prayer shawl worn by the men my grandfather Abraham prayed with in the Orthodox storefront *shuls* of my childhood.

I moved away.

My mother saw me and signed, "Yes, we go in?"

"No Momma we cannot go in. We must have tickets."

Her face fell, and then she signed with resolve, "Come we will go to pray, we will stand outside temple and be near to God, to Jewish people."

The heavy doors closed.

"It is happy New Year, look at synagogue and pray to God. He will hear us. But no sign, keep hands down, God hears your heart pray."

We stood close to one another for hours under the

September sky, until the people came out talking to one another, to those behind them, those in front of them, all saying Hebrew words I did not understand. *"Gut Yontif. L'Shana Tova."* No one explained the words, no one addressed me and I did not ask the meaning of these sounds, not then. Did Abraham say these words to me?

My mother signed, "Come we go home now. Eat lunch. It is enough time we stand under heaven. God knows we here, God understands."

Twelve

THE WEST BRONX

The lips of the righteous feed many;
But the foolish die for want of understanding.
—Proverbs 10:21

As 1941 drew to a close, the declaration of war against the Japanese filled me with terror. How could I go to school? How could I leave our small apartment? Who would protect my parents and tell them that air raid sirens were screaming throughout the city? I left instructions with the superintendent. I warned my mother, who spent her days alone in the apartment, to look out the window often and watch the movement of people in the street. I told neighbors to slip a large piece of paper under the door, which was always locked, with the words AIR RAID clearly written upon the sheet. My mother, I explained, would know what to do.

As time passed, life resumed its normal tempo. Although I was frequently reminded, by unscheduled air raid drills at school, of impending disaster, I no longer believed that New York City would be bombed. But one Saturday afternoon, when I was out with my friends on the concrete streets, I heard an air raid siren that pierced my body. In mid-sentence, I fled from my friends without explanation to our apartment building, up five flights of stairs. I ran to protect my mother. My father was out working, stuffing sofa cushions at a local upholstery shop. Nothing happened. We were safe. And I trembled.

Days became months and years. The fear of war in America was stilled long before the peace treaties were signed in Germany and Japan in 1945. I was growing up and on one rare occasion, I dared to voice a wish.

I wanted to move from the East Bronx to the West Bronx, far from the slums. The trip from the East Bronx to the West Bronx was a long one financially. My father's work was sporadic. My mother did not work. But I had seen a better place. The friends I had made at Camp Beacon in upper New York State the previous summer lived throughout the city; one of them lived in the West Bronx. When I took my first bus ride to visit her, I was struck by the newness of the buildings as I crossed the breadth of the Bronx. Instead of the usual grime- and soot-laden red bricks, the newer buildings were constructed with beige yellow bricks imitating rounded art deco forms. Alfresco gold. The wider streets, narrow green lawns and trees, shrubs in orange blossom flower, full scented, increased my longing to live near the Grand Concourse, the mighty boulevard that cleaved the borough, separating the East and West Bronx. A spacious place.

I pleaded with my parents. I insisted that the schools were better. I cajoled, wheedled and demanded until my mother finally relented. Together, we took a bus ride reminiscent of the days when my mother herded us into a trolley car looking for a sun drenched apartment. We had lived for nearly seven years in a crowded one-bedroom apartment. Each morning my mother folded the small cot, finally rid of bedbugs, on which she and my father slept and wheeled it into the bedroom in which my brother and I slept in our own beds.

It was time for my parents to have their own bedroom and for me to have a change.

My mother and I took the 170th Street bus across town and got off at William Howard Taft High School. It was a new building, white and inviting. We walked the streets until we found Grant Avenue, a long, narrow corridor. At the far end of the street, lined with red brick five-story apartment houses in tight proximity, we discovered 1294 Grant Avenue, with a TO LET sign flapping in the wind. On the top floor a two-bedroom apartment was available for rent. It was perfect, light and airy. There was room for all of us.

I convinced my mother to take the apartment by telling her that both Fred and I could walk to high school and save carfare. The rent was forty-two dollars a month, three dollars more than our three-room apartment.

And so we moved. I stayed in that apartment until I finished high school and college. I left Grant Avenue when I married.

I was a stranger in that corner of the Bronx. It was not the West Bronx as I had planned. Grant Avenue was two blocks east of the Grand Concourse. We lived at the boundary of the West Bronx. I had merely changed one slum neighborhood for one in a less advanced state of decay.

The street corner was the gathering place for the neighborhood young. On one corner there was a drugstore and on the other there was a fetid candy store that dispensed sodas, newspapers and five cent chocolate bars. In the early evenings of spring and summer after supper, when daylight still fell upon the street, we left our apartments and walked to the corner of Grant Avenue and 169th Street looking for friends and conversation. The private lives of the young were conducted in the open air.

The neighborhood was a Jewish one, but mixed in with the Eastern European Jews were Sephardic Jews who had emigrated from Turkey. These were Jews whose forefathers fled the Spanish Inquisition at the end of the fifteenth century and huddled together in Asia Minor, speaking Ladino, the language of the Spanish Middle Ages.

On the steep hill that led to the Grand Concourse, small dark shops lit by single light bulbs catered to the gastronomic tastes of the local Sephardic population. The sticky sweet smell of Turkish coffee made in small brass pots assailed my senses each time I passed. I peered in, wanting to taste the coffee, wanting to run my hands through the fifty-pound burlap sacks of red lentils, green lentils, dried broad beans and all the other beans whose names I did not know. The black olives and thick yogurt beckoned. I did not enter until I went with my friend Julia, whose parents had emigrated from Turkey.

The street teemed with kosher butchers and fruit and vegetable stands that spilled onto the streets in summer and winter. The Famous Bakery Shop made sweet-smelling heavy rye and corn bread, sticky buns and cakes. We bought the breads but not the cakes. They were expensive. Women with baby carriages stood around in clusters comparing their evening menus.

The old people collected on the sunny side of the street, warming themselves against the reflected heat of the shop windows. Jobless young men and women and school dropouts drifted to the street corner and waited for nothing in the daylight. The cats prowled the alleys where the metal garbage cans clanged and huge roaches we called waterbugs climbed from the street sewers on hot summer nights. We crunched them with our feet.

My mother and father renewed their friendships with the deaf who lived within walking distance. I was too old to regard the deaf as my family. My father fell into the rhythm of the neighborhood. Each night he collected our dinner scraps, wrapped them carefully in the *Daily News,* separate from the brown-bagged garbage, and went to feed the cats in the alley. After he deposited the trash he took his evening walk. And the cats walked with him, prancing after him with their tails in the air. Sometimes there were ten cats, sometimes twenty, and sometimes I didn't count them. My mother was comfortable in the area. She knew all the shopkeepers and within weeks she was able to deal with them alone.

I met my peers on the streetcorner. The names of my friends and acquaintances had a new ring—they were Behar and Bahamonde, Crespi and Tarragano, Candiotti and Benedetto, old Spanish names linked to Maimonides. Out of this group I met my best friend, Julia. And with her I found my first love. I was fifteen and he was sixteen. He did not live in the neighborhood. Too many of the boys and young men who lived in the area were confirmed drug addicts, even in those days. They smoked marijuana, which they called "reefer," downed "goofballs," which were amphetamines, and mainlined heroin. They were junkies and were to be avoided. These were not safe people. Safety was a primary concern of my life, and I was afraid of these people and their loss of control. Though these were bright people and I needed to connect to a group I only said hello to them as I moved on down the street to Julia's apartment.

Together, she and I planned our days after school, did our homework and decided how to spend our weekends. A bus ride away back into the East Bronx there was a park, Crotona Park, a quick walk from the Bathgate Avenue bus stop. Facing the park was a Jewish Community Center. We went to that center looking for friends and boys.

It was there that I met Sammy, standing with his back to me. When he turned, he met my eyes and said, "I've never seen you here before—I'm Sammy. And you are . . .?" His presence startled me, and his hand reaching out to shake mine stopped me. I stammered, "I'm Ruth." He was tall with curly clipped hair, and a mellifluous voice that was both deep and soft. His body had reached its full six foot height, yet it was gangly. When he smiled, his gray eyes creased with warmth. His hands were large, ready to catch a football. I watched him play ball many summer afternoons in waning sunlight on the grass in Crotona Park. He was innocent and intelligent.

We spent our evenings that summer together, walking the streets of his neighborhood and mine. We fell in love. It was a sweet love, as gentle as Sammy. He called me "Star Eyes," not "Dumbo." I was happy that summer in spite of the heat that gripped the tenements.

At night, when it was too hot to sleep in our apartment, we once again dragged mattresses and blankets up one flight to the roof and joined our neighbors in a tenement campout. In the midst of that summer's breathless August heat wave, Sammy and I, and the others, coupled off and found hillocks in Crotona Park where we could lie on the grass unobserved by our friends and hold one another in the wonder of young love.

As we lay together one night, stretched out on the cool green, with the unstarred blue black heavens above us, he reached over to kiss me. We did not move from the kiss. He rolled over slowly until his body was on top of mine and I flinched.

"Sammy, what have you in your pocket that is so hard? Is it a flashlight? It's hurting me."

He rolled off me immediately, stretched his arms out above his head on the grass and said, "I love you Star Eyes. Never let anyone touch you until we are old enough to be married."

Marriage. I was stunned. It was then that I decided to tell

Sammy that my parents were deaf. This time he flinched. It was imperceptible, but flinch he did.

Courageously, I disregarded his body message and continued, "You'll have to meet them. They are wonderful."

I saw his dimples as he smiled with his full rich being. "I'll be glad to meet them." There was not a quaver in his voice and I was reassured. Sammy would be different.

He met my parents with the usual awkwardness that confronts the stranger to human handicap. His hands were loose at his sides and he nodded graciously, struck dumb, without speech, for he did not know what to say.

"Tell me what you want to say, Sammy, and I'll translate your words for them."

He said words to me and I changed them in signed interpretation to words that I knew would please my mother and father.

My mother signed, "Tell him we are happy to meet him. He is a nice looking boy." Surreptitiously, although Sammy couldn't understand, she continued, "Is he Jewish? What does his father do?"

"I will tell you later." My hands were quick.

Sammy was just as quick. "What did she say?"

I laughed. "She wants to know if you are Jewish."

Sammy dimpled, nodded his head and mouthed the words, "I am Jewish," without sound. He did have charm.

My mother hugged him and said orally, "Good boy."

"What did she say?" Sammy asked.

I repeated her words and thought, Why doesn't he understand? Her words are so clear.

When Sammy came calling the rest of that summer, I didn't have to meet him on the street corner where the hipsters, the neighborhood drug addicts, gathered. We walked and talked the rest of that glorious summer, went to the Kent Theater and sat awed by the movie screen's magic, holding hands. I don't think we saw much of *Heaven Can Wait* with Gene Tierney or *The Oxbow Incident* with Henry Fonda. We played and laughed, full of promise. When school resumed that fall we saw each other on weekends. We were diligent students.

November came. The trees in Crotona Park were stripped of their leaves. We wore coats and gloves. When the nights were bitter, we pulled our collars up over our ears and huddled together as we walked and planned our future. We sat on the park bench and held each other closely.

As exam time neared we saw less of each other. We needed our time for study. I had no phone at home, not then. Instead, we wrote to one another. We saw each other now only on Friday nights and longed for the next summer.

The next summer never came for Sammy and me. My attention turned once more to the protection of my family.

We had new neighbors. They moved in one day when I was at school. My mother greeted me with the news as soon as I entered the apartment. "New people downstairs, they have a daughter your age. You will have a new friend."

Ina Levy was a homely teenager, bent with a gentle dowager's hump, a sweet smile of loneliness on her face. She was an only child and her parents were old. It was a family aged by Mr. Levy's premature illness. His thick white hair framed his thin crushed face. He stooped when he walked and complained little. Mrs. Levy, in matriarchal splendor, wrapped her graying black hair into a tight knot on the back of her head. Although she carefully pushed two locks of hair into soft waves on her forehead, her face remained pinched and ugly. She wore expensive clothes that were easily ten years old.

Their apartment was crowded with furniture that had graced a large house. The furniture was heavy, dark, and spoke of the family's economic collapse. There was no walking space and no light. I felt as though I were in a crammed furniture store. The curtains were always drawn, hiding the massive mahogany pieces from the sun. I did like their rugs. They were soft under my feet. They were the first people I ever knew who had a rug in their apartment.

Ina and I began our relationship shyly. Before our friendship had a chance to mature, it ended in bitter anger.

The quarrel began soon after their arrival. One early evening as we sat eating our quiet supper in the kitchen there was a loud thumping noise under our feet. My father jumped up from his chair and signed rapidly, "What's that?"

The thumping continued. I knew instantly what it was. Someone in Mrs. Levy's apartment was banging a broom against the ceiling. I explained what it was. My mother's hands were quick. "Ruth, go downstairs. Maybe something is wrong. You go help."

I walked down one flight of stairs and rang Mrs. Levy's doorbell.

She opened the door and when she saw me she raged at me, "How dare you make so much noise! My husband is a sick man. Stop your infernal noise!"

I looked at her dumbfounded. "We were not making any noise. We were eating our dinner."

She ranted, "You people are always banging on the floor. Are you roller skating up there?"

"No," I answered in a still voice, hiding my fright at her rampage.

She didn't stop. "You people are impossible. Stop making a racket. The next time I hear a noise I shall call the police."

She kept shrieking at me as I climbed the stairs back to our apartment.

"Well," my father asked, "what's wrong?"

I didn't have the heart to tell him. I lifted my eyes to his and kept my hands at my sides. My mother touched my shoulder and turned my face to hers. With her mouth she formed the words, "Ruth, tell me what is the matter."

"Mrs. Levy," I signed, "says we make too much noise." My signs were tight to my chest.

"Oh," my mother breathed.

Her face slackened. It was a look I knew well.

"It is because we are deaf," she signed sadly.

Our voices didn't and couldn't call to each other. Automatically we stomped one foot on the floor, vibrating our message foot to foot. As soon as the vibration was transmitted, my mother or my father turned to the caller. It is a common method of communication among the deaf. We did it without thinking. Foot stomping eliminated the need to get up and call someone to conversation. It was natural to us and we had never considered the shock to the neighbors who lived beneath our uncarpeted floors.

We looked at each other, my brother, my father, my mother and I.

"What shall we do?" my mother asked.

I shrugged and said nothing. My brother was silent.

"We are helpless. The hearing people do not understand that we are deaf." My mother's signs were firm. Her hands flew and she raged at the injustice of her deafness.

How would we call to one another? How could someone stop us from talking in our own home? We used our bodies, hands and feet, mouth and eyes to talk. Would we have to cut down on our already diminished speech? A rock settled in my heart. My chest tightened as my mother spent her fury. Our dinner was left unfinished. Cold spaghetti snaked over our chipped unmatched china.

My mother cried and put her head down on the kitchen table. I put my arms around her and said, "Don't worry Momma, we will tap, tap our shoulders to call each other. Let us try."

My father, who had remained impassive, flared his nostrils and hands and said directly to my mother, "To hell with them. This is our home. We finish to eat our good supper now!"

In the days that followed, I listened to the opening and closing of apartment doors until I could identify the Levys' door. I learned their schedule and avoided them. At home we made the colossal effort of curtailing our natural speaking rhythms. As the weeks passed the broom thumping stopped and we comfortably reverted to calling each other by foot.

Mrs. Levy began her broom banging again. Each time we ignored her and lived as we always did. When we passed in the hallway, she glared at me and I sneered at her. My legs were fast, and I raced past her whenever I could, avoiding her gray eyes. She snarled words at me. I ran into our apartment, closed the door behind me, and held my breath until her scathing words left my mind.

One afternoon, without a thought of Mrs. Levy in my head, I dashed up the stairs and heard horrible screams. I knew they were my mother's screams. At the third-floor landing, against a window guarded by two iron bars, my mother had her hands around Mrs. Levy's throat, screeching in a deaf soprano voice, "You son-of-a-bitch woman, son-of-bitch, go to hell!" No one would have understood her, but I did. Her beautiful face was contorted and blotched with red anger.

I moved swiftly and separated my mother from her prey. I had never seen her use physical force. She never, ever raised a hand to me or my brother. Loose from my mother's powerful hands, Mrs. Levy shouted, "You freaks, you are all freaks. You are not fit to live with normal people. You belong in an institution for crazy freaks!" She raved on.

I shuddered. I took my mother by the arm as Mrs. Levy fled into her apartment and bolted the door.

My mother, still furious, would have none of me. Her anger was cresting. "Wait," she punctured the air with her hands, "I am not ready."

I waited for her to regain her composure. I hadn't noticed the pillowcase filled with wet wash laundry. She bent down and hoisted the heavy load of wash onto her left shoulder. She washed clothes in the basement washing machine every Thursday.

She spoke the words, "Come, we go up now. I feel better."

She moved swiftly up the stairs energized by her outburst. She plunged the key into the lock and opened the door. Together we removed the shirts and underwear, socks and blouses from the pillowcase and strung them out in the small bathroom to dry.

My mother said, "I make tea and we have cookies. Go to kitchen."

I sat at our gray wooden table watching her prepare tea. We had tea in the afternoons to celebrate the day's end. She filled the dented tea kettle with water, lit the gas stove and settled the pot on the flame. She slid the unopened box of cookies on the table.

"You open!" she commanded.

I wanted to tell her that she had forgotten to turn off the tap, that water was streaming into the sink. She often left the tap running, not hearing the water. When her back was turned to the sink, she didn't know whether the water gushed or dripped from the faucet. I didn't tell her this time. Let it run, I thought. This was not the time to call attention to her deafness. Instead, I tore the cellophane wrapping from the box of sweet shortbread cookies and heard the crackle of the cellophane crescendo into the room. And I thought, she cannot hear that either. I liked the sound of the paper in my fingers, glad that I was not deaf.

After her first sip of lemon-laced tea she said to me, "You know that Mrs. Levy is crazy woman. She screamed her face at me, moving her mouth up and down, she pushed her fingers on my chest. She made the sign for *crazy* and pointed to me.

She hurt me. I am not crazy. I am sensitive woman. I try to pass her on the stairs. She stayed to my body. I could not pass her. I cannot speak. I grab her. I so very angry. I choke this woman to make her stop insulting me."

"It is all right, Momma. I understand."

"It is hard to be deaf in hearing world."

"I know," I answered, calming my own anger. I kept my anger hidden from her and from me. It was too dangerous to be angry; I had to remain her link to the uncomprehending, unfeeling world that eyed her with revulsion. I was her bridge to normalcy.

When we finished I went to the sink and shut the tap, stopping the flow of water.

"Why did you not tell me that water was still running?"

"It made a nice sound Momma."

"Tell me," she asked with childlike curiosity, "what is sound of water?"

"It sounds like it feels on your hands, soft and clean. It washes the dirt away. It washes Mrs. Levy away."

She liked that, and laughed. We grinned and hugged each other. She was feeling better.

Two days later, at four in the afternoon, the doorbell rang. I went to the door and shouted, "Who is it?"

"Is this the Sidransky residence?"

"Who is it?" I queried again.

"I have a court summons for Mrs. Sidransky."

I opened the door as far as the chain latch would permit. A strange man stood there.

"What do you want?"

"Who are you?" he asked cordially.

"I am Mrs. Sidransky's daughter."

He thrust an envelope into my hand and said, "Give this to your mother. She has to appear in court in two weeks. It's all explained in the papers." He turned and left.

Stunned, I held the document in my hands until my mother came to the door and asked, "What is the matter with you?"

We went into the living room, sat on the deep rose sofa and opened the envelope. It was a summons. Mrs. Levy was the plaintiff and my mother the defendant. I wasn't clear about judicial procedure. My knowledge of the law consisted of movie courtroom scenes.

My mother was agitated. As the family caretaker I assured her that I would handle the entire matter. I was cast into the role of omnipotence once more; the sense of power was overwhelming. I did not recognize that this power was an abuse of my childhood. No one was to blame for this abuse. It was simply so.

It continued to be so as my mother pleaded, "Who will help us?"

"I will do it," I said.

I read the summons carefully, absorbing each word. I was fifteen and in my second year of high school. I had to concentrate to get through the incomprehensible legal jargon.

"Will I go to jail?" my mother asked with fear in her fingers.

"Of course not, no one is going to jail!"

My father's only concern when he arrived home was the cost of a lawyer to defend my mother against the charges of assault and disturbing the peace.

"We have no money. We cannot pay a lawyer. We do not know a lawyer."

"I will be the lawyer," I told my father.

"You can be lawyer in two weeks?" He laughed at me.

"I will be absent from school and I will go to the library and learn to be a lawyer." My signs were courtly.

I had no doubts about my capacity to learn anything and to learn it quickly. My father caught my spirit and was about to relent, when he shook his head at the enormity of my task. I didn't allow him to soften. I demanded, "Trust me! Don't I always help you and Momma? I can do it again."

He took my hands in his heavy square hands, kissed me on the forehead and said with his voice, "Good girl baby Ruth."

That was settled.

I went to my beloved library in search of a two-week law degree. The library had no law books, just books about law. I rushed through book after book, scanning chapter headings, looking for answers to my legal dilemma. I found none. I searched my memory for the cinematic courtroom scenes I remembered and decided that if I could not learn to be a lawyer, I could learn to act like one.

The day arrived and we walked up the impressive stone steps to the Bronx County Courthouse. My father, my mother, and I were together. My father had taken the day off from work to be with us; it meant the loss of a day's pay. We were immaculately dressed. I had selected my clothes the night before with great care, choosing a black and white checked woolen skirt and a starched white cotton blouse.

When I looked in the mirror in the morning I decided that I looked too old. I wanted the judge to pity me, to pity all of us. I hated the pity I had seen in the faces of so many, but this time I would use it to my advantage. I braided my long dark hair into two thick braids and wrapped the ends with two white silky ribbons. I was ready to take on the Bronx judicial system.

We found our assigned courtroom and pushed the swinging doors into the large room. It looked like all the courtrooms I had seen in the movies. The judge sat at his bench and the court stenographer sat beneath him. The American flag and the New York State flag were in plain view. There were two long tables, one for each of the lawyers. I sighed with relief. The courtroom was familiar.

I showed the summons to the guard and he ushered us to the first row of the long brown wooden benches. Mrs. Levy and her husband arrived moments after we did, accompanied by their lawyer, and sat down behind us. We waited for over an hour until we were called to the bench.

I explained for my parents the petty cases that were heard before ours, with my hands hidden in my lap. Then I heard the names Sidransky and Levy. Mrs. Levy's lawyer rose from his seat and walked forward. I followed him.

The judge was a kindly looking man. His bifocals sat at the tip of his nose and his fat face had deep laugh lines. I liked him. His voice was firm, his manner fair. I was not afraid of him.

Mrs. Levy's lawyer presented himself. The judge peered down at me and asked, "And who are you?"

"I am Ruth Sidransky and I am here to represent my parents."

"Where is your lawyer?"

"We do not have a lawyer. We cannot afford one. I shall act both as lawyer and interpreter."

He treated me seriously. "Where are your parents?"

"They are over there." I turned and pointed to them.

"Tell them to come forward and speak for themselves."

"They can come forward, Your Honor, but they cannot speak for themselves. They are deaf."

"Deaf and dumb?"

"No," I answered, suppressing my anger at his question, "they are deaf, *not* dumb."

I beckoned to my parents to approach and they came forward. Mr. and Mrs. Levy followed behind them. We were all standing in position, my parents behind me and the Levys behind their lawyer. The lawyer presented his case, citing our continual floor thumpings and bangings. Mrs. Levy interrupted her lawyer and in a loud whisper complained that since the summons had been issued, the noise was worse.

I said nothing, but each night when my parents were asleep, Freddie and I, behind our closed bedroom door, had taken one heavy shoe and dropped it mightily on the floor. We never dropped the other.

I remained silent during the proceedings until Mrs. Levy shouted, "She's a slut, look at her, pretending to be so innocent. There are boys in and out of their apartment all the time. Damned prostitute!"

I felt myself redden at her outrageous mouthings and said nothing.

The judge said calmly, "You are out of order, Mrs. Levy. She is not charged; her mother is."

My mother looked at me, pleading with her eyes for me to interpret the words that were said. I did not lift my hands to language.

Mrs. Levy's lawyer began again, this time describing my mother's attempt to choke her to death.

I interrupted. "Your Honor, may I speak?"

"Yes, you may speak."

In a loud clear voice I recounted the story of my mother's attack on Mrs. Levy. As I spoke my hands signed the words at the same time. This was difficult to do, for the words of my mouth had to match the words of my hands. I was slow and deliberate, explaining how Mrs. Levy had goaded my mother, how she had insulted her and how my mother, in her own fright and rage, had attempted to silence Mrs. Levy's incomprehensible rantings. I paused and looked at my mother and father nodding their approval at my words.

I then put down my hands and spoke with my mouth only, and repeated Mrs. Levy's charge that we were freaks and should be made to move away from normal people. My voice dropped to a lower pitch so that the judge leaned forward in order to hear me. I continued, "We are a deaf family; we are different but we are not crazy freaks and we mean no one any harm. We are silent when we speak, but noisy when we call to one another."

The judge peered at me in sympathy.

I stopped speaking. The judge sat upright on his bench and turned his attention to Mrs. Levy's lawyer, who softened his voice and demanded that we be ordered by the court to buy carpets for our entire apartment to diminish the noise level. I turned to my parents as I signed the lawyer's words. My father looked horrified; this was something he could not afford to do.

I said to the judge, "We are poor people. If we couldn't afford a lawyer we can certainly not afford to buy rugs."

The judge ignored my remarks and asked me directly, "How did you learn sign language?"

"I learned sign language as a baby, long before I could speak orally. I learned to speak as you do when I went to school."

He motioned to Mrs. Levy's lawyer and to me to come close to him. When we were close enough that no one else could hear, he said, "This is an unusual case and has no place in the courtroom. I shall dismiss this case and refer the Sidransky family to a social worker."

He banged his gavel and declared, "Case dismissed."

I smiled deeply and said, "Thank you, Your Honor."

"Miss Sidransky, you are a remarkable girl." I had heard those words before and hated them, but this time I gloated.

My mother asked me as I turned from the bench, "What does it mean?"

I signed in small letters with my left hand at my side, "We won, say nothing, I will tell you outside."

We walked out the swinging doors together. Mrs. Levy and my mother brushed shoulders but made no attempt to communicate. I said, "Mrs. Levy, we will try to be quiet if you will try to be patient with us," magnanimous before her courtroom loss.

In the wide hallway, I explained what had happened to my parents. My father soared with delight. "So," he signed, "you are lady lawyer now."

"No," I answered, "I am your daughter Ruth."

I thought of Sammy and I wanted to share my victory with him. It was Tuesday and I had to wait until Friday to see him. Friday came and the night air was filled with the hint of springtime. The stripped trees quivered with barely discernible buds in Crotona Park's cool soft wind.

"I have something to tell you, Sammy," I said as we sat down on our park bench.

"Well, tell me. I'm waiting."

Slowly, I told him my Mrs. Levy tale. He did not interrupt me.

His face was pensive; he looked sad.

"Sammy, what's wrong? Aren't you happy for me?"

He swallowed his breath and in even tones said, "I have something to tell you."

I waited for him to continue.

"I don't know how to say this."

I waited.

"Ruthie, my Star Eyes, I cannot marry you. I do not want to have deaf children."

I sat still, wordless.

Thirteen

BENNY, MY TOUCHSTONE

Even a fool, when he holdeth his peace, is counted wise;
And he that shutteth his lips is esteemed as a man of understanding.
—*Proverbs 17:28*

*B*enny lifted me from darkness. He spoke. He made sound for me. He struck the night air tooting New Year's Eve paper horns. He pranced to the sound. Back and back into the reaches of his soul he issued sound's passion.

He patted his hand over his mouth, imitating the Indian warpath shriek he had seen in the movies. He raised his voice in mock song, straining to remember a melody, an air, a tune. But the love of sound was there, remembered in some inner space. When he brought it back he screamed in his deaf voice with undulating pleasure. His memory pulled his voice out, his sound out. He teased the thread of memory.

"Do you like my voice?" he gloated.

I flung my arms around him to kiss him, to touch him in his glory.

He flung me away. "I too busy love you now, I sing, we make a noise. It is day of New Year, new life begin, good luck to speak with voice."

He structured a V-sign with his index and middle finger, put the sign to his throat and with his nails lightly stroked his throat upward, speaking orally, saying and signing simultaneously, "I make voice."

My mother has no such recollection of voice, no joyous elation at the possibility of remembered sound; her voice is elsewhere.

"Be quiet, Ben, stop to blow your horn. Neighbors sleep."

"Let people to wake up, all to play today, to make a noise on first day of year."

She reached across to him and took the silver paper horn from his hand but she couldn't stop his trumpeting voice.

Snowflakes fluttered at the window. We stood solemnly and watched the hands of the clock tock to the New Year. At midnight my mother kissed us all and held up a tumbler of sticky sweet Sabbath wine and sang, "Happy New Year's Day to us all family." We laughed and kissed and drank a sip of wine from the single glass.

Her precise song was musical; she lost her deaf voice in that moment. I marveled at her melody, delighted in her stomping happiness.

Then, suddenly, I stopped her. "Don't bang your feet Momma. Remember the neighbors. I don't want to go to court again."

My father laughed out loud. "You will always win, baby Ruth, you very smart girl."

I welled with tears at the words. As I walked from the window to the bathroom to hide my wet face, my father shouted clearly in voice, "Where are you going? I see you cry. Cry here with Momma and Daddy Ben. Do not cry alone. It is not good."

He saw with that outside vision which sees by instinct. Everything came alive through my father's eyes. He picked up the smallest nuance of a random movement. Other parents might speak in broken English; mine spoke in broken sound.

Benny declared with his hands, "Come, we play a game!"

I ignored him, annoyed. I was reading.

He prodded again, this time softly touching my shoulder and the top of my head, and I turned away from his face, my mood serious. He walked around my body, circling me as though I were his prey and he were the cat, ready to pounce. He was playing cat-and-mouse and I succumbed to his play. I joined his drama. I darted away, crouched on my knees, and tried to stuff my head under the sofa in our living room. He caught me by the arm, kissed me and said, "You not mouse, you are person, now we go outside, play real games."

I was sixteen years old and it was summertime again. I was still his prey, still his little mouse and he stroked me the same way I had seen him stroke the backs of the mice he caught over the years, gently rubbing the gray fur against the grain.

"Feel better?" he signed. The middle finger of his right hand stroked his heart, the center of his chest twice; his face spoke. He signed the word *feel* with depth.

I nodded.

"Good, now we do real work. We invent new language. New words for hands. You and me we make words."

I knew this game. It was a creation game, a game children play, a make-believe world with make-believe language. I played this game myself without his mischievousness.

"You pick one person, or I pick one person we see on a street, and give them new name in sign. Must spell name with alphabet letters. After make new sign for name."

This was an easy game for me. And I loved it.

He pointed. It was always a fat woman with whom we began our play. "See lady in blue dress with white flowers, small feet, little thin sandals. I spell name for you, name of Minnie. You sign new word." Minnie was passing quickly, and I had to grab her essence. I leaned toward her and her free-swinging breast brushed my shoulder and she was gone.

We had one rule: we were not allowed to use already existing signs, although they could be modified.

My father said, "I wait, you slow, you stupid, too!" He smiled, goading my cleverness. I raised my arms to my chest, squeezed my hands into fists and made a circular motion, milking a cow heavy with fluid.

He clapped. "Good! Now your turn, you find for me a sign to make."

I cast my eyes down the street and saw a meticulously dressed man, blond, clutching a briefcase, rushing to the subway. I pointed to him and spelled the name Alexander into my father's eyes. He closed his eyes, lifted his head, and with delicacy, thumb and forefinger pinched together in the shape of the signed letter *a*, picked imaginary lint from his jacket lapel two times. He opened his eyes, tilted his head at me and signed, "Good name for so fussy a man."

His language was impeccable. In one stroke of the hands he communicated what oral words cannot convey.

On Saturday mornings he ate his breakfast quickly, rushing me to drink my cup of hot cocoa. A thin film of chocolate satin lay on the surface of the scalding milk below. I poked at it with my spoon and my father Ben said, "Drink all, suck up hard cream, it is silk from milk." It revolted me. The slime of the warm milk clung to my palate, burned my tongue.

"Eat egg now too!"

The egg lay on the cold plate. I didn't want it. But my father was waiting for me. I pushed the fork into the yolk, spilling it over the undercooked white mass surrounding the leaking yellow. I cut it into pieces, dabbed with a broken roll and pretended to swallow the bits of egg scattered over the plate.

"Don't want more breakfast?" he asked.

"No, I'm finished."

"Okay," he signed with a flourish, "we go buy the *Daily News*."

It was the morning ritual. He bought his paper every morning and this Saturday he was taking me with him.

He handed me the thick blue sweater my mother knitted for me, took his heavy key chain out of his pocket, put his cap on his head and said in voice, "Ready now, we go, tell Momma we come back soon."

I raised my hands to speak to my mother, and she stopped me in midair. "I know you and Daddy Ben go to buy a newspaper, to see if his horses win a race. He not bet money, but thrilling to see if he win, maybe."

I loved walking with my father. His step was firm; he greeted everyone he met with a joyous smile. The men thumped him on the back in recognition. He talked and they knew his words. I didn't interpret for him. "This my daughter, Ruth," he said. And I smiled openly at his pride. I did not speak with his men. I remained at his side until we reached the corner newsstand.

The papers were piled high. *The New York Times,* the *Daily News,* the *Daily Mirror.* The smell of the newsprint was strong, fresh, inviting.

"Before, newspaper one cent, now it is two cents, worth it. News of world important, every day we learn new information about world, new things."

At home, we sat on the couch, and the paper was divided; he got the racing section and the front page, my mother got the center picture fold, and I got whatever was left. Fred was as always immersed in his own books. We read every day. We shared language, printed language, sign language, voiced language. All talk, all human touch.

At the corner kiosk, language was not a problem. I watched him, as I grew up, mimic the stream of words issuing forth from the mouth of a hearing person. The hearing mouth insisted that he understand the flap of words shouted louder and louder from tight lips, insisted that he understand what he couldn't comprehend. My father's capacity to read lips was incomplete. The demanding stranger didn't realize that each mouth, each set of lips, speaks with unique muscle tension. It was impossible for Benny, profoundly deaf, to know the mouth movements of every hearing person. Deaf is deaf, invisible, incomprehensible to those who believed that shouting, staring down would in the end force my father to understand staccato sentences. He didn't understand every word; he caught some with his eye, but most of the sentences he watched did not convey a complete thought. He missed too many words, straining to understand the previous word.

I watched my father on these frequent occasions pull out a stubbed pencil and the small white pad he always kept in his breast pocket, and write the words, "Write what you say. Not understand all words you speak to me." The response of the speaker varied; some expressed irritation, others embarrassment, and some took his pencil and wrote the words for him, willing to take the time to communicate with him.

Mike the newspaper vendor and my father had their own point of contact. On Saturday mornings when I accompanied my father to the corner kiosk for the daily newspaper, Mike, with his winter-gloved hands, tips of his fingers exposed, asked for my father's pad and pencil so that they could discuss the previous day's events at the racetrack. They wrote numbers instead of words, indicating the dollar amounts they would have won at win, place, and show had they the courage to bet two dollars.

After they finished their discussion of the races my father and Mike began a language lesson. Benny was the teacher. He took out the slim pamphlet of silken paper that he carried everywhere, and handed it to Mike. Together they studied the diagramed hand illustrated in the pamphlet for each of the letters of the alphabet. My father patiently signed each letter for him until Mike could sign each of the twenty-six letters of the alphabet, but he had difficulty creating words out of the letters.

My father touched my shoulder and asked, "Mike not know how to spell. Why hearing man cannot spell words? Is his education poor?"

"Yes," I signed without moving my lips, shading Mike from my words. "Mike only went to school until the fifth grade. He cannot spell quickly as you do."

Disappointed, he said, "Why him? I find one hearing man who will learn to sign but he cannot talk to me in my signs, he cannot spell."

Mike and my father had their own language, foreigner talking to foreigner, a language that surpassed the connection of individual words in sentences. Between them they evolved their own syntax, a body and eye language with an occasional mouthed word that went beyond the spoken or written word.

"I leave L'Epée sign language book with Mike. I will teach him how spell. I am good teacher to him. I am like French priest who invent sign language. You tell Mike I give him book to keep for always."

"You tell him yourself, not need me, Mike always understand you."

My father handed him the book and said in voice, "Mike keep always, study learn."

They shook hands, eyes smiling at one another.

He took my hand and with the newspaper rolled up under his arm said, "I tell you story. Listen, interesting, about priest L'Epée.

"L'Epée wonderful man." He shook his head in wonder at this man who had, long ago, opened the world of language to the deaf.

I asked him in sign, "Why do we have so many L'Epée books at home?" There were cartons of them, under beds, in the closets.

"Well, see, Momma's brother Jack, when he was twenty years old, bought many, many of these books. He want to see America and make living at same time. He take little books with him. He was a hobo man. He ride trains all over America, never pay fares, he jump on trains go in freight cars. When he get off at station, no one bother him—he deaf hear nothing, good joke—but he sell books, make a living, eat foods, sleep on train free. He had good time. When he came back to New York he give to me his books to hold. Jack not need them now, so I have many books in house. I give them away to hearing people interested to learn sign language alphabet."

We walked and the story of sign unfolded.

In the eighteenth century, a Frenchman, Charles Michel, the Abbé de L'Epée, paid a chance visit to one of his parishioners and met the two deaf children of the household. The girls' mother implored the cleric to undertake the education of her daughters. Somehow he understood that the natural language of the deaf was the language of sign. This was his genius.

He sought out other deaf Parisians, studied their signs and added his own. He created new signs and codified the alphabet. And his language is used to this day. He developed a signed version of the French language.

In spite of his genius he didn't recognize that the deaf in Paris had more than the signs they used; they had an independent vocabulary and grammar. He imposed a sign language that was at times awkward. But he excited his countrymen and learned Europeans with his work. He dispelled Aristotle's claim that the deaf could not learn language, a claim that had kept the deaf without language for centuries. He taught the deaf languages other than their own: Italian, Spanish and Latin. His fame spread and scholars from Holland, Poland, Sweden and Ireland opened schools for the deaf based on his teachings.

In 1817 a school for the deaf, founded by Thomas A. Gallaudet, a clergyman, was opened in Hartford, Connecticut. Gallaudet had spent five months in Paris, studying the methods developed by the Abbé de L'Epée. Today the only liberal arts university for the deaf in the world bears his name. It is in Washington, D.C.

"I true sorry I not go to college learn better, but I learn always, in a world college. Maybe one day you go to a college, be smart, maybe more smart than Ben."

The voice of sign wasn't enough for Benny. The Abbé L'Epée's language gift left my father incomplete, yearning. He wanted to speak with his voice, with his mouth, to speak to Mike, to me, to anyone. To speak like other humans.

And so we practiced lip reading. He knew my mouth well, the shape and pattern of my words; he could distinguish my breath's pronunciation of the letters *b* and *p,* imperceptible in rapid speech to the uninitiated eye. He was quick with my mouthings. But comprehension of other mouths confounded him.

He taught me to pronounce the words I took to the first grade with me, words he learned without sound, words that sounded like babble when I mimicked them. And then, later, we practiced my words. When I was in the tenth grade, I sat opposite him and said, "Watch me, look at my mouth, I say words, you tell me what I say in sign."

Some words and sentences were simple. "Daddy Ben, I love you." He grinned and I grinned and he signed, "Not fair, too easy."

I tried another. "Tomorrow I will have a history test in

school." He understood *tomorrow, will* and *have*; he missed *history test in*; *school* was an old familiar word.

"Too hard, I not understand all. Must learn to see better speech people talk."

With some people he gave up, with others he forced understanding, but his words, although indecipherable to some, were clear to me, always communicating his thinking.

Did he think in words, I wondered; did my mother think in words? How were their internal thoughts expressed? Were their thoughts ideographs? Did they see hands in their mind's eye, spelling, signing, or were the thoughts expressed whole, visually? Was the image gray, black or did light come through? Were there any colors, reds, blues, yellows?

I asked him when I was in high school, "Daddy, how you think?"

"I think I like to win horse races make lots money, give whole family."

"I didn't ask you *what* you think, I asked you *how* you think?" I signed the word *how* slowly, deliberately apart from the others.

"How?" he signed. "You ask me funny question, hard to think."

I repeated the word *how,* spelling each letter.

"I think all at once, understand all together, sometimes I think with signs talking over and over until I know what I think about."

"Do you think with words all the time?"

He answered quickly. "No, I have inside language, my own language."

I tilted my head questioningly.

"All people have own language inside, language that see and not speak."

He waited for my response. I gave him none and he continued. "I know you have own language. I see you alone

258   *Ruth Sidransky*

when you read a book, understand something, you smile, eyes change. No one talk with you, you talk with self, no words, just see all together, understand all at once. This is 'inside language,' private to all people. Even stupid people, even retarded people have own language. Deaf too have own language, I speak with myself and I speak another language with people. Ruth, you understand my language, you understand hearing language and you understand reading language, you understand 'inside' language. Many languages you speak." He was pleased with his linguistic maneuvering. "See Ben your father know many things. Deaf but not dumb."

His wit was fine. His language more refined than great thinkers who trapped themselves in verbiage.

But his voice convoluted mine. When I was young it was a voice that said, "jubba juice." "Jubba juice" conjured the tastes and smells of the local Chinese restaurant on the Bronx corner where we went as a family on occasional Sunday afternoons.

My father prompted me when the waiter approached our table. "Tell him 'jubba juice' for all family."

I repeated his words and the waiter returned a blank stare.

"Maybe man not understand English, he Chinese man."

The waiter handed me the menu and asked me to point to the dish I had ordered.

I didn't see "jubba juice" written anywhere.

My father pointed to another waiter laden with a tray. "Tell him we want same as people at other table."

I pointed, I repeated my father's words.

"You mean chop suey?"

"Yes," I mimicked, "yes, chop suey."

"Waiter understand what we order?"

"Yes, Daddy, but not 'jubba juice,' it is chop suey." I spelled it out for him, letter by letter, with ten-year-old hands.

"Yes, yes that is what I say, 'jubba juice.' Hearing people not understand deaf words."

I blanched but he was positive that his pronunciation was correct, his voice absolute.

Fourteen

HIGH SCHOOL

The Talmud says, "Acquire a teacher. Choose a friend. These are the tasks of life."

I wanted answers. I didn't understand all the messages filtering into my mind. Why didn't the small ant make a sound I could hear? Where was the joyous yell of the eastern sunrise? And where was the sweet murmuring of sunset, of the day at rest? Was there a secret to all this silence?

I walked out into the chorus, listening, always listening. Was meaning inherent in the sound itself—in the flap of a flag against the wind, in the tone of the human voice, in the melody of coins clinking into a multicolored gumball machine? It was all sound. I was the heiress and didn't declare ownership. I waited. I marked time, put my ear to a conch shell and didn't hear the ocean's roar as promised.

I could make no sense of musical notes on a page. How did Mozart write lyrical sound from the music reverberating in his skull?

I put away my questions. The answers, for now, were blurred, hidden elsewhere.

I was a high school freshman, and I had other worlds to discover, classes to attend. A music class. It was required for all students at Walton High School in the northwest corner of the Bronx. I didn't hear music, I heard other sounds.

I heard the trees whisper, the warm stones sing, the rain fall. Sometimes it falls into a puddle. *Plat.* Sometimes it slides across a windowpane. I hear the rain on the roof; I hear pouring rain on the concrete streets. Rain is to hear, but, oh, it is to see. My mother said, "The sky is weak. It wets rain." And we laughed.

I had forbidden music's entry into my soul. My mother couldn't hear it and I put it aside. And here I was, in the large auditorium filled with singing girls, three hundred of them, and Miss Schein.

Miss Schein was a legend, a musical monster swathed in a sleek midcalf metal-gray dress, perched on black pointed shoes with curved heels. She didn't walk across the stage, she strutted, demanding attention and complete obedience. It was a tyrannical goose step. The pinched smooth black bun at the nape of her erect neck mimicked the silhouette of her behind. I watched as the roundness of her bottom bobbed in time with her bun. She was pantherlike.

She lifted her baton and we raised our voices, focusing on her bending and bowing, on her body cajoling music from our vocal cords. I was awed. I stared at this powerful short woman who elicited music from hundreds of voices. My mouth was open in song when she lowered her stick to her side and shouted at the freshman class, "Stop that noise. You are braying. We shall learn to sing 'The Star-Spangled Banner' and we will sing it together, in one voice."

She divided the auditorium into groups of thirty girls,

turned to my group first and signaled us to begin with a wave of her baton. I raised my voice high in song. She trotted down the stage and wandered near the voices.

"You!" she pointed. I turned my head to see who had the offending voice. "Don't turn around! You!" She shoved her baton under my nose. I trembled.

"You have no voice. Do not sing. Keep still, open your mouth, pretend, but do not let me hear your ugly sound!"

I whitened and closed my mouth.

I clutched Miss Schein's eyes as I raised my voice in silent song mouthing the national anthem, singing without sound. I was expert at this; I had mouthed words for the deaf with a still voice. My lips were clear with language and now I was clear without sound.

I had no fairy godmother to give me gifts. I had my voice and although it was stilled by Miss Schein, I sang. The following week I sang in full voice, almost screaming the music, defying my fear of Miss Schein's wrath and public shame.

And I listened to another song, my mother's lullaby. I had other music, deaf music. I was off in another memory, this one to protect me from Miss Schein's lunatic cruelty, her saber mouth.

I murmured my mother's tuneless lullaby. Momma rocked me and I sang; she crooned and I pretended that her voice was my voice and neither was pretty. Her words were "asha, asha," strung together syllable after syllable in the cadence of the deaf voice. She was trying to sing "hushabye baby, hush, hush to sleep." I learned the words of this song when I had a baby of my own, and asked my mother to spell out the words of her lullaby.

Miss Schein came nearer; I looked straight at her, meeting her black eyes with my own dark eyes, and never wavered. She never spoke to me again, and I know she heard my voice whenever I lifted it in song.

I heard another song as she came at me in full fury, swinging her baton, waiting for me to stop my song.

> *Baa, baa, black sheep,*
> *Have you any wool?*
> *Yes sir, yes sir,*
> *Three bags full.*
> *One for my master,*
> *One for my dame,*
> *One for the little boy*
> *Who lives down the lane.*

This was my mother's first song, the poem she learned to recite when she was six. It was my first nursery rhyme. I hummed my mother's melody under my breath as Miss Schein publicly shamed me again. I exulted in my private song, kept it close to my tongue, almost spitting it at her as she hurled her calumny upon my dark head. I brightened in my own song. She glared. And I smiled my mother's smile at her vocal abuse. I was untouchable. I retreated once more to my silent sanctuary. Impenetrable. Locked from oral harm. I had been anointed a long time ago by primal sound. And that silent anointing was my refuge. I did not listen. I did not hear her tirade. I pretended to be deaf and saw only her red mouth as I opened my mouth in song. Her voice was lost, blown away, to the back of the auditorium; it entered the wooden seats, not me. My faintheartedness turned to strength, to stone.

It was the beginning. The beginning of my voice, my own. A voice I heard, a voice that spoke, strong, without sentimentality. Almost brutal in discovery. It was mine to hear, to heed. It was the floe upon which I anchored. Not whole, not yet. I was one and I could be one like the others. In transit, no longer naked, I made my way haltingly to my destination, to myself.

I went to lunch in the cafeteria, and fueled myself with food, with the soggy tuna fish sandwich my mother made early that morning. I bit into the apple. Hard. And I grinned.

I went to my French class. Miss McClintock, lean and spare, with a pinched face and the dropped jowls of a spinster nearing sixty years, twisted her tongue and jaws into vowel sounds that she beckoned us to imitate.

"After me, class, say *'oui.'*"

We answered "we."

"No, no," she insisted, "not the English 'we.' Purse your lips, make an O shape with your mouth, push your mouth, push your throat out, and say the French *oui.*" She was pleasant, smiling at our grimaces.

"Try it again, after me."

And in unison we practiced the new sound.

Spanish was easier. "*Sí, sí!*" It all meant yes. When I wanted to say yes at home, I spelled the word; three letters formed in my hand and that meant "yes." A bob of the head was the same in every language. All these words with the same meaning.

Where did all this language come from? I listened to the foreign tones, learning language as a baby learns. I eschewed memory, lists of nouns and pronouns, conjugated verbs, masculine and feminine genders, and the subjunctive. What was that? Subjunctive? It was language.

Who put language in the minds of men? Who gave oral language to children? It was inbred, facile. Who put language into the hands of the deaf? I knew nothing of linguistics then. I knew language. I understood its presence and could speak its words, words that streamed forth on waves of sound, moving through the air in fractional time, words that bore connection, man to man, child to child.

I was learning to talk again, to speak *speech.* I was not a stone. I could speak my language and another and another. If I missed the meanings of some words, I heard my father's words: "Never mind, you will understand. Listen. Just listen. Look at the face talk. The meaning will come in the mind."

I uncovered myself for the ritual of language. It was my life lesson. I carved my mouth out of its muteness, mimic of sound, and spoke new sounds. I chipped away at nature's silence, demanding comprehension in as many tongues as I could learn.

I drifted into the words I had created when I was a child, *bertuple, sidible, larin*: God's words, another tongue, my own foreign language.

Miss McClintock's voice was sharp. "Ruth, stop daydreaming, I asked you a question."

I snapped out of my reverie and returned to my French class.

"Stand up and conjugate the verb 'to be,' *être.*"

I conjugated.

"Good. Pay attention. Don't wander away again."

I was wholly attentive, waiting, listening for meaning. Rote memory was an insult to language. It said nothing.

Language flowed. I understood it. I had entered the class as a child, perhaps as an infant, head open, ears open, ready to absorb new sounds, new meaning. Why did I have to recite nonsense? "Just speak," I wanted to shout, "I will understand." I kept still.

I was angry and could not name the anger. Speech was present. Everywhere. Stones could speak. Rivers spoke. Sand had words. The ocean lapped the shore and told its secrets. Speech was in everything.

French was the last class of the day. I went to touch the grass outside the school's bricked walls. I searched for a four-leaf clover. Perhaps it would explain speech. I never found one. I plucked a blade of grass and bled its juices into my hand. It would grow again. I had not plucked out its root. I went home, looking for speech, for language. I walked into the bedroom and saw my mother.

She said, "Time to be silent now."

And I wanted a time to speak.

She was at her mirror preening, deep into the mirror peering at herself, turning her head to the left, to the right. She stroked her face lovingly. I watched her watching herself, and wondered at her courage. I never spent hours at the mirror searching my face.

She felt my presence and turned to me. "Look at this beautiful mirror. Look at your face in mirror." She handed me the mirror from her dresser set of light blue mother-of-pearl, inlaid with rhinestones and tiny glass rubies. The comb and brush and two oval boxes for powder and hairpins lay on the tray. I flinched when she handed me the mirror. I did not peer into myself. When I looked into a mirror I saw my face, noted that my hair was combed and looked away. I did not peer into my soul. I put the mirror down immediately and closed myself from view. I couldn't touch the self that was me.

"You don't look enough at your pretty face," she chided.

"What will I see Momma, just a sixteen-year-old face? I have homework to do."

"Never mind homework, put books down here on my bed and look at yourself!"

I resisted her prodding but she insisted.

"You know, my mother, your grandmother, touch this set before she die. She gave it to me, a present before I marry Ben. Please look in yourself."

Her crooked language did not escape me; she wanted me to see myself and I refused.

"Important to know your face, your eyes, see how your mouth smile. It will tell you about your insides."

I didn't want to know about my insides, not then. I wanted to escape into my homework.

"Not do homework now. You listen to my face."

We conversed in complete silence, without hands. Her eyes asked a question. I lowered mine, hers smiled at me and in that moment of exchange there was understanding and questioning, a laugh, a second of sadness, a plan and a promise.

"Momma," I said.

She shook her head.

Up came her hands and she signed, "We have finished eye talking, face talking, I know, you know. Now we must do something. We cut and sew a new dress for you. We go out now and buy new woolen materials, a pretty cocoa color for the coming winter. I make dress for my pretty daughter!"

As we walked out of the shop with three yards of soft cocoa wool folded in a white paper bag, my mother signed, "You like materials, I cut pattern this afternoon?" I answered with an affirmative smile.

We walked home in the late light of the afternoon. We walked without words, our arms touching as we swung forth. We reached the corner, and the sky was open to view. The spring sun shone through, the clouds parted, and the sun sent pale rays nearly the color of moonbeams to the tar-papered roofs of the city. She pulled me hard, by the elbow. "Look," she said in voice, "look up to sky, I never see in my life."

I looked and saw what she saw. The whiteness of the sun's rays. The heavens had parted; we looked inside.

She asked, "You understand what we see?"

"I think so."

She opened the door of the apartment, clicked in the key. I rushed to get my English book, to read Samuel Taylor Coleridge's "Rime of the Ancient Mariner." I curled up on the couch, turned on the lamp and began to read.

The light snapped off.

"Momma," I asked, "what you doing? I study now."

"No study in electric night light. Bad light for study, for read."

I protested, annoyed.

"Listen me hard, what I tell you, light from sun is warm,

light from a blue sky is clear on pages you read. Your mind learns better in light from day. Light moves into brain, shines like rays of sun we see in street before. Make memory better, make brain to understand all meanings from words you read." She put her hands at her sides, waiting for my response.

I uncurled myself, stood up, and together we went into the kitchen, the brightest room in the apartment.

"No sit now, stand first, look at light, see light drop on a table. You study in a circle of nature light. It is God's light."

I sat down and propped my textbooks for study, opened my notebook, and focused on the printed page.

She interrupted me again. "You not listen my cooking noises, I make dinner for family, you watch light. When light stops, when light becomes dark, you stop to study, it is enough for your mind."

I continued to read into the early evening. My mother reached over the table and gently closed my poetry book. "I told you, no read now. Light no good."

I was visibly annoyed. I had been absorbed in the Ancient Mariner and his tale.

"I have a hot stammer!" she shouted at me in voice. "Listen me."

I did not want to get in the way of her "hot stammer." I closed my books and wondered how to say "hot stammer" in oral English. I knew what "stammer" meant, I knew she wasn't talking about a hot "hammer," and yet the translation of the phrase eluded me. Perhaps it was one of the deaf phrases that didn't translate. I let it go.

A friend of my mother's came that evening, a friend who articulated well, and I watched them talk in the living room, I heard them speak of anger and fury, of wrong-doings, and then I heard her friend say the words, "Do not have a hot temper Mary, not worth it." She spoke the words as she signed them.

I chuckled and never corrected my mother's pronunciation of the word *temper* from *stammer*. I kept it as my own word. She didn't need the word; I knew what she meant now.

She knew about illumination. That was enough.

She signed, "You want to still read a book, go ahead, but brain not so sharp as when you read in real light of day."

I smiled at her. She elicited smiles. She waved her hands at me, shooing me away from her presence. "Go study, go read, you love words best.

"But remember we go to movies tomorrow, after study. You remember what I tell you about light. You remember when you were little girl and I take you to movies with me first time, you were afraid of light, fire light."

I remembered.

One Saturday afternoon when I was six I walked into the movie theater with my mother. The stunning square of white moving light hit my nose. I *smelled* the light and shuddered in its awesome charge. The dusty beam crossed the theater and funneled moving, speaking images against the wall. I was bewildered. And dark fire came pouring out of the wall. I grabbed my mother's hand and screamed, "Momma, fire, run!"

She could not contain my fear. I jumped wildly, protecting her from the consuming gray flame against the wall. This time she protected me, quieting my anxiety. "It is not real," she signed in the darkened theater. "It is a fake picture on a screen, look up to the light, the camera sends a picture to the wall, see, look again."

I quieted and heard the actors speak, heard voices pouring from the wall. She held my hand, stilling my small body, watching me until I lost the trembling in my arms.

She patted my head and said, "Tell me about the story."

Cast back into the role of interpreter, I calmed to her need, listened to the voices and with my young hands I interpreted the words on the screen. We were tethered by our fingers. It was a pattern repeated on Saturday afternoons throughout my girlhood.

I preferred to go to the movies alone or with my friends. When I accompanied my mother, she kept tapping me, "Tell me what say now?" And I always stopped to translate sound into the language of my hands, sometimes missing a critical sentence, sometimes a whole scene. I would go and see the movie again, alone, undisturbed by my mother. If I saw a movie that she had seen without me, she asked questions. As always she had written her own plot; my explanations were superfluous. She created her own story line to coincide with the action of the film.

"I like my story better, your story sad. Mine happy, better ending for man and woman who love each other."

I laughed at her pronouncement and agreed with her imaginings. She wanted glorious endings, and rewrote scripts to suit her taste.

"Silent movies best," she signed. "I know everything that happens in old movies, actors move their faces to tell me what happen to them. Easy to read faces, and language was very simple. Easy for me to understand. Yes, old days are best."

On school holidays when I wanted to study, Momma invited me to go to the movies with her, to see the matinee romance.

"Come with me today, they give away dishes in the theater. Today we can get new dishes. We buy two tickes, one for you and one for me, we get two dishes."

It was not a movie I wanted to see. But I went. When the film was over, the lights went up and the women sat waiting expectantly for the gifts, one dish to a customer.

They had taken the afternoon to indulge in colorful living. They sat, row after row, in their print cotton house dresses covered by their cloth coats, their hair permanented, frizzed by harsh chemicals. They became the darlings of the handsome movie star who had passed the test set before him by the young heroine, and they glowed with the momentary promise that life could be better than their daily drudgery. I sat with them that November afternoon, freed from class by the celebration of Armistice Day.

The theater manager walked onto the stage and said, "Today, ladies, we will have our Wednesday bingo game. We have three grand prizes! A mahogany bookcase, a set of white dishes, and an electric toaster."

I wanted the bookcase. A library of my own.

The bingo cards were distributed up and down the aisles by the ushers, with small pencils to mark an X in the number called.

My mother was excited. "Good you are here, I cannot play bingo without you to tell me numbers. Stupid, he call numbers too quickly, not give me a chance to play before. Not write them fast enough on chalkboard."

As the numbers were called I signed them to my mother. Quickly she marked her boxes with an X. I was so busy marking my own card that I was stunned when she stood up after only fifteen numbers were called and shouted in her high voice, "I win!" For a second I was embarrassed. But her pleasure was so deep; she flushed, and then the redness in her face subsided. I rose automatically to be my mother's voice.

The theater manager boomed, "Well, lady, come up to the stage and claim the first prize."

She turned to me and asked, "What he say?"

"Come, Momma, we must go up to the stage to see if your numbers are right."

"Numbers are right, I am sure. I watch your hands. Did you sign all numbers right to me?"

"Yes, I signed all the numbers perfectly." I couldn't be certain but I would not spoil her moment.

She was timid about walking up to the stage to have her

card read, shy about having the nameless faces stare directly at her.

"No, Ruth, you go alone. I wait here for you."

"No, Momma, you go. I will go with you; it is your bingo card. You win the prize."

We walked to the stage, up the steps. Her bingo card was read, the numbers verified. She won. And she won the bookcase.

She asked in full view of the audience, in beautiful signs, "How we take this heavy bookcase home?"

"Sorry," said the theater manager, as I interpreted the question for his ears, "we can take it out to the front of the theater for you but you'll have to find a way to get it home."

We left the stage and followed two ushers as they carried the bookcase to the lobby. And we looked at each other.

She laughed and said, "We are strong. We carry it home together. I push, you push. We rest. We will surprise Daddy Ben and Freddie." Her signs were large, exaggerated.

We maneuvered the bookcase for five blocks until we reached our apartment. When we got into the hallway, I stopped. "I cannot carry this up the stairs."

"Don't be a baby, we will do it. We can do all things, just use your mind. It will work fine."

We lifted and pushed, shoved and pushed some more, bumping the bookcase up the steps. And with a final effort we moved it into my room. A grand bookcase without a single book, ready for thousands, millions of words strung together for me.

I went to my English class and heard the sounds of the masters. We took turns reading aloud. The poorest readers could not diminish the words of Coleridge and Shakespeare, de Maupassant and O. Henry, the music of Poe and Whitman, the laughter of Twain and the sadness of Dickens. I absorbed it, the old English and the new, the written word and the spoken word.

I thought of the African bushman who clucked his language, I heard the tonal quality of the Chinese, I felt the strangeness of the Hebrew liturgy I heard in the synagogue, I absorbed the Yiddish I heard in the streets, I moved to the Italian lilt, I bent my concentration to the Ladino Spanish my Sephardic friends spoke at home, I heard the sound of the immigrant fumbling for English sounds. This was mouth-to-mouth language and I listened. Language was imprinted. And I wanted it all.

I entered the library. I went among the stacks and stroked thick leather bindings, the bindings that held man's knowledge between sturdy covers, books on astronomy, geography, history—the secrets of the universe and the human mind, all there for me. But how could I read them all, how would I select them, how would I find the authors who spoke directly to me? How would I be able to unravel at least one secret of the universe? There were so many books and I had to choose.

I slipped back into silence, asking myself, Can I cross from one world to another? Won't *they* know that I am a fraud? Won't *they* know that I am stealing words that do not belong to me?

My words were Benny and Momma's words. And they could not journey with me through literature. I knew if they could read, as I could, they would explain, in the clearest, simplest terms, the deepest meanings of the greatest writers.

But their very muteness brought me to language, to literature. I threw away grammar. I spoke English as I heard it; I wrote it as I read it.

I opened to sound. The sound of the page, the sound of the street was audible now. I held it to me. I heard the traffic, the subway rumble. Taxis melded with trucks, nudging and rushing people along. The city was yellow for me, noisy, taxicab yellow. I practiced each day; practiced listening to the city's music, certain of every note.

I burst from silence.

I waited impatiently in the second year of high school. My teachers droned into the languor of the April classrooms. I heard the words, I could recite the lessons verbatim, but I was absent, my eyes were outside the window. In each room I made certain my seat was at the window: my mother's window. I listened to the practiced prattle of my teachers with my ears, but my soul was held in rapt attention by the first robin of spring on the school grounds.

Walton High School was a typical school of its era, the late 1940s. Three thousand girls from the borough spent their days locked into archaic academic learning that was highly structured and boring. My thirst for learning had not abated, but my attention waned.

It was May and I played hookey. I took the subway, alone, to Central Park and walked in the springtime bloom. A New York policeman stopped me as I strolled, questioned me, took my name and chased me from the green. In the morning before classes began the dean called me to her office and rattled on about truancy and the law, behavior and demerits. I shut her out.

Week after week, I sat in class after class, learning, remembering. Week after week, my eyes looked out the window, watching the springtime grow into summer. Until I was at last free of the rigid school schedule, ready to listen to my own inner ear.

School was absurd, a collection of memorized facts, a denial of questions. Learn, write, copy. Ask as little as possible. My father was a better teacher. He asked and prodded until he clearly understood. My academic asking was frowned upon, inhibited. So summertime was a good time. Together, we read the streets, the faces of passing people, created signs for their weary walks, and laughed. We observed, as my mother did through her window, but we were not silent, we chatted incessantly with our hands, gesticulating wildly, moving softly, now, oblivious to the stares of others, who peeked at us out of the corners of their eyes, who turned brazenly to stare full of wonder at this twosome, father and daughter engaged in monumental discourse. All by hand! We did not see them as we stopped abruptly in mid-block. Dialogue required our bodies. Our learning was sublime, illuminated by conversation, back-and-forth talk. He was masterful, demanding total comprehension.

"Now," he signed, "I understand, do you understand?"

That was always his last question. When I couldn't answer his inquiry at the most fundamental level, I promised to search for the answer, to question books and people until I could satisfy his wonder.

He sought light; darkness was unacceptable. And knowledge was light.

"Don't worry if you can't find the answer. God knows all answers. One day, later, we will find out, you will learn and you will teach me."

I marveled at him, and asked, "How can you be sure that God knows?"

He answered, "I know that God knows. He is my friend. We must be patient."

He took my hand, and in his deep gruff voice said, "Now we walk, we walk far, get fresh air, exercise for body. No more think. Study earth secrets later. We take subway to good place."

We walked hand in hand to Central Park, paired by our love for each other, smiling, my father and I. He laughed aloud; I shoved him with my elbow and broadly mouthed the words, "Why laugh?"

"Funny, I think of something funny."

"What is it?" I signed. "Tell me."

"I laugh because God made you to hear, and me to be deaf from meningitis disease. I want to know why, and then I say never mind to God. I know he will not tell me. I know you have my voice, my mind. So together we learn. I laugh, it is funny what God makes with people."

He found pleasure in every discovery. With murmuring hands, I confessed my escape into New York's green oasis, my confrontation with the policeman and my censure by the Dean.

His face broadened into a massive smile. "That is good, God understand that you look for springtime flowers. Stupid policeman, stupid teacher. They not understand a mind that is interesting in everything. Central Park is better classroom."

I poked him, jarring him from philosophy.

"Daddy," I said, "listen, hear noise in the grass."

He put his head to the ground, his ear to the grass and said, "I hear earth talk."

"Daddy, stop it. Earth does not talk in Central Park."

"No real, no fool, earth talk, come listen."

I put my head to the ground as he commanded and now I heard the insects and the wind in the grass and the elves spoke to me of magic and I heard the earth's dank sweet smell.

"You hear whole world, you hear China in big hole on other side of world?" he asked me, flat on his stomach listening with me.

I moved my head from his, rolled my body away from his joke and he caught my wrist. "No get up, stay listen to earth voice, tell me how earth talk."

There he was pressing me again, but this time I took his silence and laid it on yellow dandelions in the field, laid it next to my silence and said, "You hear better than I do."

"Silly talk," he signed.

"Silly to talk to earth too."

"I not ask you to talk to earth, I ask earth to talk to you. I deaf like old shoes, hear nothing. Not you. You listen. Learn earth's speech. You talk back to earth with voice, your voice."

He knew the earth's song and lifted me into its music. We shared this great sound, the silence not void after all.

We walked home from the subway without words. Our silence remained unrelieved until we entered the apartment. My mother and her friends were talking orally and signing simultaneously; it sounded like a Christmas choir gone wild. There were no hushed phrases or quiet sentences. They were arguing about their poker game, shouting that someone had not put money into the pot. Chairs scraped the kitchen floor, hands were high in the air and each distinctive voice flowed into one raging river of open sound.

Oh, I wanted my silence back. I slid into my room and opened my biology textbook. I shut the door but the deaf sounds penetrated. At last they left. It was quiet. Comfortable. I was home. Silent, with my voice. My words.

Fifteen

FANTASIES

. . . and a time to heal . . .
—*Ecclesiastes 3:3*

*I*n the warmth of my bed, I struggled once more with sound. I pulsed a mental string across the room's corners, straining to see sound, to see something. I pulled the down comforter over my head, pushed the night sounds into the corners, into the crevices from which they came. They came relentlessly through the thick quilt, through the pillow over my head. There was no escape from the invisible sound. My receptors, my ears, never shut down; I had no mechanism to rest them. My body, tired, drifted into sleep.

And I had a dream.

Celeste came, a friend, and she was my age, sixteen. And ebon-haired like me. She wore a lavender mohair sweater and an eggplant-colored fine woolen skirt. She was lithe, her arms were long and slender and they were raised high, grabbing the air into her hands. A sign. But the sign was misty, clouded. It was not her body, or her soft purple sweater, or her pale white skin that kept me riveted to her. It was her eyes. She had three. Her third eye was above her right eyebrow, centered over her sculptured nose. It was almond-shaped and smaller than the deep brown eyes, one on each side of her nose.

After weeks and months of dreaming the dream, I knew that Celeste was me. We shared the third eye. I was able to see what others couldn't. I had another level of knowing. I saw, observed, understood. I saw others free of clutter and chatter. I was quieter, the urgency diminished. And I accepted the gift of silence: my first language, a visual language of hands. A fully honed sight.

I slept and Celeste came night after night, stood beside me and said nothing, comforting me with her presence. Through the night a steady hum suffused the room, rising and falling, the spectrum of sound ever present . . . welcome. I saw a rainbow, a kaleidoscope of pastel sounds arched across the sky, sound fell like raindrops braced by an enormous iris holding the earth in place. I reached up and stroked this rainbow of falling sound, falling into luminous colors.

My father put my arm down and signed, "It is morning. What you dream with smiling face? What you touch up to sky?"

It was morning. The sun shone. The night sounds were done. Ben was there stroking my arm.

"You have nice dream. Tell me dream. You remember dream?"

I reached to him with my hands, arched my rainbow into the sky with a sign I created from sleep and described the colors. I didn't tell him it was a rainbow of sound.

"What else you dream, not tell me everything?"

"I forget, sorry about that, not remember all. But I have a new girlfriend in my dream."

I did not tell him then, nor did I ever tell him in his lifetime, of my terror of the unseen night sound. I did not tell him what my young mind could not sign. I did not tell him that I was a silhouette, dark against the light around me, a shadow without substance, alone. A non-being. I did not tell him of the silent shell that surrounded me, of my attempts to pierce it, to prick its skin. I did not tell him of the winter nights when silent snow seeped through the sealed window, so sharp that I found an old towel and pushed it against the crack of dull winter air. I did not tell him of my attempts to seal the silence in, shut the sound out.

I told him, "Poppa, I had good dream, happy dream with friend. I feel better."

He looked down at me, still under the comforter he had made for me when I was a little girl. "Up, up!" he signed, "up from bed, we begin new day, new life."

In his touch, in that moment, I was a young child again, connected to him, as he caressed my head. I was a spontaneous part of life's whole image. I was happy. I would have, if I had known how, put my arms out and encircled the earth, given it a resounding hug. I hear my father say, "Earth good, sun warm." I see Benny signing his understanding of the unity of soul and soil, his understanding that reached for God.

The black moments dissipated. But I had other moments. Lonely ones. The loneliness formed when I formed into "me," when I recognized that I was a separate being, a unique "I." I ran away from it, I took bus rides to the end of the line. I waited on the corner with other passengers for the bus that took me to the far end of the Bronx and I sat staring out the window until I lost my loneliness. I breathed the fumes of the city at each bus stop as unnamed people got off and on the bus, seeking their own destinations. As the distance between bus stops grew longer the trees grew taller, the apartment buildings receded and I saw houses with lawns, thick June roses, yellow daffodils, and the loneliness evaporated. I saw a butterfly and connected to the universe.

I pressed my head to the glass, and I was the only rider on the bus. "Fly free!" said my father, fluttering his arms imitating the butterfly's flight, its soft landing on the cream rose petal. Although he didn't travel with me on my bus journey, his hands lifted the white butterfly through the grimy windowpane onto the back of my hand.

"Last stop, girlie!"

I looked up at the bus driver, whose words were gentle, and said, "I am going back, I just came for the ride. Shall I pay the return fare now?"

"Naw, that's okay. But I'm going out for five, gonna have a cigarette."

"Can I wait on the bus?"

"Sure."

I looked out the window and the butterfly was gone.

The bus rode back to its starting point and I stared at the butterfly's image all the way home. I reentered the silence, staring at it, ignoring it, wanting an answer to my riddle. I unraveled the knots in the white cotton thread that kept me knitted to myself. I smoothed the thread with my hands and believed for the moment I restitched myself whole, free as the white butterfly, free as Celeste. I pushed the old burden of silence from my shoulders and shook myself loose. I entered another day.

I shifted. I thought, I must let go of the silence that holds me like a lover. And I can't, not completely. The obsession diminishes and the silence is peaceful, almost musical, a lilting harmony that gives me rest and ease. It is the beginning of acceptance.

And love came.

I moved hesitatingly into this new circle. My body changed, my breasts swelled, my stomach rounded, my lank limbs shaped and I fell in love. For long periods that year I put silence aside, meanings and terrors away. I fell in love with sweet Saul, whom I met the summer after Sammy. I scribbled Saul's name on every inch of my blue linen looseleaf binder. I swathed paths on lined pages in pencil, curving his name through the paper, feeling a new feeling, recreating creation. Love, new each time, was its own miracle. Our connection flourished based on unspoken childhood pain. He was a child of divorce, and I was a child of the deaf. But never did we speak of it, not even when our own children were born years later in foreign countries where people spoke in foreign sound.

It was June. The Bronx buildings, protective in winter, permitted no summer breath to penetrate the packed streets.

Julia, my best friend, who lived across the street, asked me to take the subway with her to Bensonhurst, a remote corner of Brooklyn. She had met a golden-haired lifeguard in Coney Island, had his address and wanted to find him, to see him once more. We rode the subway that Saturday, underground and overground, from the Bronx through Manhattan, across Brooklyn's belly, until we reached our destination. I recognized the station from childhood, a station just three stops before the end of the line, before Coney Island. The street was shadowed by the elevated tracks. The sound was strong as the train returning to Manhattan screeched to a stop on the opposite side of the platform. I pushed the noise aside; this was a day for fun, no time for my sound and silence query.

We searched the four corners of the intersection in this strange place, turned our heads and did not know where to walk, where to find Julia's blond lifeguard.

She said, "There must be a candy store here. I'm sure that's where the boys hang out."

I pointed to one that I saw on the opposite side of the street. We held hands and ran across the asphalt strip covered by the darkness of the elevated rails into the light, and saw no one.

"We can wait here, have a soda, someone will come."

The shopkeeper leaned over the open counter, shaded by a dull green awning, and asked, "Whadda ya gonna have girls?"

"An egg cream, please."

I watched him perform the exact ritual I had seen in the Bronx: chocolate syrup, milk, and a frothy blast of clear soda water stirred with a long clinking spoon. I wanted to ask him if he knew the candy store man on my corner of the Bronx, if they were somehow related, but Julia's dark-eyed presence stopped me.

"That'll be a nickel each, girls."

As I shoved the dime across the counter, Julia's elbow pressed into my waist and she whispered, "Some boys are coming. Talk to me; I don't want to look like a jerk."

It was the first time I saw Saul. He was tall, more than six feet, slim and dark blond. He moved with grace, sliding, talking, pushing his square hands through his pompadour. He was seventeen years old. He was with Freddie, the golden lifeguard. They stopped, claimed their piece of the corner territory, glanced at us, and resumed talking to one another, ignoring our presence.

Julia poked me and with facial gesture and pinched eyes, said without sound, "Speak to them, say something!"

"Excuse me . . ." I turned to Freddie. "We've come from the Bronx, near Yankee Stadium, we're looking for a friend at this address, just a minute, I'll get it." I took the folded paper from Julia's hand and read him his own address.

Fred's response was immediate. "But that's my address, and I live in a private house. Who are you looking for?"

Julia quickly gave her aunt's name, an aunt who lived in Coney Island.

"Well there must be some mistake."

I turned to Julia and in mock seriousness said, "You mean we came all this way for nothing? Well, let's take a walk and explore the neighborhood before our long ride home."

Fred said, "We'll walk with you. What are your names?"

The introductions done, we walked until it was time to reenter the elevated train.

I held Saul's image to me that night and for the nights that followed our telephone romance. My longing for him and our developing young love through the years before our marriage dissipated some of my frantic search for silence's meaning.

I had an inkling during the Celeste dreams that silence inappropriately sought had human disconnection as its end, but lovingly sought it could bring comfort and peace. I cast this insight aside as I cast many aside; I was in love and I now had ballast. A listening, speaking love—all mine. Someone like me, someone to share oral speech, orally spoken love.

In glintings it came upon me. I was in possession of myself away from the deaf threshold. Transposed from silence's enclave, which demanded I move in a rhythm unnatural to me, I had a change of heart. I wandered off to my own kingdom, to my own kind, listening to and interpreting my own noises. I was no longer untied, loose and alone.

I planned long absences from home. I arrived for meals, studied and went to bed early. I awakened before dawn to watch the light filter through the darkness, to listen to the morning sounds without deaf interruption. It was my time, quiet, yet filled with the noise of the rising city. I had the moments of dawn to myself, I could think unburdened by the need for explanations. I had by now identified my life sounds. And I loosened the bonds of fear.

I had a great desire to be as my father was, in total possession of myself. He was whole. I was still marred. Necessity moved in, there were people to care for, tasks to perform, school to complete. I wanted to move off into Celeste's night where no one needed me. Instead, I wrote Saul love letters and waited for the postman to bring his written reply in clear English, in perfect syntax.

Together, Saul and I embarked on a joined fantasy. We would leave America after college, go back to Europe from whence our ancestors came, redefine ourselves, our lives. We plotted and planned our lives, recreating them from childhood scarrings. But that was in the future and the present was now and I was still, in spite of Celeste's presence, encircled by my quest for silence's meaning.

I dreamed of escape to foreign lands, to new languages to shield me from my mother tongue, the tongue of hands. It was to be an escape from the language of hands to the language of voice alone, where no one would ask me to speak with my fingers, where instead I could ask the meaning of new words with my own voice.

I denied my own language. My hands did express a universal language. Translation wasn't needed, superfluous. The language of hands has its own feelings, its own tone. It was and is exquisite. But I wasn't quite ready to accept its beauty. I was waxed into myself, the wax warm, keeping me to my primary language. It was touch that connected me to people, connected me to myself. Sign language was rich, my attempts to be rid of it futile, foolish.

And I remember Ben, my father, who said repeatedly, "I not a fool." *I* was the fool.

I walked the streets of the Bronx and on the blue air clear as winter snow bells I heard his voice. "Hands everybody's language. Make to understand all people who cannot understand different language from the mouth. Not necessary to hear sound."

I saw the curve of his hand enjoining me to touch another as he had touched me. I taught Saul sign, and we played in another language. His signs were young, awkward, almost comic. And I reached for my native language, my hands.

Sixteen

COLLEGE

Take fast hold of instruction, let her not go;
Keep her, for she is thy life.

—Proverbs 4:13

There was a betrayal of the words I had stored, of the dreams I had hidden from myself. My father refused to allow me to go to college.

"You are seventeen now. Now you must go to work, help support me and family. I am tired. I work hard. Now it is your turn."

I looked at him with loathing, not caring, not understanding the burdens he carried within his soul. He too wanted to be free of the weight. And he wanted me to help him. I wanted to shout, "Leave me alone! Haven't I done enough? I want to go to college. I want to be somebody, I want to be myself."

I turned without a word, without a sign, and walked out of the door of our apartment determined never to return.

I was angry. And anger was a forbidden emotion. The word *no* was just as forbidden. *No* meant incurring displeasure and I was raised to please and nurture.

This time I wanted what I wanted.

I ran away. Not far. Just across the street to my friend Julia's apartment. I stayed there until night fell. I wanted to enter college, where there would be no parents' nights, where there would be no pitying eyes and heartfelt sighs from teachers who were shocked by my parents' deafness. I didn't want delicate treatment by my teachers, I didn't want my classmates to stare at me.

My mother came looking for me. She knocked at my friend's door, and I heard her voice inquisitively sound my name when the door was opened.

When she saw me she said in voice, "No hot stammer now Ruth."

I smiled, remembering my discovery of the meaning of her words.

"You never angry, why now? Stop. Not nice, be so angry. Come home, you go to a college, I promise you."

"I am a girl. And it is not important for girls to go to college, just boys. That is what Ben said. I hate him. He does not understand. I want to learn. I want to be a teacher."

"Come, we explain all to your father. He is sorry. He tell me it is okay you go to college. Say good-bye to your friend Julia."

We walked slowly down the street. My father walked toward us. I pulled away from him. He touched my shoulder and signed solemnly, "No be angry at Ben. I love you daughter Ruth. You graduate high school now and in September you go to college to study, do what you love best, always to study to learn. I go to college with you, you teach me."

He signed his language as an ancient stylized scribe. The calligraphy of his hands startled me with its fluid precision.

The signs punched the air, the language accurate. He saw what I heard, I heard what he saw and we understood one another. And we did not understand; our language sense split us apart, separated us. And I was to be his teacher.

While I was still at Walton High School, I watched the Navy women, the Waves, dressed smartly in blue and white, marching in formation on Hunter College's campus grounds from my classroom windows. Now, with the war over, the Bronx campus was once more the domain of young civilian girls, and the school opened its doors each semester to another group of students.

The first day of class I walked over winter grounds feeling the snow underfoot, for the moment buoyant, thrilled to be part of this new world. And then I entered the college gymnasium. I was alone, the piano flush against the wall. I was early and my new ballet shoes scuffed across the floor on my way to the black upright. I looked around, saw no one, and with my finger I stole a note. Plunk. I could dance but I wouldn't play the piano. I plunked again and another note. I was making music. Bang.

The dancers came in, dribbled into the gymnasium. The dance instructor was late. A raven-haired aspiring ballerina approached me at the piano.

"Here," she said. "See what I brought. Hold it."

She turned a key. It was a music box, a box with a voice.

I heard voices. I separated them, I attached them to hands. They'd jell and melt, thaw and harden. I didn't have the power to grab hold, to identify each voice alone, to unify voice into the flow of all earth sounds. The ground was firmer. The closer I got to my own voice, the closer I got to myself, the more competent I became in sorting out all voices, even those musical voices I denied my whole childhood.

I read. I read the writings of others, read the allusions to silence, the descriptions of deep silence and wondered how writers used the word.

What did these writers mean when they addressed silence? Did they understand what it meant never, ever to hear sound, any sound? Years and years of silence, silence forever. Did they know about long moments of silence when no miracle occurred? Was the miracle silence itself? Did it have its own teachings? I waited for an answer, an answer for my father.

I read John Keats' "Ode on a Grecian Urn," and he wrote, "Heard melodies are sweet, but those unheard are sweeter," and I shouted internally, "Liar! What do you know of silence's dumbness? Can you quantify the infinity of silence? Mr. Keats, how do you transcend silence and find it so sweet? It is the sound of sound that is the sweetest of all. Do you hear me Mr. Keats?"

I was angry at the great body of literature that played romantically with sound and silence, with speech and language. The anger rose, and with each rising, I began to heal, began to find my hearing path, my hearing-speaking self.

I went back to my books. I looked for books at home, and there were none we owned except the *World Almanac* my father bought every year to titillate his collection of facts. There were no cookbooks for my mother, no history books for my father; there was a pile of comic books left over from childhood in the closet, the last issue of *Life* magazine in the living room. My college texts were stacked on the hall table, our old mahogany dining table with its massive carved legs. It was another remnant of the past, and it held my keys, scarf, gloves and my latest library books.

My father shook his head at all the books, in the hallway, on coffee tables, on my nightstand, in the kitchen propped up behind the sink and said, "Too hard to read so many books, so many words together, long, long pages."

The recital of his limited literacy broke my heart. He so wanted language's pleasure, language's flow of ideas, laid one on top of the other like cans on a grocery shelf, neatly labeled, neatly laid out with the occasional imported erotica, the caviar, thick white asparagus, oysters dripping in pure olive oil.

"Tell me," he signed, "who is best writer in world?"

Stunned, I signed an opening paragraph for him, word for word, propping his fluency with the author's pen. He watched my hands; I watched his eyes until his concentration flagged, until the words joined together for him in one mass. I wasn't speaking sign language, I wasn't speaking our language. My hands obscured a flow of words too difficult to sustain in my father's language. I interpreted Mark Twain's words, I abridged the novelist's polish and lost the tenor of the writer's music.

I recited words, I recited single poems.

He brushed me aside. "Too many words, fall everywhere, like rocks coming down mountain, too fast. We forget to read now. You explain me better."

Defeated, I dropped my eyes and he said with his fingers in the air increasing and decreasing the width of space between his thumb and forefinger, "Next time we read thin book, not so thick, and I sure to understand every word." His grin was huge.

He made me laugh again. With his fingers he lay the stripe of my childhood across my back: my language was mine and his was his, and I alone crossed over, back and forth.

The college years were wonderful, fulfilling the promise my father had made when I was a child entering school for the first time. He asked me, "What you ask professors today?" still demanding a questing mind, for me, for him.

But I grew too busy for his questions, for teaching. I was absorbed in the passing years, absorbed in work, in study and in my love for Saul.

I gave up working in Macy's book department and got a job as a wrapper, nearer to Hunter College, at Alexander's department store on Fordham Road. I was on my feet four hours every afternoon beside the cashier, sliding lingerie, over-sized bras and small lace panties, sweaters and skirts into thin brown paper bags. I listened to the clack of the cash register, mulling my studies over in my head, ignoring the world as I sealed bags, wrapped packages and lifted coats into boxes as my fingers folded and unfolded cartons. I handed the merchandise to each customer with a frozen thank you, a smile, and waited for the hours to pass, so that I could return home, to my books, to my mail.

Christmas came and lines grew longer, the press of wrapping more intense, and I grew stronger, totally absorbed in my book life, reading until I needed new glasses, straining now, for words in books that were no longer just words I had strung together as a child. Benny sensed my concentration and stopped asking me the meaning of this word, that word. He felt my happiness and said, "Maybe you stop to work now, take a time off, have more time to read, to learn more, later you teach me, not so busy when you work too."

I smiled at his acceptance, at his love, and went on working and waiting for Saul's letters to arrive from the Ross Sea. He had joined the Navy and was on an expedition with Admiral Richard E. Byrd in the Antarctic. The letters were widely spaced, sometimes there were none, and then there were three all at once postmarked from the bottom of the world, stuffed into the mailbox where my mother left them for me.

My dreams were sweeter now; Celeste no longer came.

I dreamed another dream. We were riding in a 1932 "tin lizzie," a restored relic, painted dove gray with a thick white line painted around the car. We were in it, Saul and I and our friends, riding merrily to a picnic, the car crowded; the sticks of crunchy sweet-smelling French bread fanned out tall in the rumble seat, the bottles of wine clinking with each turn in the road. The picnic's laughter, the sun-filled happiness stopped abruptly as we swerved to avoid a line of birds, white, yellow beaked, waddling like emperor penguins. The driver hit a bird. We scrambled out of the car. Someone, a male, bent over the stunned bird lying on the ground. In unison we lifted the bird and gently, gently extended its enormous wings; the bird's eyes opened. I stroked its head. It did not move. And then it shook itself off, stood up on its webbed feet, moved in a waddle and joined the column of birds on its stately march down the poplar lined road. It was an albatross, freed, alive.

And I awakened smiling, freed, alive.

Home on leave, Saul asked me to marry him, to follow him from naval station to naval station until his discharge. I wouldn't give up my dream, my college life, until graduation. But in the last year of college, after his tour of duty was over, we did marry secretly, agreeing that we would tell no one and live apart until I finished college.

We drove up to White Plains on Armistice Day, a Friday. I had no classes and took the day off from work. We stopped at a phone booth and searched the yellow pages for a justice of the peace who would marry us. When we arrived in the early November afternoon, he refused to perform the wedding ceremony although our papers were in order. I was only twenty. He said, "Only a minister, priest or rabbi can perform a marriage when you are underage."

The afternoon was darkening; sundown would be upon us soon. This was the only day we could do this, and no rabbi would marry us after sundown on the Sabbath.

We went back to the car and decided to try the yellow pages once more. The first rabbi we called invited us to his home on a hill and tried to dissuade us from our plans. When we promised that we would let him remarry us with our parents present, after my graduation, he consented. And he did so, one year later, in December of 1950.

"Hurry!" he said. "We must do this quickly, before the sun sets."

His white-haired mother, slim and elegant, played the piano as he recited the vows, and we repeated them. His wife served as my matron of honor. When the ceremony was done, he poured wine and we drank to our delayed tomorrow.

We drove back to New York, Saul to his part-time evening job as a host at Rosoff's restaurant in the heart of Times Square, and I went home to spend my wedding night with my mother at a neighborhood movie, interpreting once again the film's love story.

We lived the year apart and although we saw each other on the weekends and spoke daily on the telephone, my life resumed its own rhythm—work and study.

We had a second wedding ceremony thirteen months later, and our parents were present. They never knew about the first ceremony.

A month after our first wedding, I rushed home with joy in my heart, pushing the subway faster, faster to the Bronx from Manhattan, from Hunter College. I had ecstasy to share; I had something to tell and this was not a secret, but no one was at home when I arrived. My mother wasn't at the window.

I see her now. Younger. She enters the room within her margin of silence and I am in awe of her quiet beauty. She is my mother, always my mother. Her complexion immaculate, the first ripening of summer fruit, delicate and unblemished. Her smooth chestnut hair is gathered into a bun on the nape of her scarred neck. The December sun lights her face. I am overwhelmed by her beauty. She sees me, breaks the spell and sopranos my name: "Ruth, Ruth, you are at home, good. I need not wait for you at the window."

I smile at her as I always do. I do not move to kiss her.

"Why you home so early from a college?"

"I had exams today and I finished early."

"You first to finish to write tests?"

"Yes, Momma, I was the first to finish."

"Always, you finish first. Will you to fail a test?" She laughed, teasing me with her hands.

"No, Momma, I will not fail. I have something to tell you."

"About your college?"

"Sit down and I will explain you all," I signed in her vernacular.

As she sat, she smoothed her skirt, focused her eyes on mine, searching my eyes for a clue and signed, "I wait, you tell me all, I ready to hear news now."

"I win a prize Momma, I earn a gold key for my college work. Name of key is *Phi Beta Kappa*." I spelled each Greek letter for her; there are no signs for the letters of the Greek alphabet.

"It is important prize. It is honor for daughter?"

Our eyes met in a long smile.

"You work hard many years. I proud on you."

And in a rare moment, she reached across the table, took my face in her hands and kissed me.

"Tonight we tell Ben, your Daddy Ben, he proud, very proud too."

Unable to contain her pleasure, my mother pulled my father into the living room the moment he opened the door, waving her hands at him.

"Ben, I have surprise."

"I take off coat, hat, wait."

"No wait, I tell you now. Ruth has Phi Beta Kappa."

"Funny words, I never heard. What you tell me Mary?"

I watched their hands from the doorway, my father's back angled just enough so that I could see his question.

Sensing my presence, he turned to me and asked, "Momma not spell right. Funny language. What she talk about?"

"She spelled the words right." I repeated the spelling, letter by letter.

"Okay, okay, you both smarter than me, tell me what words mean now."

"They are letters of the Greek alphabet, *p, b,* and *k.* It is the name of an honor society for best students in college."

He made the connection at once and shouted with his voice and hands simultaneously. "We have a good luck. Tell me again how to spell honor club words."

Once more I spelled the words and he etched them into his hands.

"How I know real you receive a prize?"

"Take off your coat, Daddy, your cap and I will explain."

"Coat wait, you tell me now!"

"I will receive a golden key with my name on one side, and Phi Beta Kappa written the Greek way on the other side. There will be a ceremony soon and you and Momma will come and watch me receive a key."

He sat down on the sofa, pulled me down to him and rubbed his mustache across my face. Then he took me by the shoulders with both hands and in oral words said, "Congratulations to daughter Ruth."

We laughed. And the scripture of his hands praised me as he lifted them and stroked my head in blessing.

"I am hungry, now I take off coat, now we have our dinner. Momma get wine and we drink to God, thank God to honor our daughter."

Although it was my father who refused my entry into college, it was he who received its ultimate gift of excellence. It was he who had touched me with the primal conquest of language. It was he who taught me to be direct. It was he who taught me to be watchful, to listen with my eyes and then ask with my mouth. It was he who never put up the barrier walls. It was he who taught me the power of speech. It was he who led me to the deliverance of my voice. It was he who pointed me to sound, to select it amid the silence.

Part Four

VOICES

Seventeen

MY DEAF FAMILY

Hear attentively the noise of His voice,
And the sound that goeth out of His mouth.
He sendeth it forth under the whole heaven,
And His lightning unto the ends of the earth.
                                    —*Job 37:2–3*

I listened to the road talk, to the subway talk, to the country talk, to the city talk. I was eager to speak with my voice, with my hands. I was eager for the touch of talk. But there was a time when deaf touch revolted me.

When I was eight years old, I saw Helen Keller—in reality, in fantasy, in film. I am not sure, even now, but she was real for me. I heard her flat-faced voice and was repelled. I felt her touch and moved away. A monotone voiced shuteye. I reached for my father, put my hands up and said, "I want go home, don't like this lady, no eyes in face, no real voice."

Sensing my fear, my father took me by the hand, saying

nothing until he found my mother in the crowd of deaf assembled for this special meeting and then said, "We take Ruth home now!" His hands were absolute, speaking without hesitation.

It was a time before I met Helen Gribbs in the early 1980s. An adult now, involved in deaf-community affairs, I had heard about this Helen from the others; another blind deaf woman. I didn't want to see her. I didn't want to meet her. I didn't want her hands on mine, listening to my voice. I avoided her presence, until one day a deaf classmate of my father's, in his eighties, rushed up to me, signing, "Come, I have surprise for you!" He led me to Helen.

She was standing alone. Sentinel still.

My father's friend deftly put his hand under Helen's and signed his introduction, pulling my hand to hers so that she could touch my words.

I stiffened and signed awkwardly into her hand, "I am happy to meet you."

She barely touched my fingers. And because she had once been sighted and her blindness had come upon her, shutting out the light slowly, she signed in open sign, "I am so happy to meet you." Helen was born deaf.

Relieved that the formality was over, I moved away from her and turned my back, glad to be gone. She tapped my elbow; I turned once more to face her and she signed fully across her face and chest, "Do you know Mary Bromberg?"

I reached my hand quickly into hers and signed, "Yes."

Before I could finish my sentence she signed softly, "You have the same hands, the same speech, the same touch."

And I continued with my fingers in her hand, "Yes, she is my mother."

I shivered in her tactile knowledge, in the memory of her hands. She lived in darkness, she lived without sound and she lived alone. She was seventy-seven years old. And she was funny. Very funny. In some ways like Benny.

We became friends and she told me of the days she and my mother went to school together. She told me of the days when she could see, told me of the fading light, of the blackness. We touched an orchid and she said, "What color?"

"Purple," I signed into her delicate hand.

"What color purple?"

"Dark with a white throat."

"Elegant," she answered.

We both smiled. She stroked the orchid throat.

"You know I am blind and that is stinky."

"Stinky?" I asked, spelling the word into her hand.

She pulled my thumb and index finger to her nose, pinching in the universal sign for a foul odor. She touched my face and we both laughed.

When I come upon her now, I barely touch my fingertips to her hand and she jumps with glee. "Ruth, Ruth, it is you, right?" I throw my body weight against her tall, slim form and hold her tight. Our bodies speak their own voice.

It was the Jewish New Year, September, I heard the blowing of the *Shofar*. And the deaf congregation broke into spontaneous applause as the sound was imitated in long flowing movements of the arms and hands. And Julius, my father's friend, Helen Gribbs's everpresent interpreter, described the call of *Tekiah* into her hand. I saw her bland face speak as a smile entered her soul and rose to her lips until she was filled with listening in the darkness, in the soundlessness. Her body lifted from the chair, she removed Julius's hand and she applauded, unaware that all around her were applauding with her. The congregation was on its feet, filled with the sound of the blast they did not hear.

They fulfilled the obligation of listening to the music, to the ram's horn heralding in the New Year. It was an obligation from which they were exempted, yet they listened. I rose with them, one of the few present in the synagogue who could hear the *Shofar*'s trumpeting. I too heard with my eyes and saw the imperfect sounding of the perfect *Shofar*.

The services were over and I went to greet Helen, to stand before her and wait for her to recognize my breath before I touched her arm. My mother pulled my arm and said, "Talk to Helen later, she now know you are here. I want you to meet Rose Davis. Your father Ben know her since they are children."

I looked at Momma's face, still beautiful at seventy-six. Her hair, almost white, was smooth across her head, gathered into a bun, as always, at the nape of her neck. She wore the same shade of coral rose lipstick I remembered from childhood. Her eye were clear green, her skin unwrinkled, her smile enchanting. And she still wore the same scent, soft and sweet.

"Stop to stare at me. I am your mother. The same, never change!" She was pleased by my attention.

I returned her smile and she tugged at me, ignoring my reluctance, forcing me to follow her across the room to meet Rose. She was small, white-haired, and at eighty-six, she wasn't frail.

My mother addressed her and signed, "Do you remember my daughter, Ruth?"

"Yes, she looks like Ben, same dark eyes. I know your father, he sat on my lap when he was a boy."

I shook my head, my father dead five months now, and she so alive, so eager to tell me how it felt to bounce my father on her knee. She pointed to her lap, signing rapidly, as though it were a miracle, "I had him on my knee here, here I held him."

Our eyes exchanged the meaning of her words.

"My father and your grandfather were best friends. My father had a bottling factory, your grandfather Morris had a cork factory, long time ago, 1907 or 1908. Your grandfather tell my father about his deaf son Ben, and my father told him about me, his deaf daughter Rose, who goes to a deaf school. That is how your grandfather took your father Benjamin to the 23rd Street school for the deaf."

And another piece of my father's history fell into place.

She laughed, poking her upper thighs with her cane astride her leg muscles. "See," she repeated, "this is where I held your father, and I was only eleven years old." And I knew she was telling me that she was the first one who understood him back at the turn of the twentieth century, that she had been blocked from the world as he was, alone and isolated. But she had begun her passage to language and had passed that gift to Benny by giving him her lap for solace.

My mother said, "See interesting news about Daddy Ben," clinging to his memory.

She endowed me with her smile and signed, "Go talk to Helen now."

The deaf were on their feet, in circles, arms and hands alive, talking to one another. I skirted the groups, walking around them, out of sight until I reached Helen. I touched her and she sign smiled, "Go see everyone Ruth, Julius is here with me, go and say hello, come back later and tell me who is here."

I turned to the noise of the uncommon voices rising as one cacophonous shriek. I made my way through the crowd, discerning this voice, that voice, separating deaf sound, male and female, receiving shy greetings, wet kisses and blank stares. I received the touch, always the touch of the deaf in language. I threaded through their raucous parliament surprising them with my unheard presence, seeing each familiar eye, seeing those who teased me about my childhood habits, those who knew me by name alone and nodded my reserved greeting in return. I pressed on until I acknowledged each person. I was at home here. Familiar.

I lingered within each circle waiting for conversation,

news beyond the salutation of hands. I waited for the common exchange among people. I waited to hear, "How are you? What are you doing these days? It's been months since I've seen you."

And I waited as they turned their heads from me, turned to each other and continued their rapid signing. I moved from exclusion to the next group, and the next, and the next. They signed and they spoke and their voices followed me in a narrow strip across the room. I lurched across the room, weaving as some deaf do, balance awry, my inner ear assaulted by the lunatic sounds spoken without definition from group to group.

I turned to look at the faces, turned my eyes to the assembly collected in pantomimic clusters and saw silence amid the crowding noise. This was not lunacy. This was the collective voice of the deaf, polyphonic sound.

Then I lifted my arms to speak and there was no one in front of me, no face to address; there were backs of heads, arms moving, people breaking into conversation, pushing their hands into the group, vying for armed dominance. I could have spoken to the air with my hands; no one would have noticed. I sought Helen's face and she was expressionless. Blind.

Again I looked down the length of the room as they prepared to leave, conversations completed. I looked across the room at this softening choir, saw their voices, heard their voices, one hundred voices melded into a single strident soundtrack. It may have sounded like bedlam to some; to me it was home. I wasn't one of them, I didn't speak with their voice. And when they were done with me, they were done. And still it was home.

I made my way to Helen. And she touched my face.

Eighteen

BENNY DIES

The hearing ear, and the seeing eye,
The Lord hath made even both of them.
—*Proverbs 20:12*

*I*n the last year of his life, my father spent the month of December in intensive care, attached to a heart monitor. He was eighty-one or eighty-two years old; the date of his birth was never clearly established. The records had burned. Was he born in 1902 or 1903? He insisted it was 1903.

"No matter," I said to him, as he lay there shining his eyes upon me.

"Matter, we must to know always perfectly."

"Matter that you are alive Daddy, and I come to see you every day."

And every day he asked me to speak to each patient, to each of the six men, and ask if they needed anything.

One afternoon there was a new patient, a black man, long

and skinny in his narrow bed opposite my father. His face was the color of melted chocolate hardened into crevices. His kinky hair was white, raised on his head in the manner of fright. His eyes were big and brown and clear. He sat up, leaning on his elbows, and the nails on his elongated fingers curled in their mandarin length. The blankets on his bed were disheveled. His bony feet were capped with nails so long that no shoe would fit him.

He pointed at me and said, "Is that your brother? My name is Thomas. See that bed your brother lay in? My wife, she died in the same bed nine years ago."

My father asked with his hands, "What say that black man?"

I repeated Thomas's words.

"Is his mind gone?"

"No, Daddy, he is just old and thin and he forgets much."

"He does not eat today, Ruth. Give him my banana to eat. You bring me another tomorrow."

I walked to the other side of the room and touched Thomas's hand. "I brought you some dessert."

I handed him the banana and turned my back to him. My father's voice shouted at me, "Go back, look at him eat banana."

Thomas was unable to bite down on the unpeeled banana. I took it from his mouth and peeled it for him, breaking off small pieces and feeding him by hand. He licked my palm.

"Like feed children, remember you little girl, we feed alone animals to Bronx alley, near garbage cans?"

"Yes, I remember, Daddy. I go outside few minutes to walk."

I walked into the waiting room, into the fading December sun casting winter's pale light on the tar-blackened rooftops stretching from Queens to Manhattan. I went to the window to stare into the sky, freeing myself from the oppressiveness of the intensive care ward. The men lay there, decaying, waiting for death or reprieve.

A young patient in a rumpled hospital gown interrupted me, pleading, "Miss, have you got a cigarette?"

I turned my head to accommodate his request. "Sorry, I don't smoke."

"Oh," he said, "I'm sorry too."

He walked into the phone booth stripped of its telephone books and sat on the seat, staring at the paint flaking from the wall.

I went back to the window. The sky faded into a bland pink and the streetlights came on, coating Queens with electric dazzle. The ugliness was hidden. And I lost the final moment of daylight.

I went back to my mother, seated, quiet, watching my father's breath. I sat beside her and we did not speak, in this room at Elmhurst Hospital in Queens. My mother stared at the young Korean lying in the bed next to my father, his eyes closed, a sky blue respirator breathing for him.

Certain that my father was sleeping, she said to me in minced hands in her lap, without moving her lips so as not to frighten the small Oriental woman at the Korean's bedside, "Man will die tomorrow, maybe next day. No, he will die tomorrow."

I looked at her, waiting for an explanation.

"I know," was all she said with her lips.

And I knew that she knew.

She asked me, reflection of her knowing light, "Will Daddy Ben, your father die?"

"No Momma, he will not die. Not this time."

The thin female resident, ashen faced, eyes ringed, entered the intensive care unit, saw me sitting at the window with my mother and asked with a twitching face, "Why do you stay, hour after hour?"

"I stay to be my father's voice."

The twitching stopped, her face relaxed.

"What doctor say?" my mother asked vocally.

I repeated the exchange.

"Yes, better, we are here, no one understands deaf hands."

The next day, my father—rested, alert—asked where the young Korean had gone, why the bed was empty.

My mother was quick. "He die. I tell Ruth yesterday, he die."

There is a legend that tells of the unborn child who knows everything, but at the moment of birth all knowing is erased by an angel. Do the deaf keep this knowledge?

My mother said, "I am tired, hungry, time to go home and have a rest."

We walked into the rain, after the long day, found a taxi and my mother signed, "You tell him my address. Glad I do not have to show a driver paper with my street number."

And once again I was my mother's voice.

"Air smell wet, good with so heavy rain."

The ride home was quick; we ate a simple supper. And then we sat, tired by the day.

The storm gathered force, thunder shook the windows. The panes rattled in their grooves, loosened by years of city grime, by soot that hid in the sealed crevices. My mother rose from her chair, moved by the vibration.

She made the sound of the loud explosion with her hands. She created the thunder boom by making a fist with each hand, tensely bringing one fist over the other, holding the explosive sound of thunder at chest level as though she were ready to strike someone. The signed substance of nature's noise took but one second to manually express.

"I hear noise!" It was a spoken thrill.

"Momma," I repeated as I often had as a child. "Did you hear that or did you feel it with your feet?"

"No, no. I hear. Maybe now, almost eighty years old hearing I lose come back!"

"Momma, you did not have hearing, how can you lose what you never have?"

"True, what you say real. I think what must be to have hearing and then to lose. I do not remember hearing, never hear, never lose. Daddy Ben, lose hearing when he was so little a boy."

I tried to imagine a sense of loss; there cannot be a remembered sense of a sense that never was. I put my hands over my ears, forcing sound out, but life's sound entered as it always did.

"You cannot be deaf, you do not know how." She was angry at my posturing.

"I do not want to be deaf, I just want to understand more."

"How many years you try, forget it, be hearing woman. Maybe when I die I hear. Maybe when Daddy Ben die he will hear."

My father came home and lived some more. Eight months later I was called to another Queens hospital. This time he did not speak, did not ask me to inquire after the other patients. I saw him with his wrists tied to the bed, his hands immobile. And I was angry. The doctors had removed his language. He flickered his eyes, unable to sign-speak his last words. He died within the hour of my arrival, cut off from his greatest love, language. He rests now within the shade of silence, grinning at me, I am certain, prodding me to learn more and more words that "make people to be close."

When I said to my mother, waiting in the corridor outside the intensive care unit, "Momma, Ben die. He was past eighty-one years old. He will not suffer anymore. It was his time," she pulled her summer hat down over her ears, protecting herself from the unheard sound of death. She raised her head and slowly signed, "Who will make me laugh?"

The day Benny died the house was silent, the laughter gone. I closed the door to the apartment. Momma went to her room. I sat in the wingback chair, looking across the narrow street and the red brick of Queens, which hid the moon's rising and falling, its movement behind clouds and its miraculous appearance, in, out! Imprisoned by my father's space I waited for my mother's voice to call me from the single bedroom. In the meager moment alone, I smelled roasting chicken down the hall seeping under the doorway, through the crack, filling the apartment with burnt garlic. I could see the shape of my face in the falling light. I could see my father's face smiling at me from death. His face was beside me in the window; he entered the room draped in sienna silk shantung. The lights switched on in the apartments, votive candles flickering on the last day of my father's life, embers speaking to ecstasy.

And I heard his voice as it was in life. And I saw the gentle lamellation of his signs.

I rose from the chair, no longer imprisoned, and went to the kitchen and touched the seven day candle commemorating my father's passage.

And I said, aloud, "I'll feed the sea gulls for you Daddy."

Deliverance came. I lay hold to the language he taught me, fiercely moving to an unknown depth that tied us together as a family, broken by death. My father dead now, my daughter praising him in her words and mine at the chapel. All oral. I could not stand before my father's bier and sign my last words to him publicly. I would have had to sign-speak them simultaneously and I would not, not on this warm August morning.

I heard my brother's tears, but not his voice. I held my mother's hand, and my son was somewhere in China. And I knew he knew, that the knowing had been passed on.

I sat with my hands in my lap, signing funny words to my father. I lay hold to the lyric of hands and felt my tears sting.

His younger brother Irving rose, shook his fist as he stood before my father's coffin and shouted, "God, do you know who you are getting?"

The interpreter couldn't lift her hands to repeat his words to the deaf assembled in the chapel. The pause was long, and then the signs flowed. Once more, for Benny.

We followed the hearse in a rented black limousine over the George Washington Bridge into New Jersey. My mother said softly with her hands, "Ben and I walk many times across this bridge in spring days. Now he goes like king in a big gray car."

The coffin lurched into view and she waved to him and said, with her lips slowly moving, "Hello Ben, I am here."

I turned my face away, numb, not wanting to see the rest of her farewell.

As we pulled up to the cemetery, to the section reserved by the Hebrew Association of the Deaf, the driver cautioned, "Stay in the car until we bring the coffin to the gravesite."

All I remember now is the mahogany coffin I selected the day before, lowered into the ground. The rabbi prayed, a short prayer, turned, and said, "Let us leave."

"No," I said, "I must do something first."

I bent down, filled my palm with some of the earth that had been displaced and tossed it onto the coffin.

"Good-bye Poppa," I whispered. "Momma wants to know, can you hear now?"

* * *

He can hear me now. I know this with my mother Mary's light.

He hears what he has seen. He hears with all the magic of my childhood fairy tales, my childhood dreamings, with the legends of yore.

Benny re-created the world for me. And through my tears, I smiled as my mother signed the last words she saw him say as she left the hospital the day before he died. "Don't tell Ruth I am in hospital. Let her go to Sweden."

He let me go, and I returned to the source of my life, again and again, to Benny, the inventor of the chuckle, of the deep laugh, smiling at life's biggest joke. He was deaf and his deafness turned language into music. His was the voice of passion, his was the voice that gave me my voice.

And I laugh Benny's laugh, his laugh at life's pleasure.

Once I was fugitive from sound, from my own senses—not now.

Lungs detonate sound, send it blasting into the ether, blessing life with human expression. I look at my father, alive, I stare into him, transfixing my gaze at his vocal expulsion of words. I see his lungs inhale, exhale, breathe language, and he does not hear himself. I do not believe this.

He says, "Why you look at me so hard?"

And I say, "I want to catch your words from the mouth at once."

And he smiles at this enigma, this daughter, and shakes his head, talking and signing away at me nonstop.

Laughing!

Nineteen

MARY

And Miriam the prophetess, the sister of Aaron, took a timbrel in her hand; and all the women went out after her with timbrels and with dances.

—Exodus 15:20

One day in June Momma had a stroke. One day in June Momma lost her language.

The phone rang. I was listening to music, quiet, at rest. A strange woman's voice said, "I was with your mother, sitting on a bench in front of the supermarket. I touched her to tell her I was leaving, tapped her shoulder, and she fell over. I screamed for help, the supermarket manager came, he called an ambulance, they took her away. I have her purse, that's how I have your number."

"Where is my mother?"

"I don't know. Maybe the manager knows."

I swallowed fear, wrote down the woman's phone number, called the police, the local hospitals, until I found

Momma, conscious, her white hair streaming down her face, her teeth missing, intubated, thrashing her right leg, her right arm tied to the bed, her left side inert, paralyzed. In the days and months to come, the fingers of her left hand curled into her palm, rigid, useless. She was left-handed.

The young emergency room physician at the University Hospital at Fort Lauderdale gently said, "The CAT scan shows that your mother had a massive right-brain stroke." I was silent. He continued, "The best is that she will be in a wheelchair; at worst bedridden, a vegetable."

"Will she be able to talk?" I hesitated. "She's deaf, from birth, sign language is her . . ."

His clear blue eyes flickered, interrupting me, his words carefully chosen, "If she survives the next few days she may be able to use her right hand as a communicator."

I didn't tell him that we spoke to each other left hand to left hand. I looked into his tired face and saw Momma tell me, as she did so often, "I want to die, I want to sleep with Ben."

And I said, "Please do not resuscitate my mother. Be gentle with her."

He answered, "I will write the order. Go to her, take any valuables home with you."

"Momma," I wanted to shout with my hands, "wake up, see me, tell me you know me." I removed the restraint, took her right hand in mine, and slowly removed the rings my father had given her. I put them on my hand. I stayed with her, soothing her, hoping that at some unconscious level she sensed my presence.

The next day, Friday, I was in her hospital room. I took her limp right hand into mine and signed my name, pushing my fingers into her palm as I would push them into a blind deaf person's hand. Over and over, I signed her name: Mary, Mary. Momma, Momma. She opened her eyes. I looked for a sign of recognition. There was none.

The nurse placed a suction tube in her mouth. "This removes the phlegm, we don't want her to aspirate." Momma protested, banging the air with a chop, hard, in the deaf way that demands, "Stop at once!" Her hand flailed against mine. A word. She was in there, alive.

I drove home in a rush hour storm, the sky so black, the water so thick on the road, sheeting from the heavens that I pulled over, turned on the radio and heard Beethoven's crashing Ninth. His deaf symphony. In this first moment of calm, in the downpour blocking all visibility, I saw Momma's hands in the windshield, talking to me, asking me something. I was tired, dizzy.

A police siren screeched, wailed into my ear. I turned on the ignition, pulled out. There it was, an overturned car, blue lights flashing, visible in the wet charcoal light, blocking the street. Cars collected in puddles, water splashed. Visibility was dangerously limited. The only open path, narrow. I cried.

I made nursing home arrangements, funeral arrangements and planned her way back to life, to speech.

Monday. I walked into her hospital room, the silence deep, heavy. I signed, "Hello Mom," and touched her head. Her green eyes squinted a smile. I signed my name into her hand. I signed the word *hospital,* the word *stroke.* I said aloud, "Do you understand, do you know me?" Suddenly she grabbed my hand, opened her palm flat for words, for language. She moved my fingers. I asked, "Do you want to sign?" I took her fingers and attempted to form the letters of her own name. She pulled away. Tired, her expression blank.

I signed and signed, words, phrases: "eat," "warm,"

cold," "love you," "come tomorrow," "see me Ruth," "Ben," "try talk." My signs were broad, exaggerated, penetrating her brain. I sat down beside her, smoothed the wrinkled blanket and felt her move. She raised her right hand, I raised mine and we tapped hands, we tapped fingers. She touched my face, signed the letters *y* and *s*, the word *yes*—her first word. Her eyes knew me, her hand wiped my tears.

There are no coincidences. There is God.

And so the long trek back to speech began, successful days, frustrating days, days of speech and days of anger. The months passed into September. I put Momma in a nursing home and never told her. She believed she was in another hospital.

And I began. I taught her what she never taught me, her own language. I signed to her humor and courage. I asked, "Momma, do you understand me?" Each time I added a word to her limited vocabulary, careful to catch the comprehension in her eyes.

One day, as soon as she saw me in the doorway of her room, she pointed her finger down, down into the bed. Her index finger stood straight up, the sign for the number one. I had to reach into her mind, reach into my own intuition and speak her words for her. "Momma, you want to say you only have one good hand, one good leg?" She shook her head up and down, a small smile on her mouth. Yes, that meant yes!

Talking rapidly, she repeatedly punched the middle of her chest with her index finger, held it up again for the number one. Her eyes were speaking, willing her thought into me. "You are the only deaf person here?" I asked slowly, tentatively. She signed the word *yes* twice, without any prompting. She lifted her index finger, placed it softly over the center of her lips and drew it in a straight line down her chin. The sign for *lonesome*; she was lonesome.

And out of nowhere came her first spontaneous speech.

I ignored her words, fingers flying. "Momma, you talked by yourself, alone, your own words. Wonderful!"

"You out, forget." Her signs were soft.

"Not forget, you are Mary, queen, my mother." My hands rushed on, "All your language is in your brain, a closet full of words; you can never forget. Never!" It was too much. I stopped my hands, took her right hand in mine, looked at her staring green eyes empty behind her thick cataract lenses, and mouthed her name.

We waited and her delicate hand slid out from mine, her eyes danced as her fingers spelled the letters of her own name. "Mary." Perfect. Her fingers were perfect. Fluent.

But the days were not all the same. I walked into her room, past the men and women who lined the hallways in their wheelchairs, ill, most beyond recovery. I held my breath. I walked into her room and sensed the heavy institutional stupor. My unspoken words wanted to shout, "Momma, talk to me!" but my hands said, "Hello Momma, it is me, Ruth, glad to see me?"

No response.

I touched her head; her eyes smiled.

With playful fingers I commanded, "Come, Mom, spell your name for me. Remember, Mary?"

After so many weeks and months, she knew what to expect and lifted her hand, but she was tied to the bed and I had forgotten to untie her. How could she talk to herself, how could she think with her wrist knotted to the metal bed frame? I removed the strings, loosened the sponge-lined bracelet that shackled her. She raised her arm over her head, shook it, and I massaged the red marks round her wrist. She pulled away, reached out, patted my hand; she wanted something. To talk, to tell me something.

And once again we began that great struggle for language: the guessing, the facial, spatial speech. Her hand rose,

ready, poised—she fumbled a letter, she tried. I didn't understand. My hands quickly asked, "Do you want water, ice
cream? Do you want to go out, a new robe?" Her eyes told
me, "No." She waved her hand at me, waved away my words.

I began again. "Momma, do you want to go home?"

Her eyes shone, her face alive with connection.

Her hands shot up from the bed. "Yes, when go home?"

I lied. "When the doctor tells me you are better."

I could not take her home. I could not lift her. I could
not move her weight from the bed to the wheelchair.

She looked out her last window to a small view of the
green lawn, resigned.

It was March, her birthday. The cake was on her tray,
nine candles. "Your birthday today, Momma."

"Old?" she frowned.

"You are eighty-one years old today."

Her feeding tube had been removed; the white gauze pad
covered the large cancerous wound on her scalp; the trappings
of incontinence surrounded her bed; the four-pronged cane she
had used after she broke her hip stood in the corner and she
ignored it all.

She insisted, "I want get well!"

Delighted, I teased, "I am Mary!"

"No!" she signed. She pointed to me and signed the
letter *r*.

I clapped my hands. It was time. I took her hand, placed
it on my throat and said, "Mary, Mary," the syllables vibrating
through my skin. I opened my mouth wide, her name on my
lips. I laid my open palm on her throat. "Talk Momma, say
'Mary,' use your voice." My fingers pried into her lips.

She understood. She squeezed her mouth shut, forming
the letter *m*, Mary. The word perfect on her lips. But there

was no sound: the sound never came, no speech, no oral singing, no memory of her trained voice.

She waited for my response. And I said with my hands, "It was perfect. You say perfectly 'Mary' with your mouth."

Happy, she was happy.

She closed her eyes. And I imagined I saw my mother shimmy, bounce her young body to the rhythm of the Charleston.

A short holiday, a moment's respite, more than a year had passed, and I was in Santa Rosa, California. A housefly rested in the kitchen window's summer warmth. I watched this little black insect buzz helplessly at the windowpane that framed the garden vista: the huge lavender lilies of the Nile, the royal-blooded dahlias, the neat lush roses. He kept falling into the same crevice, struggled, moved higher towards the sun's heat and then slid down. This housefly repeated the journey, a continuing up and down motion, reflexive. The distraction clarified my role.

I returned to Florida, to the nursing home, to Momma.

Two months before her death, I put on Benny's hat, a lush brown fedora, and felt his bellylaugh. I fondled the hat, pulled the brim down, careful not to bruise it—he had barely worn it before his own death five summers past. I looked at my face in the mirror, adorned by Benny's hat, and smiled—smiled at the familiar scent still in his hat, at his touch, at his words that told me, "All is fine."

I sauntered into Momma's room. Benny's hat was cocked on my head, and I saw her speaking hand tightly bound in a padded mitt, her pallor gray. She was propped up in bed, dressed in a peach and aqua robe, her eyes vacant. I slid into the room, pressed my nose to hers, lifted my head and grinned. I pulled off the thick white mitt and she stroked my face.

Her words, her incomplete sentences came rushing at me. "Why me here? How long here? Food terrible! Home, I want home."

I answered each question slowly, watching her face, and when she nodded, her eyes riveted to mine, I continued, "You are here fifteen months."

"Too long time. No more!"

I reached to console her and for the first time she signed my father's name: "B–E–N."

I placed his hat on her head, gently.

Her hand touched the hat, and then she shook her hand, urging me to sign the thought that she could not initiate. "I want to sleep with Ben. I want to die. Life over. It is enough."

She sighed, relieved. I said her words. Her aphasia healed for the moment by my hands.

I changed the mood. "Momma, look, see what I have, pictures of you, Ben, friends, me and Freddie from many years ago." And one by one, I placed them in her hand, pictures of her youth, of her wedding day sixty-one years before, of Fanny and Abraham—her mother and father, her brothers, of me on a pony, of her friends Sadie and Ruben. Her face beamed as she held her life in her hands. And then her tears came, in silence. Simultaneously I wiped the tears from her cheeks and handed her a picture of Louis K. Her face lightened and the old smile returned as she signed the phrase "Fool around!"

"Yes, Momma, he always fooled around. Made us to laugh so hard." I completed her sentence, saying her words as she would have said them to me.

I dropped all the photographs on her bed. Her startled face stared at me as I pirouetted Louis K.'s dance around her bed, and when no one was looking, I tossed my wide summer skirt over my head in a gesture typical of Benny. And I heard her laugh. Once more I heard the sound of her voice. I dropped my skirt. She kept on laughing at my crude antics. I gathered the pictures on the bed and threw them at her. Motioning me to stop my play, her hand in benediction signed, "You hold my memory strong!"

"Yes, Momma, I hold your hand words strong."

Benjamin Sidransky: September 26, 1903–August 4, 1984

Mary Sidransky: March 6, 1908–November 1, 1989

EPILOGUE

*. . . wherefore should God be angry at thy voice,
and destroy the work of thy hands?*

—*Ecclesiastes 5:6*

*T*here is a legend that tells of a young man named McCarthy who had a speech impediment, a man without song on his tongue. One day, walking on the grounds of a grand Irish castle, he saw a damsel in distress. She had fallen into a swift stream. Rushing to her aid he pulled her from the churning water. She was a witch and offered him a wish, a single wish, as a reward for saving her life. He asked, without hesitation, in his mumble, to be able to speak properly. She directed him to Blarney Castle's parapet, where he would find a stone . . . and he was to kiss the stone. So goes the tale of the Blarney Stone. So goes the gift of gab, the smooth talk, the Irish lilt.

Not so for Benny, for Mary, there is no stone for those who have never heard a birdsong, the lark on the wing, but there is melody. There is melody! The sounds may croak and grate, screech and shout to the hearing sense, but there is melody. There is an aria for every deaf hand, a swell of tuneless music for every deaf voice, but there are no witches, no fairy godmothers, no stones to kiss, no blarney . . . no imperfect sound to make perfect. It is. It is another language, another dance: its own ballet, its own strut, its own gorgeous expression.

Benny was my Blarney Stone, my fairy godfather. The elocution lessons he gave me were confined to the grace of my hands, to the curve of my neck, to the tilt of my head, to the lift of my eyebrow. He cautioned me to be clear, to speak with open hands, with an open heart. He showed me exquisite arrhythmic sign, punching and dropping words into the air, patternless poetic creation. No, speech did not perish in his hands. They spoke to stone walls, to people, to animals, to me. He taught me how to make my hands laugh, to flutter them in snowfall, to press down with them, pouring rain onto the city streets. He taught me to turn my wrist in delicate slow motion, to pray to God with supplicating fingers. His hands jumped, mocking their fine expression, to humor me.

There was no silence in his hands. They were his literature.

But when I was younger, I waited for my literature. I believed that my voice was stuck dumb by deafness, that it hid in silken corners, purloined, waiting, always waiting to emerge. I waited for my life to start with real language, void of hands. My tongue would speak and not lie inert in my mouth as I spoke with my hands. I listened to strange voices practicing melodies I would imitate. I wanted to enunciate sounds that would place me among the hearing forever. I wanted to erase my hands.

And then, in time's passage, I caressed my hands, my first voice. In the end, words, volumes of words, all signed, were the eloquent metaphor of my life. It was the language born of hands that was my beginning.

I pay homage to the language I spoke as a child, to the language I still speak, not a patois, but words richly defined, sibilants and vowels, signed and spoken in deaf voice, a strong binding cohesive voice linking me to life. The astonishing word power unleashed by sign is at times epic. An immense power, a cantata curving with rainbow clarity.

Great mystery resides within the crucible of hands. Within the hand that speaks is the hand that touches. It is the hand that heals, the hand that pats away the tears that slip down the cheek. It is the hand that clasps with pleasure. It is the hand that comforts, the hand that wipes the perspiring brow, the hand that cups the chin in thought. It is the hand that teaches, that reaches for the butterfly, that speaks when words fail. It is the hand that doodles and scribbles, that computes and calculates. It is the hand that plucks apples from September trees. It is the hand that waters the plant, that diapers the baby, that massages and soothes. It is the hand that fires a gun, draws a saber, reins a horse. It is the hand that blesses, that creates, that paints, that writes and types. It is the hand that touches another.

Hands have stories to tell, tales of anger and love, of pain and pleasure, of youth and age. Hands clutch the head in woe, in grief. Hands wring with unresolved tragedy, lift with joy. Hands shovel the earth and bury the dead. Hands construct skyscrapers and mine the earth. Hands soothe and demean. Hands hug a child. Hands bang, slam, ball up, curse and cause fright. With my hands I have quieted an angry child, a frightened human being. I have prayed with my hands.

When I smooth my hand over a caged yellow canary or pet a rambunctious collie, my hands know the difference in texture, the difference in the life beneath the hand. When my stomach hurts I rub my belly. When I fondle the crimson rose petal and bring it to my nose to smell its sweet aroma, it is my hand that carries the aroma.

My hands are my messenger. They tell me the state of another when I shake hands. Is that a limp dead hand I receive or is it a hearty hand that pumps my hand in joy? When I meet a new person, a person that I think may play a part in the orbit of my life, I look for discovery in the hands. We have learned to veil our eyes, fake the voice, but we are not so adroit in hiding our hands. They are open.

"Do not sign in the street. Nobody to know we are deaf. Not nice, not safe."

This was my mother's command, repeated throughout the years. Speaking hands contained shame. I bit my nails to the quick, kept them ugly and out of sight. I acquiesced time after time to my mother's need, keeping my hands still in public places, protecting us from the peering stranger. And then I rebelled. I sign openly now, my nails trim and manicured. My hands bring me joy; they are the talisman of my life. They are my first gift, my first contact with language, my first connectors to human touch.

I know my hands at play. My mother threaded white cotton string between her fingers and created a horizontal ladder. She held my fingers in her hands and spoke with her voice, both hands occupied, removed from sign: "Watch, I make you wonderful, a magic."

She threaded the string through each of my fingers, lifted the design deftly from my hands, looped loops around her thumbs and said in voice, "See, I make another picture." We played for hours and in our play she taught me the miracle of string sculpture.

I showed my friend what I learned and she said, "That's the cat's cradle. I know how to do that!"

"Cat's cradle, cat's cradle." I rehearsed and rehearsed the words with my tongue's breath.

I went home and signed, "Momma, I know name of string game. It is 'cat's cradle.'"

"Never heard so silly a name. Cat has no cradle. It is a game I learn in school for the deaf."

I dropped the name and kept the game we played in the voice of our hands.

I lay my hand against the window of my own house now. It vibrates. I flatten my palm against its surface and it resonates with the sound of Momma's song. I hear the echo of voices, hand voices. The echoes strike the center of my chest. I stretch out my hand, hoping to hold fast. I can photograph a signed utterance, but not a word sound. Inaudible, the signed words arrive at my vision uncluttered with wind song, or birdsong or man's song. No single sound distracts me from the intention of the hand's meaning.

Hands in motion. "Why," I ask, "are they so beautiful?" I stroke the pads of my fingertips, eliciting perfectly perfect speech. No impediments. Language in motion. I touch myself when I speak, I feel my body in speech, not oral speech; I have another way to say, to utter, to tell: I have Benny's way. Language nests in the cup of my hands, ready to explode with word song, I am bursting, I must tell you what I have discovered. My hands vault, one over the other. My hands are loud, so great is my excitement. I am pushing you on the shoulder: "Listen, listen to what I say . . . see what I see."

And the stranger stares at me. He doesn't understand what my signs say. He doesn't understand my hearing-deaf hands. I try my throat: "Look, look!" I say, and the stranger turns from me. His face tells me that he thinks I am mad. I am only speechless, not handless.

It is another morning. I hear a bird. The bird insists, demanding I listen to its whistle, its rise to life, hearkening all within range of its call. He shouts. Who is this bird that stops me from my moment? I go to find him, to see him, to join his song. A strident red cardinal, his red flame muted by the morning rainwash. He sits atop a wire, screaming now, and his voice flows across the air into my bedroom, into my pen, relentless in his cry for his mate. Or is it the cardinal's own *Shema,* shouting, repeating for me the words, "Hear O Israel, the Lord our God, the Lord is One."

I know the cardinal's music. I have heard his canticle, his symphony in one pure voice. And I know the symphony of Benny's hands. I have seen it, and I will always see it.

I see Benny, my father, with the sea gulls on the beach, standing among them as they fly towards his outstretched hands tossing dry bread into the air. They hover over him, squawking another song, pecking at each other in their attempt to pluck bread from him. The birds come into his hand, one by one, unafraid, pointing their beaks as though they are diving pelicans, and swiftly flutter their wings to the pewter sea, their bread prey safe.

"Open bag, more bread for gray gulls."

The bag is empty. I shake it out in the sand. The gulls come but they do not linger at my feet, they snatch the crumbs and fly off, circling my father's palms lifted to the sky. His hands, although empty, receive the gulls; they alight and then they screech away. I cover my ears with my hands.

"What is the matter? What you hear? Bombs?

"No, Daddy, the gulls are angry. They make so much noise, they all scream at once."

"Sea gulls have voice? I think they make noise with wings, talk with wings, like deaf talk with hands."

"Yes, sea gulls have voice. All birds have voice," I answered.

"I think only parrot talk and canary sing."

"Some birds sing, some talk, some whistle."

"You whistle?"

"No, Daddy, I don't like to whistle. Too hard to do for me."

He spread his cheeks with his fingers, took the breath from his lungs, pursed his lips and expelled the air. No whistle came forth.

"Well," he asked, "I whistle air, not feel sound. Teach me whistle."

I tried but I could not teach him, then, or ever, how to whistle. I could not teach him the beauty of sound as he taught me the beauty of hands.

ABOUT THE AUTHOR

RUTH SIDRANSKY was born on Clymer Street in Brooklyn before moving to the Bronx. She now lives in South Florida.